Giving
Their
Word

Giving Their Word

CONVERSATIONS

WITH

CONTEMPORARY

POETS

Steven Ratiner

University of Massachusetts Press
Amherst & Boston

Copyright © 2002 by Steven Ratiner
Printed in the United States of America
LC 2002003125
ISBN 1-55849-357-3

Designed by Jack Harrison
Set in Adobe Garamond & Monotype Bell
Printed and bound by Sheridan Books, Inc.

Library of Congress Cataloging-in-Publication Data

Giving their word : conversations with contemporary poets /
[compiled by] Steven Ratiner
    p. cm.
Includes bibliographical references.
ISBN 1-55849-357-3 (alk. paper)
1. Poets, American—20th century—Interviews.
2. American poetry—20th century—History and criticism—Theory, etc.
3. Poetry, Modern—20th century—History and criticism—Theory, etc.
4. Poets—20th century—Interviews.   5. Poetry—Authorship.
I. Ratiner, Steven.
PS325 .G58 2002
811'.5409—DC21

                                        2002003125

British Library Cataloguing in Publication data are available.

All photographs of the poets are by Steven Ratiner except William Stafford, courtesy of
the Estate of William Stafford; John Montague by Rachel Brown;
and Marge Piercy, courtesy of Marge Piercy.

For my two constants:

my mother, Anne

and

my wife, Karen

CONTENTS

PREFACE

Beginning in 1979 and continuing for over two decades, I was a monthly contributor to the *Christian Science Monitor* newspaper and their syndicated radio programs. I wrote reviews on contemporary poetry for their "Books" page and essays and poems for an eclectic two-page section called "Home Forum." My editors at the Forum usually allowed me great latitude in the subjects I could tackle and this included Alice Hummer, my editor at the close of 1990. I had just completed a year-long series centering on my work as a poet-in-residence in Massachusetts schools. The stories had been quite well received and perhaps that emboldened my thinking. So one morning I visited her office with a new proposal.

I envisioned an open-ended series of poetry interviews featuring both the prominent names in contemporary writing and emerging talents. I said I intended to explore some of the enduring themes within each poet's work and to make the connection between a poet's creation and the daily lives of all readers, not just the small percentage who were brave enough to visit the poetry section of their local bookshop. I listed a host of such essential experiences: the family and the importance of relationship; the natural world and our sense of place; the province of memory and the recording of living history; the imagination and the power to name. These poetic concerns were in fact human concerns and played a significant role in shaping our daily lives. I argued the position—easily refuted at the time by book sales and magazine circulations—that poetry would matter to people, if only they could be coaxed into the difficult work of reading carefully and thinking daringly. Perhaps I threw in William Carlos Williams's much-quoted lines from "Asphodel, That Greeny Flower" that poets are fond of brandishing:

> It is difficult
> to get the news from poems
> yet men die miserably every day
> for lack
> of what is found there.

All that our readers might need, I suggested, was an invitation, a place to enter the material—something these interviews would provide.

I finished my ten-minute pitch, realizing how quixotic and overheated I probably sounded. After considering for a moment, Alice's response was a simple question: "Who do you want to do first?" It was only through an act of great will that I maintained my professional demeanor and reserved my wild laughter and cheers until I was safely in the parking garage. But in her office, I calmly ticked off a wish list of half a dozen names and, borrowing some *Monitor* letterhead, promised to get started that very evening.

In each letter I laid out what I saw as the scope of the series and explained to each poet why his or her work played an important role in my thinking. I spoke of Rilke's idea that a poem is born not from a single thought or perception but from a life lived with attention and intensity. I suggested to each writer that their life might represent such an example (and because of the impressive and diverse talents I had to choose from, this was something I could claim in all sincerity). Much to my astonishment and delight, nearly all the poets I contacted granted my request—though not every one agreed completely with the concepts I'd put forth. Joseph Brodsky, who was the poet laureate of the United States at the time, accepted my invitation but took ill and died before we had the chance to talk. In his letter, he disputed my premise with more than a little wit: "One can survive [the] bombard-ment of Hiroshima or spend twenty years in [the] camps and produce not a single line. Whereas a one-night stand can give rise to a deathless lyric." I was chastened by the comments and tried to make clear that I was not at all suggesting that experience equaled art, nor was I recommending a return to a biographical interpretation of a poet's work. Indeed, several of the poets with whom I spoke carefully asserted the primacy of the imagination and the freedom to follow language wherever the poem led. Yet, in the end, none of the conversations were without compelling moments where the bond between the poet and the landscape in which he or she worked was not clearly evident.

Only two of the thirteen interviews were conducted over the telephone. John Montague—both a wonderful poet and the mentor of a generation of Irish poets—was my first subject. Our conversation began in Boston after a marathon reading of Irish poets that Seamus Heaney had arranged, and continued over a long phone session. I met with Bill Stafford in Boston as well but recorded the interview with him over the phone from his home in Oregon, one of the last he gave before his death. On the recording, I can hear the rain that was falling simultaneously on his coast and mine.

Whenever possible, I'd visit the poets in the places they lived and worked, curious as to whether something of that terrain would manifest itself within the poetry. We would sit together at a table sipping coffee or tea and I could observe the way the words animated their faces. Mary Oliver, who has granted precious few of these interviews, sat with me in her living room as a wild Cape Cod storm pounded the roof. While she spoke of her daily walks along the shores and dunes of Provincetown, it was possible to smell the salt carried in on the rain. It was quite a different situation when I sat with Charles Simic in his dining room. I detected at first the wariness that comes from having been questioned too many times by literary reviewers like myself. But after the first five minute give-and-take, I knew we'd established a rapport when he went to the kitchen and returned with blueberry muffins his wife had baked. An interviewer has to earn his place at the table.

There was, of course, the tedious task of producing an exacting transcript of the long recordings, listening to certain sections a half dozen times to ensure I'd gotten down each reply correctly. But the most difficult work involved editing a ten- to fifteen-thousand-word document into a compact twenty-five-hundred-word piece that somehow preserved the tone and flow of the actual conversation. While generous by newspaper standards, the *Monitor*'s two-page spread had to make room for a brief introduction, the text of the interview, a photograph of the poet and a one- or two-poem sample of the their work. Again, Alice provided invaluable support, helping me with the final trim, often done under the pressure of a compositor's deadline. Once the final layout was set, we were presented with a line count so exact that only a greater power than ours could alter it.

But again and again our effort was rewarded by the overwhelmingly positive responses we received from readers and from the subjects themselves. What's more, each interview seemed to build upon earlier conversations, with ideas from one talk reemerging in the next. It felt to me like a vast weaving where the design, appearing of its own accord, was larger than I could view all at once. It was easily one of the best learning experiences a writer could ask for.

In preparation for each talk I would read through, not just the recent material, but all of that poet's published work. In this way I gained an intuitive feel for the themes and patterns that threaded their way through the texts. I would prepare a sheet of questions and another containing numerous passages quoted from the poems that I might want to draw upon. But always, it was my goal to follow the flow of the conversation, to listen hard to each response and allow that to guide the course of my questioning.

This project was always challenging and not without its share of surprise turns and unforeseen obstacles. But I left each visit feeling such exhilaration, such a hunger to reread the texts in light of what had been said, to this day I view the years that the series ran as the luckiest job I've ever had. If my editors at the *Monitor* had informed me that I would have to pay them for the privilege of doing this work, I'd have reached for my checkbook without hesitation.

I've now gone back to the original transcripts and restored to each interview all of what seemed most relevant. Whenever it was possible, I allowed the poet to go over the newly edited text to correct errors and grammatical lapses. The writers were not only generous in their efforts, many were quite excited to finally view their conversation in its entirety. In a single case I decided to conduct a follow-up interview. At the close of 1997 I re-interviewed Donald Hall because, more than any of the other subjects, his life and work had undergone a dramatic change, brought on by the early death of his wife, the poet Jane Kenyon. His new circumstances and the book that arose from them seemed a compelling contrast to what we'd discussed years earlier. This new conversation turned out to be one of the most honest and emotionally wrenching talks I've ever had with another artist.

The novelist John Gardner used to be fond of saying that the real impetus behind his writing—and perhaps that of most writers—was the desire to be a part of "the great conversation" that is at the heart of our literature. Taken together, the diverse group of poets presented here provides us with an insight into what that conversation was about at the close of the twentieth century. It is my hope that this material will offer writers and readers of poetry much to consider as we make our way into the twenty-first.

First, I would like to thank the poets who took part in these conversations and allowed me to quote extensively from their work. In addition to Alice

Hummer and the *Christian Science Monitor,* I'd like to express my gratitude
to my editor at the University of Massachusetts Press, Paul Wright, for the
faith he displayed in this book, and to Craig Triplett, who copyedited this
manuscript with exceptional care. Several poet-friends—David Raffeld,
Marilyn Zuckerman, Jean Flanagan, and Tam Neville—helped me with the
introductory material through their careful reading and commentary.
Lastly, I am inexpressibly grateful to my wife Karen for the support she
offered in every stage of this project, and for the caring she brings to all my
efforts.

STEVEN RATINER

Giving
Their
Word

INTRODUCTION

Songs are thoughts, sung out with the breath when people are moved by great forces and ordinary speech no longer suffices.

Man is moved just like the ice floe sailing here and there out in the current. His thoughts are driven by a flowing force when he feels joy, when he feels sorrow. Thoughts can wash over him like a flood, making his breath come in gasps, and his heart throb. Something, like an abatement in the weather, will keep him thawed up.

And then it will happen that we, who always think we are small, will feel still smaller. And we will fear to use words. But it will happen that the words we need will come of themselves. When the words we want to use shoot up of themselves—we get a new song.

—ORPINGALIK, Netsilik hunter, shaman, and poet

I celebrate myself,
And what I assume you shall assume,
For every atom belonging to me as good belongs to you.

—WALT WHITMAN, "Song of Myself"

I BELIEVE IN THESE MOMENTS: the curiously intimate communion between mother and son, a bucket of water between them as they peeled potatoes for Sunday dinner—"her head bent towards my head, / Her breath in mine, our fluent dipping knives— / Never closer the whole rest of our lives."[1] Or the young black girl with her family gathered on a "forbidden" beach in Fort Myers, an open fire, crabs boiling in a pot, fearing that "they" will appear at any moment and chase them "back to the colored-only shore / crisp with litter and broken glass."[2] And then there's Bess, the small-town librarian, walking to work every day past "the secure houses," diligently attending to life's simple duties—all the while attempting "to keep her friends from knowing / how happy they were"[3] by not letting on that she was suffering from cancer and that her time was running out.

I trust these moments and the poems that brought them into my life in much the same way I understood the truth inside certain family stories I heard around the dinner table as a boy—that is, suddenly and in my very bones. Their basis is not something I can verify by a comparison with "real world" events, though part of their foundation does in fact rest upon the actuality of lived experience. (This was certainly the case with the three poems I quoted from earlier, taken from the work of Seamus Heaney, Rita Dove, and William Stafford.) But in the end I must trust the integrity of the speaker and my sense that, as Mr. Heaney put it, the writer is "clued in, knows the score" about how the world and our lives within it are put together.

To my mind, this is one of the crucial factors in the work of the most powerful shapers of language—their ability to stand on two grounds simultaneously and be grounded by both. The first involves an experience of the shared world, the same streets we both might walk down, the same fields or shorelines. These writers are so carefully observant of their environment, they are able to draw upon its imagery with both a clarity and a heightened sense of the mysterious shimmering just beyond it. But the second is a more inward place where the new poem inexplicably erupts. This impulse to respond to some intensified moment brings to bear the poet's complete understanding—about language and the world—and lifts both into a startling focus. To such a writer, this wordspring is not so much a choice but very nearly an autonomic response.

I believe it's the power of this grounding shared experience that ultimately convinces a reader, allows the poem's linguistic elements to work their spell. There remains in these creations the utter necessity of their provocation: it must be so. And that necessity, working line by line and image after image, establishes a bridge across which we may enter that moment, bearing the weight of our own memories and preoccupations, arriving at a place of clarity and order. It's quite an astonishing gift, even if it endures only for the time it takes to read the poem. But in fact, with the most powerful examples of this work, when we cross back to our own lives, when we find ourselves sitting in our own houses or walking on familiar streets, the truth of that poet's moment continues with us, a marker we may use for considering and navigating whatever lies ahead.

I've long felt that the finest poets have had some signifying experience, a moment that became for them a measure of truth-telling to which they were committed and by which they assayed all of their own work. Sometime in their formative years, they must have come upon that supreme bit of alchemy by which mere words were able to establish a world, vivid and tangible. The eruption of this pure song might have been in response to some emotional event or seemingly out of the blue, an answer to a question they didn't even know they'd been asking. Stranger still, that word/world was not limited by the actuality of the commonplace, yet not wholly independent either. A curious harmonic would exist between the two—and by each, the other was illuminated, even transformed.

Such a moment might embody the first sense of promise that ever appeared in their writing lives—in fact a twofold promise. One promise emanated from whatever source experience offered that initial spark. There are as many varied territories for this as there are poets: family, love, the natural world, solitude, the spirit of place, or the condition of loss. I am never surprised to discover artifacts from these territories arranged prominently on studio desktops and bookshelves: old family photos, seashells, a picture postcard yellowed and worn, talismans from an ancient culture or the curious bits of flotsam discovered during a beach walk. This promise involves the hoped-for reoccurrence of that wonder: "If I persist in my deepened attention, new mysteries will continue to unfold."

The second promise involves the writer's own spirit and a feeling of indebtedness—to the abundant world now being revealed and to the past masters in the genre who served as models for the aspiring poet: "All this was given to me; I must be responsible for giving it back." Seamus Heaney captures it beautifully in the preface he wrote for a special edition of his early poetry. He describes coming upon the work of Patrick Kavanagh and Ted Hughes shortly after college and the sudden sense of liberation they provided. "The poetic voices I had just discovered were more in tune with the actual voices of my own first world than the ironies and elegances of MacNeice and Eliot ever could have been. At last I had discovered sounds in print that connected with the world below and beyond print I had known early on in County Derry."[4] And writing two decades later, he found himself "still surprised and grateful that the liberating, appeasing gift of utterance happened, happened to *me!* I hope the poems that follow show the gift being embraced with delight from the moment it disclosed itself and being exercised with gradually deepening responsibility."[5] It's as if, in this unexpected opening, the poet was offered both the gift of his native land and his native tongue.

And though the precipitating events vary widely, Heaney's experience is not unique among writers, nor is his reaction to it. Pablo Neruda often spoke of a moment from his boyhood that carried a similar transformative power. One day a child's hand appeared through a hole in his backyard fence. It was offering him a gift—a toy lamb. Neruda rushed into his house and came back with one of his own prized possessions—a pine cone. He passed it through the opening to whoever was waiting on the other side. The poet says he learned much from that childhood moment where, anonymously, the most precious elements of our lives can be shared with a stranger. "This exchange of gifts—mysterious—settled deep inside me like a sedimentary deposit, and perhaps all my poetry came from that."[6] Like a catalyst, such a moment seems to have the power to reorder an individual's previous impressions, even forging from them a new lens for the self—one that just might come with the self-bestowed title of *poet*. I imagine such an event as the sealing of an unwritten bargain which the young writer could implicitly rely upon (long before anyone around them might lend credence or support), and one which they dared violate only at the risk of dispelling the charm.

Of course there must be talent involved—some natural inclination toward the territory of the imagination, the musicality or even muscularity of speech, the exacting task of making the language work. But whether that artfulness was innately present in what we typically call "a gift," or achieved only through arduous practice and great emotional determination, talent alone does not guarantee that an individual will achieve a unique creation. My suspicion is that such accomplishments are driven by the compelling force of that sense of promise. These poets will steer their lives by it, sacrifice material advantage out of respect for its requirements. Tirelessly, their practice is to explore the multiplicity of ways its pledge can be honored: "If I speak the words *so,* the world opens."

Robert Pinsky points to that self-enforced bond as one of the necessities for an artist in any discipline. In his essay "Responsibilities of the Poet," he writes: "An artist needs not so much an audience, as to feel a need to answer, a promise to respond. The promise may be a contradiction, it may be unwanted, it may go unheeded, it may be embraced but twisted . . . but it is owed, and the sense that it is owed is a basic requirement for the poet's good feeling about the art. This need to answer, as firm as a borrowed object or a cash debt, is the ground where the centaur walks."[7] There are many skilled writers whose work leaves the mind unconvinced, the heart unmoved. The need to abide by that early promise—now so deeply embedded in the writer's consciousness, he or she may rarely be aware of how each new poem reflects that earliest inclination—may provide the additional impetus that marks the most successful body of work. Perhaps that is what demands more clarity, more discovery from the twentieth or sixtieth draft before the poet releases the poem, fully empowered, out into the world. And conversely, the absence of this standard is what surely leads to the abundance of mediocre and unrealized verse that pours into literary magazines. In the work of the poets I most admire, I cannot help but feel that they were writing as if their lives depended upon it—and not simply their careers.

As I prepared for these interviews, I envisioned an arc running between the world, the poet, and the text, one that provides an extra charge on the poems derived from this vital relationship. This was, in the age of deconstructionism, hardly a fashionable concept, yet not an original one either. Hadn't poets like Gary Snyder, Robert Bly, Wendell Berry, and Jerome Rothenberg compared the poet's work to the ancient tradition of the shaman whose songs were responsible for the tribe's well-being, who connected the community to the earth that sustained them and the powers beyond them? Weren't there numerous accounts from modern poets who viewed their own work as an essential tie to something larger—community, tradition, the dignity of labor or the spirit of the land? I developed a great curiosity about the various permutations of the word/world connection, especially concerning the poets whose work I return to in my own reading again and again. And during the years in which I conducted these interviews, I watched as my conversations with these remarkable writers refined or reshaped my understanding of how poet and poem are trued by this bond.

I've come to believe that our current critical postures are simply too narrow to appreciate what is most vital in poetry today. Many of these concepts have attempted to sever the relationship between reader and poet, between poet and the world. On the one hand, we've limited the province of meaning-making to an island that contains only the reader and the printed page. On the other, we've untethered our poets from the common ground and focused instead on the interaction of language and idea. For both the maker and reader of poetry, the result in many cases has been a diminished experience.

To be sure, in asserting the primacy of the written text, this notion made way for a pure poetry, radically liberating the poet's language and imagination. And not surprisingly, many poets (several of my subjects included) have spoken supportively of such creative freedom. But there seems to be a clear divide between the writers who actually work as if their responsibilities lie exclusively between the opening and closing lines and those whose work reaffirms aspects of the poet's traditional place in the world: the one who invokes, reveals, praises, bears witness, gives voice to our collective experience.

In a recent essay entitled "Warning, Witness, Presence," the Irish poet Eavan Boland fleshed out this old dilemma: "Where does the poet belong; where should the poem be rooted? Within or without? In public or private worlds?"[8] Her concern focuses on the last few generations of inward-turning poets "crafting a language to reflect a reality rather than seeking a reality to inform a language."[9] Of course Boland comes out of a bardic tradition that has not lost the memory of what it's like to have the very ground beneath you repossessed, to have your poetry (and even your language) suppressed by a conquering army. Honoring her predecessors, she writes, "It was not just that their words were written in the shadow of the gallows, or the darkness of history. It was also that they had touched the heart of their people. Their poems were remembered, recited, kept alive in an oral tradition. Despite the tragedy of their decline, they proved that poetry could keep company with the ordeals of a people."[10]

I think it too simplistic to assume that these recent developments mark some sort of cultural evolution, as if at the close of the millennium we'd suddenly entered a new stage of human consciousness. Writers like Gary Snyder remind us that poetry's role as a bridge between the personal and the communal is a fundamental one. "Poetry must sing or speak from authentic experience. Of all the streams of civilized tradition with roots in the Paleolithic, poetry is one of few that can realistically claim an unchanged function and a relevance which will outlast most of the activities that surround us today. Poets, as few others, must live close to the world that primitive men are in: the world, in its nakedness, which is fundamental for all of us—birth, love, death: the sheer fact of being alive."[11]

When the poet opts for the idiosyncratic language of the self, it becomes more, not less difficult to attain that authenticity let alone to communicate something of the experience to a reader. The truth of the matter is that too little of the work being done today could ever hope to claim the heart of its people; sadder still, much of it fails at poetry's most elemental requirement: that of being memorable. Quite the contrary, the language of much contemporary poetry evaporates from the mind with the turning of the page.

I think it is the thirst for this very authenticity that makes readers today willing to work through the challenging text of a poem. They trust that the poets they value have explored recesses deep beneath the surface—on ground where they too make their homes—and have returned with a vision. In this Internet age, when it feels as if we can easily acquire a thimbleful of information on a million different topics, the poet must be the one who has dug down to the wellspring and brought an elemental music bubbling back up into the light.

I should make it clear that most of the poets I talked with would probably never make such grand claims for their own work, and were in fact quite reticent about examining too closely the mysterious underpinnings of their poetry. But as they spoke to me—with passion, humor, and delight—about the elements and practices that informed their work, I began to sense the way some of those fundamental promises still provided fuel for the creative fires.

This sense helped guide me in the arrangement of the interviews in this book, which became thematic rather than chronological. In the conversations with Stafford and Oliver, the focus was the daily discipline the individual undertakes in order to achieve that necessary solitude from which the poem is born. Continuing with Montague, Simic, and Heaney, we see the work of the individual set against the horizon of public and political forces. A small personal poem conveys quite a different impact when events on the world's large stage hover quietly in the background. In their own ways, both Hall and Kumin explore the intimate connection between the imagination and the life of the land in which it is rooted. Central to the Forché and Espada interviews is the idea that the poet is a historical witness, one who provides a voice for people and experiences removed from the public eye.

The poet's bardic role is broadened to include spiritual, racial, and social concerns in the Piercy and Dove conversations. And then, coming full circle, my meeting with the Chinese exile Bei Dao depicts a poet who was thrust early on into a public role and now struggles to reclaim the spiritual home that he lost. Reflecting the desire of many contemporary writers, he is searching for a language that cannot be blunted by governments or co-opted by the cultural and commercial marketplace. The closing interview, a return visit with Donald Hall, not only reconsiders several of the earlier themes, but it is also a painfully honest demonstration of poetry's enduring power in the face of profound loss. We witness a poet using the tools of his craft to come to terms with his present reality and to construct a tentative passage toward his future.

What does all this say about the reader's place in this relationship between poet and text—especially for those schooled in the theory that the poem is a universe unto itself? I don't envision their active role in establishing the reality of a poem as having changed at all, with the exception that they might not have to conceive of themselves as alone in the effort. And, in fact, I would argue that this more closely resembles the experience of most readers today. Do we not look for some common ground upon which the poem is to unfold? Is the person and personality of the author completely beside the point when we are mulling over the deepest implications of a poem? Is there no expectation or emotional accumulation from a poet's previous work? Do we browse the book aisle simply by sampling poems from each text, without regard to the author's name on the dust jacket? Understanding a certain critical stance does not necessarily mean our intuitive response proceeds accordingly.

When I spot a new title by a poet I'm fond of, I always think, "I wonder what he or she is up to these days?" Having followed the evolution in a writer's work, I can see how each successive volume adds a fresh chapter to that growth—and I don't think it's too great a stretch to say that these developments extend beyond the newest permutations of language. A spirit is at stake in a poet's work, as it is in each of our own, no matter the occupation. The poem is a report from the frontier where the latest changes are taking place.

To my mind, the experience of reading a poem has more in common with receiving a letter than viewing a museum exhibit. We are not cordoned off behind a velvet rope, examining the pure object on display. We sit in our favorite chair and open to the first poem as if Mary Oliver or Seamus Heaney were about to address us personally. Within the solitary act of reading we are aware of the voice and the mind who first shaped the creation, its history and affinities. Each poem is a part of an ongoing conversation, one that, in the finest work, touches on the continuous dialogue at the root of all culture.

Similarly, the poet maintains some conception of a listener, either real or imagined—and if it does not always come into play when first speaking onto the page, it certainly does as the poem is being revised and prepared for publication. An interrelation between poet and listener is involved in this meaning-making process that is difficult to pin down yet vital to the experience. When readers say of a poet, "I love his (or her) work," they are confirming the intimacy of that bond—one that almost all of the poets I talked with held in high regard.

So perhaps the arc that I've been describing is broader than I first imagined: from the world to the poet, from the poet to the text, from the poem to the reader, and then, once it has imbued the reader's memory, that energy moves back out into the world again in whatever small or great way that experience has altered our perception, spurred our imagination, re- stored some fragment of personal history, or simply instigated a hunger for *more.* And that more involves the people around us, the places in which we make our home, and the practices that help us with the next opening, the next step onward.

Language, both poetic and mundane, helps us to lay claim to our past and map out our future, to envision who we once were and who we are becoming. The poet Wendell Berry was right on target when, in an essay examining the language we use to frame such discussions, he wrote, "I come, in conclusion, to the difference between 'projecting' the future and making a promise. The 'projecting' of 'futurologists' uses the future as the safest possible context for whatever is desired; it binds one only to selfish interest. But making a promise binds one to someone else's future. If the promise is serious enough, one is brought to it by love, and in awe and fear. Fear, awe and love bind us to no selfish aims, but to each other. And they enforce a speech more exact, more clarifying, and more binding than any speech that can be used to sell or advocate some 'future.' . . . We are speaking where we stand, and we shall stand afterwards in the presence of what we have said."[12]

Standing here, the gift was given (and even the poet cannot say precisely from where it arose). Shaped as a poem, the words are given again. We receive them with a deeper listening than the words to which the ear and the mind are normally attuned. And, when the poet's words strike home, we cannot help but carry them forward. As the shaman reminds us: fearing we are too small, we rejoice in coming upon the largeness of spirit and the resonance of song.

Who would not want to be a part of such a conversation?

NOTES

1. From "Clearances" by Seamus Heaney, in *The Haw Lantern* (New York: Farrar, Straus and Giroux, 1987), 27.

2. From "Crab-Boil" by Rita Dove, in *Grace Notes* (New York: Norton, 1989), 13.

3. From "Bess" by William Stafford, in *Stories That Could Be True—New and Collected Poems* (New York: Harper and Row, 1977), 152.

4. From *Poems and a Memoir* by Seamus Heaney, selected and illustrated by Henry Pearson (New York: Limited Editions Club, 1982), vxii.

5. Ibid., xviii.

6. From an interview with Pablo Neruda conducted by Robert Bly, in *The Sullivan Slough Review*, no. 1 (1969): 63.

7. From "Responsibilities of the Poet" by Robert Pinsky, in *Poetry and the World* (New York: Ecco, 1988),85.

8. From "Warning, Witness, Presence" by Eavan Boland, in *Poets and Writers,* 28, no. 6 (2000): 53.

9. Ibid., p. 52.

10. Ibid.

11. From the essay "Poetry and the Primitive," in *Earth House Hold* (New York: New Directions, 1969), 118.

12. From "Standing by Words" by Wendell Berry, in *Standing by Words* (San Francisco: North Point, 1983), 62.

1
William Stafford

—OPENING THE MOMENT

Linked by more than the phone line, we were connected by weather. I sat in Massachusetts listening as a warm July rain pelted the garden. William Stafford—one of the most vital and open-hearted modern poets America has produced—sat in his workroom on the other side of the continent and looked out on "a typical Oregon day. Can't tell if the water is coming from the ground or the sky. It's just *wet!*" Though he'd lived in the West for decades, the Kansas lilt persisted in his voice and his laugh. After several hours of conversation, the distance between our two windows seemed surprisingly small.

Stafford's many collections of poetry and essays earned him numerous honors including the National Book Award, a Guggenheim Fellowship, the Shelley Memorial Award and the National Endowment for the Arts Senior Fellowship for a lifetime of "extraordinary contributions to American literature." During his years as a professor at various colleges and writing centers, his beliefs about the process of poetry writing were both popular and controversial. He emphasized a relaxed spontaneity, free from prejudgments or literary standards. He was unique, not so much for the approach, but for the extremes to which he carried it and for his daily commitment to its practice. Listening to this conversation, it was easy to sense the light and daring spirit that animated all his writing. At the same time, it was hard not to be challenged by his passionate attention to the inner and outer weather of our lives.

Stafford's work is a reminder that, contrary to certain critical pronouncements, poetry indeed has its usefulness, has earned its place in the world. One clear example occurred late in the poet's life when he was commissioned by the U.S. Forest Service to create a unique project celebrating the Methow River and the geography of the Northwest where he made his home. He created a sequence of poems that explored both a sense of place and its connection to the imagination. The poems were then constructed into a series of roadside signs so that the poet's work might serve as a companion for travelers along the North Cascade Highway. They are an excuse to stop the car, walk along the river valley and allow the poet's words to provoke your own quiet response.

When William Stafford died in 1993, he left a void in American poetry that will not likely be filled. We do have his distinctive voice to rely on—both in the older books and in posthumous collections like *The Way It Is* (from Graywolf Press)—and, more importantly, the utter confidence he had in the generative forces moving around and through our lives. This was his gift and now it is ours.

SR: Since you talk so much about the daily process of writing, can you set the scene for us: If we were eavesdropping on the start of your work day, what would we see?

WS: My morning writing would begin for me by getting up about four o'clock. Every other morning I take a run, about three miles, and on such mornings as that I would still get to my writing by about five. On the alternate times when I am not running, I would get to my writing around four or maybe four-fifteen or so. Then I would have an uninterrupted time until about seven or a little later at which time my wife would naturally get up. Our house where we have lived since mid 1950s is now pretty quiet. . . . We had four children, but now my wife and I occupy it alone. It is very quiet here. Our neighborhood is absolutely quiet until the birds wake up—and in the summer they wake up pretty soon, but they are not very loud. The crows are the loudest, but the whole symphony of other birds are in the trees. I lie down on the couch in the living room in front of a big, I guess you would say picture window which looks out on our quiet neighborhood. The giant fir trees, some other shrubs and trees, rhododendrons and so on outside. I'm lying there relaxed. . . . I have a blank sheet in front of me. I put the date on top and I start letting whatever swims into my attention get written down on the page. . . . I probably have as relaxed an approach as anybody does. I welcome anything that comes along. I don't have any standards. I know that I'm the only one that is going to see this, unless something eventuates that I think might be helpful to an editor. I put it this way because I am not trying to contend for a place in magazines or in books. I'm just letting my attention flow where it wants to flow. When I say "flow"—that's a new image for me to say—but it's easy like water, it seeks its own level, it doesn't have any ambitions beyond its source, and so on. And the relaxation of it is part of the charm for me.

SR: It's a purely private place.

WS: Yeah.

SR: And then where do the beginning points come from: from within the room, the imagination?

WS: I immediately think of really barefoot beginnings of poems. I think of one that starts, "Walls when they meet, / hold each other up, / the ceiling goes out. . . ." So I mean, I'm looking at the room I'm in. Or it may be the sound of the birds outside, or it might be the residue from a dream I just left from my sleep. It might be something from a recent experience. I don't try for being relevant to current experience but if it invites itself, I welcome it. The feeling is of greeting anything at the door and saying, "Come on in."

SR: As both poet and teacher, you've been more open and generous than most about the process that produces your work. What does such extreme receptivity give you as a writer?

WS: For one thing, I think it's a defense against being stampeded by current, intentional engagement with what other people think is important. It's very subjective but it is the kind of subjectivity that makes you available for what is [making] a valid, actual individual impression on a human being: yourself. I almost cross my fingers—I *do* cross my fingers when I am talking to you like this, because I don't want to be caught up in trying to conform to somebody else's priority in terms of value or relevance or style—and I think if you begin to get your stuff published, you begin to be induced to seek out where you can get approval again. And getting approval outside [of yourself] is something other than what it takes to be a coherent human being.

I'm afraid that getting published has often pushed me toward trying to repeat what has succeeded, and I don't want to do that. I want to stay as trusting and innocent as I was when I first started to write, and I don't want to have presumptions that what I write will be accepted. . . . Instead I want the door to be open.

Oh, I was going to add one other thing just because it struck me while we were talking. The other room in which my writing takes place, in which a lot of the revision takes place, is a room my wife and I built in the double garage which is attached to our house. We put up walls, furnished the inside, put in a big window at which I'm sitting right now looking into our back yard. The front yard is the one I look into for the delicious hours of the early morning. This is in the afternoon out here. By the way it is overcast.

SR: Yes, and raining here, too where I am. In fact it made me feel more like my memories of Oregon, perfectly appropriate for our talk.

WS: It's a typical Oregon day. Can't tell if the water is coming from the ground or the sky. It is just wet. As we were talking a hummingbird came fluttering up here to the vine in front of my window. I am looking out past the rhododendrons again toward holly trees, fir trees, yew trees, maple, some laurel, the flowers my wife tends in the garden. I see a couple of corners of a roof straight ahead of me but it is obscured by the trees, between me and there. A typically Oregon look, like being in the clearing of a forest.

SR: Is it in town or the country?

WS: It is in town but it's at the edge of town. About one bow's shot [in the distance] is the beginning of a big wilderness park and we just stroll over and go over the paths where there is some wildlife. In fact, I've got to figure later today what to do about a raccoon that keeps coming over here and raiding our little pond in the backyard.

SR: So it is nice you have access to both worlds then. You can be in the town but you can take a short walk and be away from the human community.

WS: That's right. I can walk or ride my bike or, if I'm really lazy, I can get into the car and go down to the town library which is a half mile.

SR: I've read your poetry for many years now and it seems to me that you are not only willing but almost take pleasure in allowing yourself to be *lost*. I was not surprised to see in the new collection, *Passwords,* the poem called "The Day Millicent Found the World." Millicent kept pushing further and further into the woods until finally she knew she was "Lost. She had achieved a mysterious world / where any direction would yield only surprise." What is it in being lost that it holds such allure for you?

WS: You know it's true that I have thought about this often, but never exactly this way about what it means to me as a writer. I believe it's a kind of an emblem for that deliciousness that I was trying to get into my explanation earlier about the "delicious writing" of the early morning. That if you're lost enough, then the experience of *now* is your guide to what comes next. And in several poems—I think of another one called "The Preacher at the Corner," in a collection of mine called *Stories That Could Be True*—the old man who is preaching there suddenly catches my eye with the crowd listening, turns to me and says, "You!" Just like this: "You can't get lost. That is exactly the trouble with you." And that's an accusation. Those fallible human beings who are sure they *know*. . . . It's a quaint position to take. It's an arrogant position. It's understandable, forgivable, I know the feeling— but I don't believe in it. None of us knows what comes the next second. We manage to survive in our lives by staying inside the bubble of our assumed self-sufficiency. That's nice, cozy—but as a writer, as a thinker, as maybe a meditator—I have a sense of being in a set of circumstances that's much more wilderness than most people assume.

SR: Much of the time, we are willing to do almost anything rather than face the unknown, the wilderness. Without realizing it, we retrace the same exact paths through our daily lives. When we drive in our cars, we'll go on for endless miles, refusing to stop, rather than admit we're lost. We move headlong through our lives that same way until a crisis stops us. But that fear of the unknown, the uncontrollable, blunts our experience of the world, doesn't it?

WS: Yes. That sense accompanies me all the time. One of the metaphors I have thought of before—oh, we had a dog, an Airedale, who would stick his nose out the window when we we're driving. And I would see that eager sniffing, inhaling experience the dog was having and I would think, "If only I could get the world like that!"

SR: This daily practice of being present, of accepting what comes—how long has this regimen been a part of your life?

WS: Well, I became vividly aware of doing it regularly in about 1942.

SR: After more than five decades of this discipline, can you say how this has shaped your life's experience?

WS: I give a sigh, because I realize that the first thing that occurred to me was that it's made it lonely. In a sense it has been lonely because nobody else is up. . . . Someone was talking about Joseph Conrad, in his novels he gives the feeling of—I believe it was Clarence Day who had this—in the novels you get the feeling of [being] on a ship where they're all below celebrating. And there is someone up there at the bow of the boat who realizes how deep the ocean is down there, and where they are going, and that around them is this mystery. So getting up early and being receptive like this, day after day, is a reminder of the depth and mystery around us. And it's recurrent enough to give you the feeling of being alone on deck like that. That's one thing.

I think another thing is, your life gets centered all over again every day. The daily practice is enough to take you out of the current of your obligations and the current of the experiences of others that have been impinging upon you—and put you in relation all over again to something that feels like the big current outside of us, the tide of the eventfulness of being alive.

SR: For most of us, it's only the rare moments, often the moments of some surprise or emergency, that make us feel so fully awake, present to our experience. It requires an act of great will. What would life be like if you didn't have that practice?

WS: On the campus where I was teaching, someone said to me about the time I retired, "Well, Bill, you still writing as much as ever?" And my impulse was to respond, "Yes, but I'm trying to taper off." The person who was asking me was thinking, "Oh, this is someone who has to nerve himself to do it," but I turned it around, thinking, "I'd have to nerve myself not to do it." It is sort of like Newton's law: anything that stays in uniform motion—which I am in—it takes a strong external force to stop it. So when someone says it takes discipline to do that, that word always gives me little jolt. I think, "Oh, it sounds so grim"; because to me it is not a discipline, it's custom, it's a habit. . . . to some people this seems surprising, even other writers I talk to. They say, "Oh, Bill, I haven't written anything for months," or something like that. Sometimes they say, "How 'bout you?" and I don't want to look them in the eye because I'd have to say, "No, I never go that long without having that experience."

By the way, maybe my circumstances have helped or hurt me into this. Let me explain what I mean. When I said I could remember vividly starting in 1942, that was when I was drafted, right after Pearl Harbor. I was sent off to a conscientious objector's camp, and in that camp your life was suddenly drastically changed from outside.

SR: When you say, "camp," was it like a prison camp?

WS: It was like a work camp or prison camp. You know, I could say, in a careless way, I was in a concentration camp for four years. But, you know, some concentration camps were more pleasant than others.

SR: For example, was it a place where you expected to do community service or was it purely a detention place?

WS: Well, we thought it was more detention really than it was community service. The law says—I can quote it to you—"Those [who] by reason of religious training or belief are consciously opposed to war in any form may be sent for alternative services of national importance." We tried to make it as if we worked for the Forest Service or Soil Conservation Service, but we were not like other . . . forest service workers because we were not at liberty to leave the camp. We were under orders of the government during work hours. We were under the same constraints as those drafted into the military about visiting, leave, furlough, etcetera.

SR: So how did that prompt the beginning of this writing method?

WS: Well, it made me want to preserve a part of my life for my own. And the early morning was free time. The government never thought of harnessing us at four in the morning. They thought they were being cruel if they harnessed us at seven-thirty. Well, that gave me three-and-a-half hours of freedom.

SR: It brings to mind the situation of many women poets—Sylvia Plath comes to mind—who, because of their commitments as mothers and wives, would get up early enough that the children would still be asleep in order to have the time to work on their poems.

WS: Yes, in fact, often when I meet people and they talk about not having time to write, I have to avert my eyes, not to look accusingly at them.

SR: Let me play a bit of the devil's advocate here. It's clear your commitment is more to the process than the product of writing. But if this pure spontaneity is a proper orientation for writers, what does that say about the university that wants to hand down the traditions and the critical standards?

What about Literature with a capital *L* and the great models by which we were taught to measure our worth?

WS: Well, it seems—at least on the face of it—there is a conflict here. I don't think that there really is because, in the best kind of education, there is a leading forth of what is available to the individual human being. It is not so much like putting an overlay, some kind of grid on the developing person. So that the kind of education I am interested in, the kind of education I think I profited from, has been the welcoming process, allying the self to what is available to that self . . . at that time. But there are many people who teach in the university who are *professors* of writing, not writers. There are professors of philosophy, not philosophers. Wittgenstein made a big distinction concerning this. When I first read him, it was like a breath of fresh air, by the way, and I thought, *"Yes!"* That's the way I felt about Nietzsche, Kierkegaard.

There's something else—you could call it tradition, I guess, or another kind of method for forwarding the explorations of the individual soul in this life—that is different from the one who says, "Now I will give you the standards, now I will give you the marks to shoot at." . . . Recently, I read someone's article that said, "You can't be a writer now, if you haven't read . . . ," and then he named off a certain bunch of our own peers, you know, current fashionable writers—and I thought, "Poor Sophocles!"

The professors I have valued the most have been the sort who would listen in a kind of limber way as conversation was going on and they would embrace the possibility of confessing to whatever ignorance they felt, at the little nuances that were going on. Then there is the other way, that is to try to be invulnerable, to put on the armor, to wear your Phi Beta Kappa button and lecture others.

SR: And that way props up the little self, the little ego, and probably makes you feel better when you go to bed at night—and it actually impoverishes you.

WS: I feel it does. Armor is fine, but it keeps you from knowing what the weather is like. . . . I feel that one [must] stay flexible, stay a participant. A writer is not a person who has a fixed position from which to expound to others, but one who is—I guess this is the process-attitude—one who still knows how to swim.

SR: This is quite interesting to me. I teach in my state's artist-in-residence programs, working with teachers and students from the high school level right on down to kindergarten.

WS: Yes, I've done that, too.

SR: And it's very refreshing in a way, because the students are not coming at the practice of writing the way college-aged students might—looking for tricks of the trade, the current fashions—all with an eye toward future careers. If I come and tell them that writing is about living, about using language to discover who and where in the world you are, they are not only willing to try this approach on for size, they are delighted in this freedom. They feel too oppressed by the constant shadow of "standards" and the fear of not measuring up. But I worry about the dangers inherent in the system of writing programs in colleges today. Are we giving license to young writers to explore their creative freedom without providing some sense of what a life is about, what is crucial in experience that gives weight to their expression?

WS: Again, in answering this, I want to be several people at once. One is that, I went through the Iowa workshop; I have gone to many workshops, I taught at Breadloaf, and all over the country on this kind of thing. And I really do think that the so-called workshop poem is not an example of this lower-your-standards-and-keep-writing method that I've been preaching— but it is all too much paying attention to the leader of that workshop and the people around you. That's not people who are up in the early morning getting the breath of heaven, that's people who have been dipped in the workshop and have become encrusted immediately with the standards, the styles that prevail among people around them. In other words, they are not independent, they are not without standards; they've got too many standards. That's one way to look at it, but those standards are picked up from all sorts of places.

Then I believe that those who are more accomplished, or more trained, are even more in need of this relaxation. Kids learn to talk before they go to school, and they learn in a way that I believe in—that is, by immediate association with those people and circumstances around them, they get innumerable signals—not from great professors of language, but maybe from their mothers who either smile or wince when they talk. They are learning these immediate, tactile, what-does-it-mean-to-me kind of experiences that I would urge people to cling to. Even after they think they have learned the language, they haven't really learned it, you know. It's got them to a point at which they can survive, pick up the standards of the society around them, but they become ossified. If they could stay as flexible after they learn, they could keep on learning. And I think of those scholars who have become masters in their field—but meanwhile the whole dazzling

universe lies all around them, and they become insulated from the invigorating possibilities of further exploration.

SR: That reminds me of the quotation from the Zen master Suzuki that
says, "In the Beginner's Mind there are many possibilities, but in the expert's
there are few." You paint the picture of the expert as someone who tends to
pace back and forth on one small patch of ground while the beginner has the
whole universe before them.

WS: Oh, yes. I realized that after I retired, and I went to an academic
gathering.

SR: How long ago did you retire from teaching?

WS: I retired about eleven years ago.

SR: I didn't realize it's been that long.

WS: I hadn't either, until you asked me. But I remembered that I was sixty-
five, and I'm seventy-seven now.

SR: I always underestimated your age. I'm impressed by how sturdy and
hearty you are at seventy-seven.

WS: Well, you know, we lead a pretty easy life, yours and mine. The jobs
I had early on would make you grow older, faster. Working the crops, the
sugar beet fields and so on—it's harder.
  Where was I? Oh, I went to an academic gathering and I listened to various
people talking, and I suddenly had this awful feeling that the professors were
not conversing—they were giving lectures to each other. They each had their
field, their specialty. You could just see them get turned on when the topics
came around they were ready to propound on—and they propounded them
all right. There wasn't a tentative note; there was the same kind of
assertiveness that we all probably were panicked into adopting when we had
our orals [for the doctoral theses]. You were supposed to have read all this
stuff and, by God, you had better be able to give some kind of positive
reaction to them.

SR: After all you've said about your approach to writing, can you say
something about how this might affect a reader—especially a reader who
happens not to write on their own? It seems as if you're granting a similar
authority to your readers as well, challenging their sense of wakefulness,
asserting that "your thoughts are as valid as mine." There are two or three

poems in *A Glass Face in the Rain* where you address your readers directly. One of them, "Sending These Messages," begins,

> Over these writings I bent my head.
> Now you are considering them. If you
> turn away I will look up: a bridge
> that was there will be gone.
> For the rest of your life I will stand here,
> reaching across.

WS: Well, this kind of consideration comes up often for me. For one thing, I feel that these surprising experiences are available for readers, to have them on their own. Insofar as you can enter into it with another person, you are capable of it yourself. You can't assume that your reader can pick up everything in the language just by having gone through some kind process of learning to sound out the words on the page. Reading is not like that. It's an active thing. It's a participatory thing. So that I look for participation from readers, and if it isn't there I can't take seriously criticism from readers. I mean, I don't meet readers on one hand and writers on the other. I meet human beings who are swimming in this realm of possibility together. And the assumption that there are those of us who are writers who know what it is all about, and then there is the ignorant multitude—that doesn't appeal to me. For one thing, you get your surprises from those readers, just the way you do from your students in a class. Who knows whether there is Emily Dickinson or Sophocles in the front row? You can't tell. To assume that you know is to preclude the possibility of the enrichment of experience. So I encounter readers ready for surprises, and ready for surprises myself—so far as I can keep my fingers crossed and not succumb to the role society tries to frame me into. That's how the bridge is formed.

SR: I'm sure you've already experienced this from your teaching and readings, but very often I'll share some of your poems with a class—perhaps graduate-level students or a class of sixth graders—and in each case, they instantly seem to enter the poetry and bring their own life experiences to bear. I was thinking about what an open invitation your poems are.

WS: That's great, I really like to hear that. I think that the other situation, the one I feel a hazard from, is based on the assumption that one accumulates information in order to become a professor, to be able to profess. The process is much more fluid than that.

SR: I'm curious about what you feel lies at the heart of this process. There is a line in one of your essays that says, "It is as if the ordinary language we use every day has a hidden set of signals, a kind of secret code." Well, a secret code implies a message from someone or somewhere. Can you tell me about what you're tuning into?

WS: Let me give you a quick, dangerous, probably not-to-be-used answer: it's coming from God. That is just the shorthand way of getting at it. I think, by that "secret code,'" I was reaching for a formulation of words that would do a lot in a hurry. What's coming to you has the developing realizations of a pattern or code, but it wasn't made by anybody; it just happens on its own.

So let me try it another way. I think that what is there in the language is the history of the language. Sort of what Nietzsche was getting at when he said, "Any word with a history can't be defined," or that "every word is a prejudice." . . . I have this feeling of wending my way or blundering through a mysterious jungle of possibilities when I am writing. This jungle has not been explored by previous writers. It never will be explored. It's endlessly varying as we progress through the experience of time. The words that occur to me come out of my relation to the language which is developing even as I am using it. . . . I am not learning definitions as established in even the latest dictionary. I'm not a dictionary maker; I'm a person a dictionary maker has to contend with. . . . I'm a living element in the development of language. Not a person who's learning it, I'm building it. Others are too. I am not separating myself from them, but I am just realizing a different assumption about what it is like to be a writer. I do think that it is different. And I am willing to take whatever buffeting comes.

SR: Sometimes, to me, it feels like my past self is beginning to unwind within the language and sometimes it is like a future self being formed.

WS: Yes, well, that's tantalizing what you say to me, sort of the culmination of the past or the anticipation of the future. When I'm writing, it feels like the anticipation of the future, but I wouldn't like to contend with anyone who would like to convince me . . . that what it feels like to me is a delusion. It doesn't make any difference to me if it is a delusion; it's the experience that I'm having. And I'm a valid part of whatever is happening to us all. In fact today, someone asked me to give a speech at a gathering of writers, and I looked at an old poem of mine. It's called, "The Poets' Annual Indigence Report." It has something in there that says, "we all" . . . that is, we writers or poets, . . . let me find it:

While we all—floating though we are, lonesome though we are,
lost in hydrogen—we live by seems things:
when things just *are,* then something else
will be doing the living.

Doing is not enough; being is not enough;
knowing is far from enough. So we clump around, putting
feet on the dazzle floor, awaiting the real schedule
by celebrating the dazzle schedule.

And, whatever is happening, we are here;
a lurch or a god had brought us together.
We do our jobs—listening in fear
in endless, friendless, Jesus-may-happen fashion.

Our shadows ride over the grass, your shadows, ours:—
Rich men, wise men, be our contemporaries.

I work by the impressions, fallibilities inherent in being human since I don't have anything else.

SR: But my reading of the poems seems to point also to a certain gravity, a coherence at the heart of all these explorings—one that's quite separate perhaps from the self we dress every morning and accompany to work. Is this consciousness creating a second center inside the individual?

WS: One way to put it into language would be to assume that there is one center and another center. One way that occurs to me, at least tentatively now, is that the process of writing, of being creative inside language is essentially being available to what is developing as you carry out your life. The process of doing these repetitive tasks, these jobs that others get us to do—you know, the boss can tell us exactly what to do and we can do it like a robot, but we are robots with dreams. We are not restricted, nobody is. We do have dreams, we have these other impulses—slight glances and sometimes stupendous insights. I assume that maybe all the insights are stupendous but that people are not open to the realization of what they are doing.

Maybe I have a way to get at it: When I was reading student papers day after day, at first I had the perception I'd learned in the school of education, that I'm grooming these people toward some kind of acceptable communication so that others won't be stumbling over their odd punctuation, and so on. But another part of me was beginning to realize that every student talking and writing is wonderfully individual. Then the writing changes from being communication to being evidence, evidence of a being that I am privileged to be associated with for the duration of my attention. . . . So when a student used to tell me, "I'm not sure you understand what I mean," my impulse would be to say: "I not only understand what you mean, I understand more than you thought you meant."

SR: Which is a startling statement, one that salutes something unacknowledged in that student.

WS: I'm saluting the individual, rather that the trained robot.

SR: One of my favorite poems in *Passwords* has that delightful combination of attitudes: pride, wonder and utter humility. In "The Way I Write," the poem seems to declare that this activity is absolutely crucial to the universe and, at the same time, is completely insignificant. As if Dante, Jefferson, and Emily Dickinson are hanging on your words—"important / additions but immediately obsolete, like waves."

WS: But this makes me think that if you write the way we have been talking about—the way I think I do, accepting what comes—then many of those poems will seem insignificant and they are insignificant, and even ludicrous and grotesque to those who have "standards." [I'm] willing to look awkward when I try to catch one that can't be caught, to stumble because of the inability of language to get there from here. So I don't feel protective of the poems. . . . I am trying to operate without making myself vulnerable to the kind of criticism that tries to hold every effort to some kind of model.

SR: Yet there is that assured and perfectly matter-of-fact acceptance that following those word-trails is your job!

WS: That's right, I'm washing dishes!

SR: But, as readers, we can't easily dismiss this impulse as insignificant, maybe because we feel it within ourselves, maybe because you take the work so seriously. The poem goes on to say:

> The ocean and I have many pebbles
> to find and wash off and roll into shape.

> "What happens to all these rocks?" "They
> become sand." "And then?" My hand stops.
> Thomas Jefferson, Emily Dickinson,
> Pascal, Dante—they all pause too.
> The sky waits. I lean forward and write.

WS: Yes, I think it is possible to take a stand that will enable you to laugh them off, but I guess what I'm saying is that the ocean finds them important. Me too.

SR: But there is that crucial pause in your poem, a questioning that stops your hand as it writes.

WS: Well, maybe I'm learning from our conversation how to find entrances into some of these things. The impulse I have is to say that my hand stops, and I don't put into the poem what could be after that question because I'm not in the same universe as those people who think there's an answer. It doesn't stop arbitrarily, it doesn't stop whimsically; it stops necessarily. Well, Wittgenstein said, "Some questions shouldn't even be asked," and the implied answer that's in that space: there's nothing there. I don't know; that's the next poem.

SR: Although the miracle of it is that from that absence, that pause, suddenly something issues. And it carries some connection to Jefferson and Dante, to the universe looking over your shoulder.

WS: That's right, we're the pebbles.

SR: There's a line I've remembered from an old profile of the novelist John Gardner. The interviewer asked Gardner what he wanted out of his writing, his work. His answer was that he just wanted to participate in the great conversation. And the implication went far beyond the literary canon; he just wanted to get his voice into that great sounding—right down, I think, to the ocean and the pebbles.

WS: I think he had a good one there.

SR: Many of the interviews I've been working on examine the interrelatedness of a writer's inner and outer landscapes. I wanted to ask you about the people who end up in your poems. You give your characters so much breathing room, I'm curious about their fictional or nonfictional roots. One of my favorites is an old poem that I share even with very young students: "Bess" the librarian, an early one from *Stories That Could Be True*. That title almost begs the question and precludes it at one time. Do the real people in your life and in your community end up finding places in your poems? Is Bess real in that way?

WS: This is one that's easy for me to be direct on. Bess was in my world. She was the librarian at the school next to our house. I can look over and see into the school building from here, through the trees, where my wife taught. So

I knew Bess. She lived a steady life in our community. She found she had cancer and it progressed fast and she died. So I wrote this poem in the circumstances of knowing her and of her death and the kind of person she was. So that's very close. You mentioned earlier "The Day Millicent Found the World." I chuckle, because I'm thinking how wonderful and various writing is. When I began to write that, I didn't know anything, not even the name Millicent. I guess the syllables of that name made me feel I was talking about an old-fashioned kind of girl. I just began to write without knowing what was coming. There's no Millicent in my life; there was just this kind of person who went farther and farther into the surroundings, a person who found her way from the structured life that she had been living, into the realization that there is a wilderness, that life is richer and greater than those formulas, formulations, dictionaries, encyclopedias, and advanced degrees, that there is something swirling, and generous and maybe dangerous—but maybe not.

SR: And in fact, in my world, a continent away, it really doesn't matter if Bess walked your streets or if Millicent lived, because I'm only receiving the message, just the words on the paper—and I took them both with equal seriousness. It doesn't diminish the emotional experience because I don't get to live next door to any of them. I only get to live next door to the poem.

WS: You and I and others in our situation—it may be what we are glimpsing is that occasions and actual encounters in our lives seem to be what they are partly because of the readiness that's in ourselves. Bess was known to many people. She got into one poem and maybe that's because my way of meditation or my receptivity made her "Bess," not just the librarian of the school.

SR: So the people who live around you now in Lake Oswego occasionally find their way into your poems?

WS: That's right. I have to change the syllables of their names often— because they are still present, right? This would be a clue that we writers might share. Sometimes the new name rhymes with the old name.

SR: So that you carry over as many of the syllables as possible, right? I'd like to ask you about the section of *Passwords* that's called "Elegies,"—and, again, this may be territory that you'd rather not comment on at all. But "For a Lost Child," and the poem "Going On" that follows it: these are poems of extreme tenderness, extreme loss. Are these based on experiences from your life?

WS: Our conversation now verges on something else. "Elegies" got its place in *Passwords* because, it is true, recent experiences had led me to write quite a number of poems recognizing tragedy. A tragedy did occur in our lives three years ago. Our oldest child. There was in *The American Scholar,* about two years ago, a memorial poem to our son Bret. It is about him. I didn't include that poem in "Elegies" because I thought it had too much voltage. I thought it was okay as a poem, but it seemed—maybe I can do this by extrapolating from how we started. You asked me, "I wonder about some of those people in your poems. Are they real?" This was too real. . . . So I found myself writing elegies—"For a Lost Child," "Memorial, Son: Bret,"—quite a few poems like that.

But even when it happened to us—and it was like a bolt of lightning—in a way my practice of writing over the years prepared me for this. I had written some things like this in my poems. I suppose you would say, when someone has an experience like this, "it is must be over overwhelming." Well, in a way it is not over overwhelming. Not because it doesn't have the same valence, the same human seriousness about it, but it is not new. It was anticipated. Do these things happen? Yes, they happen—something like this.

SR: It's a curious human response, that we tend to assume such poems must be biographical. But I have to say, I was surprised by the intensity of grief I felt from these poems, and it made me want to know if this was the situation for the poem's maker. It's not that, as readers, we are vicariously living our lives though yours. It's more that we are somehow allowed to feel our own lives with a greater depth, that such poems are an invitation into that intensified concentration.

WS: Yes, you make me think that, as a matter of fact, not only are we allowed to live our own lives, but that's the only way we can, mirroring the method of the poem. Our relation to it is our way of deep reading, of realizing the poem, so that a response that we make is indeed our own, and its validity depends upon our own participation. It doesn't have to be congruent with our lives to somehow create meaning in terms of our lives.

[Note: At this point in the conversation, we recalled an earlier discussion by letter concerning a new poem Stafford had sent to me. I caught a typo or two in the text and had asked him whether his wife proofread his work as mine did for me. The thought prompted a (mistaken) biographical reading of the piece, and the poet now thought to set the record straight.]

WS: By the way, about having your wife look over and check for typos. That's not the case with me at all. Nobody reads my stuff.

SR: Nobody at all?

WS: No. And recently I was traveling in the East, to the University of Maine, and somebody said to me, "Who's on your committee?" What do you mean?, I asked. "Well, you know, writers who publish have people who read their work and guide them." He picked up a current collection of poems and said, "I'll show you who is on this person's committee," and he turned to the page that says "Special thanks to, etcetera, etcetera." You see this in most collections. And while I was there, he received a book-length manuscript from Donald Hall, asking him for his reaction. And later in my trip, I saw Robert Bly, and I was telling him this story; and he said, "Yes, Don Hall sent me that manuscript, too."

   I explained that was not the case for me at all. Out West, for one thing, there aren't that many of us [poets] close together. But I got to thinking, "Well, I guess there are that many because I know a number of writers who have others who read their work before publication." But nobody sees my stuff.

SR: And does that use of "a committee" seem like a mistake to you?

WS: Well, I can tell you the thought of it gave me a real jolt at first. A mistake? First I'll try to be doctrinaire, from my nondoctrinaire position that is. Yes, it's startling, because it means these writers don't trust what is coming to them. On the other hand, as a human being, it's not startling; I guess, in a sense, I always realized that people did that, and I realized that an editor does this as well. I've long had this as a definition: prose is what an editor edits; poetry is what they don't touch. I got that from practice, not from theory. Hardly ever does a poetry editor enter a poem. It's either yes or no— even those who read from the big publishing companies. But it shows that the product we read today quite often is synthetic; it's been modified, altered. And this comes out of the influence of professors, thinking that art can be made by following rules. So when I read Sophocles, I thought I was reading Sophocles. Now I realize when I read Donald Hall, I'm not reading Donald Hall, I'm reading Donald Hall, Robert Bly, Wesley McNair. . . .

SR: Doesn't it depend on how the poet deals with the comments or how specific the comments are? Supposedly Robert Lowell was famous for incorporating whole lines and images from the suggestions of poet friends.

So you're right, in such cases you might not be reading a solitary mind but several voices intertwined.

WS: Yes. I don't really have a very neat response to this, because I was thinking that, for myself, if someone has commented, tells me that I really shouldn't do this or that in a poem, as a human being I listen alertly. And I do, I learn—but almost always what I learn isn't relevant to what the poem is going to be. It's as if you're putting up a tent and someone says you should change the position of the stake. They don't realize that changes the position, the tension of all the other stakes. Critics usually enter a poem and they see certain gross things about it, but they don't realize that there's a bulge in the ground. They don't realize that, to make a change, you've got to make the earth over again. What I have draped over the earth, or draped over human experience or human life, is shaped by human life, not by critics' insights into what kind of contour they find appealing.

SR: And you're willing to be the sole authority and the sole sensibility to form that?

WS: I'm not only willing, I'm afraid I have to be. It's just like that.

SR: Aside from journalistic reasons, one of the motivations that prompted me to begin this interview series was simply as a furthering of my own education. I've been talking to writers whose work I admire enormously, but each has staked out a different position concerning the substance of this creative work. As a poet, I've found my own beliefs challenged again and again. And whether I agree or disagree with some of the ideas in these talks, they always sharpen the focus of my outlook and provide me with food for thought for the weeks that follow.

WS: Yes. I think I sort of want to clear a space for myself on this. For one thing, like you, I think conversations like this are great. I take it in. I digest it. It's a part of me. It will be a part of me from now on. When I write a poem, it will be with the totality of myself that has digested this conversation. It is not the same thing as taking advice. It is more like being nourished. And the self that writes the poem is the result of all the previous experience. Critics think that their contribution is crucial. It is almost erased in my experience; it's part of it, but it's not guidance. It's more like part of the melody that I hear form the world.

SR: And so you don't feel you have to somehow turn away from criticism or screen it out?

WS: No, I read it and I write it too, as a matter of fact. But I realize that when we write criticism, we enter into someone else's work . . . and we may immediately have all kinds of judgments to make—but in comparison to the time the writer has spent on it, our time is trivial, very small. Since writers spend so long writing their books, and critics then spend, if they're generous, maybe a day reading the book before telling the writer what all is wrong with it—wouldn't it be a lot better if critics just wrote the book in the first place?

SR: Certain critics will spend the first eight paragraphs of a review discussing their own ideas before they will even mention the book at hand.

WS: You're right. As some interviewer once asked me when the tape recorder was going, "What help do you get from critics?" There was this long, long pause.

SR: Was there any answer at the end?

WS: No, I just let the pause go on. I remember years ago I wrote this poem, "Traveling in the Dark," and we had a group that met back then, stirred each other up about writing. And so I read this poem and the whole group said, "No, no, Bill, you can't end it like this! You can't end it pushing the deer over the edge into the river." And right away, I thought, "Oh, I can't, eh?"

SR: In fact, I always thought that the power of that poem was that I didn't want to accept that ending either; my heart resisted. And I realized I had not read a poem that forced such a large counter-response from me. Before, I could agree or disagree, smile or not smile—but with "Traveling" I had to wrestle.

WS: Well, good. You see, if I had followed my committee. . . . And they were quite emphatic, and they were writers and they were perceptive—but they didn't realize that the tent stake that they were trying to move was going to make this tent really grotesque.

SR: When you were a younger poet, starting out, did you feel as confident even then that you could simply follow that inner voice, and not necessarily be swayed by the helpful or the unhelpful comments of friends and writers?

WS: Well, for one thing, by the time I went to Iowa, I was already incorrigible. I remember Paul Engle rolling his eyes at some of my poems. But it didn't make any difference to me at that stage. I guess I always thought that what I was doing was discovering something that other people hadn't discovered. And when someone said, in a way, "You didn't discover that,"

I'd say, "I got there. I'm telling you what was there." Oh, I've thought of a neater way which I've put in print somewhere: Someone goes to visit Dr. Freud. Freud says, "Tell me your dream." The person says, "Well this is the way my dream was . . . ," and Freud interrupts and says, "No, no, not like that." So the people who tell me, "No, that isn't the way it's done. Haven't you been to Breadloaf?" All I can say is, it's my dream; I can't help it. In fact an editor I knew well, Michael Cutty, asked me, "Bill, I want you to write an article for a special issue of *Ironwood* coming out about your craft of writing." He said, "I don't want some of those dreamy things about relaxing, I want you to tell how you really do it." So, I said, "Okay, Michael." And I wrote, "How to Improve Your Dreams." I tried to sound as serious as possible about having worthy dreams. Because for me, improving your writing by making it worthy is like improving your dreams before you have them.

SR: Was he pleased with what you gave him?

WS: Well, he called me up and he said, "Okay, Bill, I'll publish it if you can't give me anything more concrete." He did publish it.

SR: If I could, I'd like to run a couple of other ideas by you to see how you react to them. There's a book of essays by Wendell Berry called *Standing by Words.* Do you know that one? I was really impressed by it because it solidified a number of concerns I had about what was ailing poetry, especially American poetry. Berry is arguing for a certain kind of responsibility for writers, that they be able to stand by their words, vouch for them, in a sense, by their actions and experiences. I believe he sees poetry as grounded in an experience of land, a knowledge about the human contact with a piece of this earth. He's setting this in opposition to poetry of pure imagination and the sort of verse that is a closed system—language about the art of language.

One of the metaphors he used struck me: if you were walking through the woods and you questioned a local farmer, chances are you could put your trust in his directions; his knowledge of place could steer you onward. But this is hardly the case with many contemporary poets; the world they write about bears little relation to the one you and I are walking through and you don't place the same sort of trust in their language. It's just words on paper—beautiful words, perhaps, but nothing you'd stake your future on. And when I interviewed John Montague, the Irish poet, he gave me a Gaelic term for this sort of confidence: *dinn shenchas* which means "place-wisdom." He commented that an Irish poet had to possess place wisdom before he or she could dare speak about something in a poem.

How do you react to this idea of having to stand by your words, that they are backed up by the real territory of your life?

WS: Well, I think you really have nailed me on something where I feel vulnerable. But in order to be honest, I have to tell you how vulnerable I am. Wendell Berry's *Standing by Words,* and also I'm thinking earlier of Orwell's "Politics and the English Language" and his ideas about "purifying the language of the tribe." I'm a witness for a more oblique approach to this topic, and that is the easy way of saying, "I don't quite subscribe to this." Orwell, for instance, used this as an example: when some official said "pacification of boundaries" they really meant "kill all the old inhabitants." He says how awful this change in modern language is. Orwell is more optimistic than I am about human beings. I think if they have to say "pacification of boundaries," that is a gain over saying "kill all the inhabitants."

SR: Why a gain?

WS: It's a gain because it shows that they are sensitive to what they are doing. A real villain would just say "kill them," but someone who has a tiny little nudge of conscience would say "pacify the area." It's a concession to the human need to become more kindly. And so a person who lies is in some scales better than a person who doesn't feel the need to lie. I don't know if this makes sense to you. For me, those who think they are going to improve the validity or merit of human beings by getting them to "tell it like it is," are naive. There is something more pervasive, more fundamental than the resolve to "tell it like it is." Poetry lives by the slipperiness of words. I'm not trying to establish a language. Do you remember the place in *Gulliver's Travels* where the people carry with them anything that they're going to refer to? If they want to say "rock," they've got a rock to show the listener. I think language is different from that, that it's glory is its slipperiness—and so when someone says that the language has deteriorated now because words used to mean this and now they mean that, they are talking like a conservative dictionary maker. They are not talking like a poet. The poet uses the language the way it is, not the way it ought to be. The way people hear it. So when I do a poem about something present, about the war in the Gulf, I would think my poem would be doing something much more devious or subtle, maybe much more central to the human psyche than applying geographically correct terms for the war in the Gulf.

SR: It seems what you're referring to is the accuracy of the language—and you're arguing for a different measure of accuracy: you're not demanding that these particular syllables correspond to this hill of sand. But Berry is also describing the use of language where the poet feels his full self behind the words, investing them with his experience. At least it sounds, from your own comments, that when I read a Bill Stafford poem, I'm getting nothing but Stafford. The responsibility for the life of those words rests with you alone.

WS: Well, I feel inadequate here, and I don't think that we're going to be able to corral this idea in one session. But my own feeling is that those who choose the heroic stance about language as Wendell Berry does, or as Ezra Pound did—they're deluded. The self that they're positing doesn't exist. If a reader thinks that the validity in my poem depends on the rectitude of Stafford, they're making a mistake. I'd argue that my rectitude, in the sense that we've been talking about, is a different kind of rectitude. I mean, I'm loyal to my poems. . . . Berry, Pound, and others have an idea of integrity or rectitude that is too antiquated. They're knights in armor and the time for that is long past. The kind of integrity that I would seek is the commitment to the emerging richness of what occurs to me when I write. . . . But that kind of integrity cannot subsist with an integrity that depends on a political program or a moral code or an allegiance to a country or anything outside of itself. It is totally inside itself. Maybe it is a kind of integrity that Picasso would have. Looking at his paintings, you say, "That's not the world!" Well, what's happening to him is some kind of titanic revolution of perception while he is engaged in it. That's the kind of integrity that I would have. And those who would stand outside the poem, and say, "Well this is a good person, so somehow you can rely on his words to tell us where the streets are in Lake Oswego"—they're making a mistake. You can't rely on my Lake Oswego. You've got to rely on my poem *about* Lake Oswego. Does that make any sense?

SR: Yes. But sometimes I become dispirited, reading through some of the work that is held up for inordinate praise by the critics today. I think we're allowing the waters of poetry and the language itself to be polluted by work spurred on by commercial considerations, by popular trends and the insatiable desire for the new. Recent poetry seems haunted by that pervasive, flattened, dispassionate voice we've come to associate with modernity. It strikes a pose of intellectualism that cuts it off from the rest of humanity. I will confess to a certain naïveté here, but when I was younger, I believed poets were truth tellers—that their work, at the core, was rooted in a fundamental commitment to the veracity of their experience. Now I see poets sometimes like businessmen, selling whatever voice or vision they think is marketable at the time.

WS: I see, I think, two strands of what we are saying and I want to make sure I get myself on the correct one. I have the same feeling—that those who would guide their talk and their poetry by some kind of already-achieved orthodoxy are not poets. They're not entering the experience of creating the new thing that the poem must be. The kind of integrity, the kind of guidance that you can get from poetry is that a poem is not just congruent with something that is achieved by society; it is the next stage of society. I am a participant in history, not an interpreter of history. So if there is something wrong with my poem, there is something wrong with my time. I even have a quote from Wittgenstein on that somewhere in my notes here. He says, "I'm addressing this book to a kind of reader that hardly exists anymore. If my book has validity, if my book is to be corrected, I myself must be."

So I would like to be so pure a tuning fork that my poem would tell you, at this particular time: this is how it is. And I just can't help it because I'm a participant in the process that made this poem. That process is what you're participating in when you get my poem and you shouldn't assume anything more than that. . . . My poem means what it does, not what it says, if you notice.

SR: You don't take that as a responsibility then, as Pound implied: to somehow purify the oceanic language in which we work or to move the tribe in one direction or another?

WS: This perhaps will sound too abrupt, but I am not a propagandist. I am a poet who is a victim of the language of my times. I am not a captain of my fate. I am confessing my fate in my poem. I'm not kidding. If my poem is confused, I'm confused. If you feel confused, we're both confused. Those heroes, those knights in armor, they're not touching the world.

SR: This presents quite a challenge to me personally. It makes me realize that when I first began writing poetry in my teens and twenties, I clearly was casting myself as a knight in armor. It makes me want to re-examine the voice in those early efforts and see how it maybe haunts me still.

WS: There is a mitigating effect for me about confessing confusion. . . . The authority of a leader is based on the shared fallibility with the followers. They concur because they too are lost in the same way the leader is. Thomas Mann said something relevant to that. He said, "A national hero is a national calamity." Of course with his experience in Germany, that statement carries a lot of force. But the people in England also had a national calamity named Churchill. He won, but that doesn't make him a guide. I mean a person who has dashed across a crowded freeway blindfolded, come out on the other side, and says, "See, I was right!"—is not right. You don't want to do that again. Montaigne said this, "People assume that history comes out a certain way and that proves that the principles adhered to, to get there, are right"— but he argues it's more interesting and devious than that. That is what I feel about human life. It is more interesting, devious, problematical than the professors and heroes would have you believe. [President George H. W.] Bush says of the Gulf War, "See, I was right." Well, he just ran across the crowded freeway blindfolded.

SR: But let me use an example that emerged into the common language from that very war: *collateral damage*. It sounded like a term a banker might use to describe some investment scheme. What offended me the most is how powerful a veil language can be, obscuring the destruction and loss of life behind so sanitary a phrase. And, oh, the sorts of things these busy hands can be doing behind such a pretty veil! In some way, I have the belief that the poet's language strips off that barrier and lets us see the hands and their handiwork with fresh eyes.

WS: Right. Those managers of words are interesting, but they are specimens to me rather that poets—even those who flourish and thrive and become celebrated. They become so through a kind of pitiful inadequacy on the part of us listeners and readers. I feel that every poem has a chance to be something that is not just a conformation of some idea that has been discovered, but a revelation. And there are people who are unwilling to take it as a revelation. Maybe they should, but on the other hand, maybe they shouldn't. Maybe what I write is not welcomed or recognized or valued. It doesn't have to be. It is just a certain shape of rock I have found, that's all. But I must decide how to respond. The editor says in his [rejection] note, "Sorry, this is not for us." Should I assume it is indeed "not for us?" I don't recognize it. I think, "I've got to find a better editor."

SR: But if the language accepts everything those "managers of words" would like to offer—everything from the latest McDonald's slogan to the most inauthentic poem—won't this make it harder for you to use this same language to get at something true?

WS: I think this might help us. I think of something Coleridge said, "I don't ask if something is true, I ask what it means." And that is the way I feel about political speeches, poems, articles, Ezra Pound's propounding. I don't ask, "is it true?"; true is a function of our limited awareness. But what does it mean?

SR: And then how do we take meaning from it? What does that expression—"what does it mean"—even ask?

WS: What it means is not a fixed position, but an event. A poem is an event. Reading is eventful, not progress toward truth. It is an experience. As a matter of fact, living is an experience. When I enter into the realm of art, I'm doing something that is more interesting, more contemporary, more explosively possible, than when I enter into the realm of truth—which is, by conception, dependent upon something that has happened already.

SR: So the poem is not a thought-vehicle to get you someplace.

WS: No, it's an event.

SR: It's the place, the destination itself?

WS: Yes. . . . Practical people think you learn all the technique and then you make the art. I don't think so. I think art springs out of total experience—not art experience, not craft, not explanations from professors. Studying art is different from participating. . . . If you study a novel, you are not reading a novel. A novel leads you by your appetite for reading. So when a novel is assigned, it immediately turns into something else. . . . Your graduate committee assigns you to read *Paradise Lost* and what results is something other than the appetite, the hunger, the excitement of the writer.

SR: You're describing a poetry that propels us—writer and reader—right into the heat of experience, into the sort of hungry thinking necessary to take life to heart. It makes me remember that little poem you sent me, "How You Know." Let me get it:

> Everyone first hears the news as a child,
> surrounded by money-changers and pharisees;
> then later, from gray trees on a winter day,
> amid all the twittering, one flash of sound
> escapes along a creek—some fanatic among
> the warblers broken loose like a missionary
> sent out to the hinterland, and though the doors
> that open along the creek stay closed for the cold,
> and the gray people in their habitats don't look out,
> you—a homeless walker stabbed by that bird cry—
> stop mid-stride because out of a thicket
> that little tongue turns history loose again, and holy
> days asleep in the calendar wake up and chime.

There is a joyful acceptance of what is, and a tacit warning against remaining behind our locked doors. Would it be far from the truth to say then that—whether we're talking about the elegies or the love poems—William Stafford's work is a poetry of praise?

WS: Yeah, I would be ready for that. I immediately begin to adjust myself to all sorts of concurrent feelings about it. Praise in the sense that it is an embracing of emerging experience. It is a participation in discovery. I am a butterfly, I'm not a butterfly collector. I want the experience of the butterfly.

2
Mary Oliver

—A SOLITARY WALK

WHEN MARY OLIVER TALKS about her work—something she is quite reluctant to do, fending off interviews and media proposals—there is an austerity, a quiet determination to her thought that brings to mind an earlier century. The discipline of her writing life might seem more natural in a time before every living room was plugged in to the perpetual tide of images and ideas, when an individual cultivated the solitude and curiosity of the inner life. This is not to say Ms. Oliver's poems aren't thoroughly contemporary in style, voice, and motive. It's just that, during our conversation, I kept getting the idea that Emily Dickinson would have found her a most agreeable next-door neighbor.

As a young writer, Ms. Oliver was not crushed by the intense isolation and general lack of support peculiar to the poet's vocation. Nor was her equanimity dramatically altered when her book *American Primitive* burst on the national scene, winning the 1984 Pulitzer Prize. In 1992, her *New and*

Selected Poems was honored with the National Book Award as well. The poems and prose poems of her last collections, *The Leaf and the Cloud* and *What Do We Know,* continue her long exploration of the Cape Cod landscape—Provincetown has for many years been her home—but are infused with the sweet and dark strains of a new presence: a meditation on the ineluctable losses of the mortal, and a consideration of what may yet endure.

All the while, Oliver's audience has steadily grown and she has become sought after as a speaker and a teacher; she was the Banister Writer-in-Residence at Sweet Briar College in Virginia for several years until she returned to New England to serve on the faculty of Bennington College, a position from which she has recently retired. She continues to thrive on the simple necessities of her daily routine: time to be alone, a place to walk and observe, and the opportunity to carry the world back to the page.

Like Dickinson before her, Mary Oliver focuses on the luminous particularities of experience, savoring both the simple and the astonishing occurrences of the natural world for the wisdom embedded in beauty and for the mysteries hovering just beneath the glittering surfaces. Her poetry is also an extended investigation into the nature of the self. But in her vision, the self is a much more open and encompassing concept than the succinct identities to which we affix our names. The "Mary Oliver" of these poems has rain passing through her, contains swans and gannets, pine groves and waterfalls, and the uncanny sense that, at any moment, the world is poised on the verge of speech.

❖ ❖ ❖

SR: In reading through the advance copy of *New and Selected Poems,* I was most impressed by the utter consistency of the book. I'm assuming that what we have here is at least twenty years of poetry, correct?

MO: More than that. Twenty-seven.

SR: And yet in some ways it reads as if it were a single volume.

MO: Oh, that's wonderful. That's very pleasing.

SR: But that's not true for all writers. Some, like painters, go through clearly recognizable periods—changes in style, subject matter, vision. This book seems like it's just one, long unfolding. Is that what it feels like to you?

MO: It's very much what it feels like. And it's what I intended. If I started over, I think I just would write one book and keep adding to that book. The first two very early books are, I think, more formal and properly derivative, as much early work is. The voice in which I try to speak and want to speak begins with *Twelve Moons*. The poems of *New and Selected*—the four single books and the new section of poems—certainly have a consistency of intention. So that's pleasing to hear.

SR: Developing out of what then? If it's not merely literary style that unifies them, what's the force that's steered you in this one smooth direction?

MO: Well, style I guess is no more than the apparatus that you try for in order to say whatever it is you wanted to say. So if style is an apparatus, it leaves the other half. Emerson said (he used past tense in the context in which he was speaking)—he said that the poem was "a confession of faith." You have to have some sense of overall vision in your work, or upon what does the work feed? What does it mean? What does it matter? What's its impetus? I have always had *that*, that sense of vision. That wish to—what? Show, I suppose. The wish to demonstrate. The wish to demonstrate a *joie*, I think. In this country, if one speaks of another poet as a nature poet, it seems a narrowing. Certainly I love and honor nature for its own sake. I also understand it as emblematic. But I don't really see it as separate from our own lives. For example, how could you understand metaphors without understanding the natural world? How could you understand "It is the east and Juliet is the sun" without having your own firsthand experience of this light descending and vanishing and coming back?

SR: How did you keep from the trap most younger poets fall into—the sway of imitation, the pull of literary fashion and the desire for approval— influences that might have kept you from discovering your own personal voice?

MO: I think a couple of things. For one, I never, myself, was in a workshop setting.

SR: Never?

MO: I was slightly, chronologically, before that era. I decided very early that I wanted to write. But I didn't think of it as a career. I didn't even think of it as a profession. I thought of it merely as something I wanted to do. It was the most exciting thing, the most powerful thing, the most wonderful thing to do with my life. And I didn't question if I should—I just kept sharpening the pencils! I didn't want an academic career, I didn't want to teach. I teach now part of the time—I like to teach. In fact, I'm writing a book on teaching the writing of poetry. But for most of my life, I didn't think of doing more than getting up and going out and seeing what I find and trying to set it down in words.

SR: You never had the insecurity of, "Am I doing this right?" or "Do I deserve to be doing this?"

MO: Oh, I never have felt yet that I've done it right. [*Laughs.*] This is the marvelous thing about language. It can always be done better. But I begin to see what works and what doesn't work. I begin to rely more on style, which is, as I say, apparatus or method, than on luck or prayers or long hours of work or whatever. That is, of course I'm more adequately verbal now. And I've certainly worked long hours. . . . My school was the work of the great poets—I read, and I read, and I read. I imitated—shamelessly, fearlessly. I was endlessly discontent. I looked at words and couldn't believe the largess of their sound—the whole sound structure of stops and sibilants, things which I speak about now with students, until they don't simply look at the word in terms of sense but also in terms of body, in terms of sound. All such mechanics have always fascinated me. Still do!

SR: So you created your own school, then, that way.

MO: I certainly went every day to my own school.

SR: I've asked many of the poets in this interview series how they feel about the workshop process and the proliferation of writing programs, and some have expressed a certain sense of danger—that we are creating whole generations of young writers who speak in similar voices, produce what has come to recognized as "a workshop poem."

MO: Truly most poets are doing such work, not out of love of teaching, but simply out of the necessity for a monthly check.

SR: Yes, exactly. Right.

MO: I do think the workshop is here to stay. I mean, there are workshops not only for poetry, there are workshops for everything from ceramics to computers to group therapy. Everything now is done in a group. Support systems.

SR: But the solitariness that was central to the way you discovered poetry— this is largely ruled out by the university workshop model. Are younger writers missing this essential experience?

MO: It was *central* for me—I don't know if it was essential, really. It's the way I happened to do it. Also, I take walks. Walks work for me. I enter some arena that is neither conscious nor unconscious. It's a joke here, in town, because I take a walk and I'm found standing still somewhere. This is not a walk to arrive; this is a walk that's part of a process. Donald Hall takes short naps. Naps work for him. They open the door to the "vatic" voice, as he calls it. Something else will work for somebody else. It's a matter of trying everything you can try, just to see what will work for you. Working alone or in a group. Walking. Napping. Whatever!

SR: And the moment when someone would find you, standing still—is that the onset of the poem? Would you begin to write at that moment?

MO: Well, sometimes. Sometimes. I keep a notebook with me all the time—and I scribble. You begin to respond verbally when you work with words every day for so many years. You begin to get your felt reaction in a phrase, perhaps. But, you know, I've said before that the angel doesn't sit on your shoulder unless the pencil's in your hand. . . . And so I consider it absolutely a responsibility, to be ready. If this is my line of work, it's my responsibility to catch what is given. And in truth that given is only given after years of desiring it, being open to it, and walking toward it.

SR: Do you think of your writing more as a thing that you build, or as a gift? It sounds as if you're describing it as a gift, and if so—from whom?

MO: I'm not sure I do, no. I think of my interest in writing, my wish to write, as a gift. But truly I do think that most people could be better writers than they are. Most people could be *writers,* in fact. Most people will not put in the incredible years of effort. I could walk to the moon three times and back if I followed the little path my pencil has made over the years. And reading also. Thinking about writing, thinking about language. So it's—I don't think of it so much as a gift. I'm sure it is, I mean, but I don't think of it that way.

SR: Actually, I was thinking of "gift" in its other meaning—not like, "Oh, she's a gifted writer. She's born with this gift." Some writers talk about the sweat and strain involved in creation—they "built" this poem, do you see? Like the pride a craftsman might take in building a house that stands straight. But Bill Stafford describes his mornings of sitting at his desk being prepared to receive whatever his imagination brings him that day—as if he was merely the recipient and the poem was coming from some other source.

MO: Yes, but I don't see how you can separate the pleasure from the work. There is nothing better than work. Work is also play, children know that. Children play earnestly as if it were work. But people grow up and they work with a sorrow upon them. It's duty. But I feel writing is work and I feel it's also play—bound together.

SR: But you said before that it was your responsibility, your job to receive it when it comes?

MO: Oh, yes, I have to do it. It's my responsibility, if I choose to do it, to write as well as I possibly can. I believe art is immeasurably important. It is one of the things that could save us. We don't have to rely totally on experience if we can do things in our imagination. We can, in imagination, live lives that are not our own lives.

SR: Tell me what you mean by that. That's curious.

MO: Well, art is not only cathartic, but an example. It's life that you imagined but you do not experience yourself. But imagination *is* experience. It's the only way in which you can live more lives than your own. You can escape your own time, your own sensibility, your own narrowness of vision.

SR: You can experience a death or birth in a poem that you may not have confronted in your own life.

MO: You understand it. You reach a level of understanding.

SR: And then, walking away from that artwork, your perception, perhaps even your behavior may be altered?

MO: Yes, yes, yes, yes. So, you know, it's important. It's soul-saving. Men die every day from the lack of the good news of paintings and poetry—how does that quote go? I'm serious. I'm utterly serious, though art must be playful too, even when it's most serious.

SR: Stafford's description of this process almost makes it sound as if the poems were being broadcast from some other source—internal or external. And the poet's job is just to be the receiver.

MO: Sure, sure. And Blake was top dog in that reception line, surely.

SR: Do you feel like your reception involves something inside or outside the self?

MO: I'm not sure, I'm not sure. I don't dwell on it much. What I meant about the notebook and so forth was that you do not recall it so well—ever— as when you first hear it or first think of it or whatever it is you do. I will scribble in my notebook and come back days later, open the notebook and not remember having written it. But the words will carry me right back to where I was and what I was thinking.

SR: And that's pointing to the power then of the sound and the breathing and the rhythm that accompanied that moment—not just the idea. You might recall the idea days later, but a whole host of elements would be missing.

MO: Yes, yes. And so often, for me, it's what I have seen. There are very, very few poems that I've ever written which take place indoors. If there's half a dozen I'd be surprised. This is something I only realized recently. But it's true, I live to wake up and get out of doors. I think that's where my house is, outside there somewhere. So I go out everyday and wonder what I will see. And then when I see something, that's the business, observing it and getting it down in some kind of language so that it can *rehappen* for the reader. I worry about it later. What does it mean? What emblem of our own inner lives have I found here in some simple thing in the world?

SR: One of the consistencies I felt throughout the poems involved something like a three-step process, a natural progression into the experience. The first stage involved seeing, a careful scrutiny of the subject. But that seeing evolved into a deeper focus, a heightened awareness. Suddenly we become present to the moment. It's almost like a meditation. But inevitably there comes a seeing beyond? Can you tell me what that involves?

MO: It's like an epiphany. I see something and look at it and look at it. I see myself going closer and closer just to see it better. As though to see its meaning out of its physical form. And then I take something emblematic from it, and then it transcends the actual.

SR: Yes, it's that ineffable moment of transcendence that's at the core of so much of your writing. I think of the lines from "Peonies": "This morning the green fists of the peonies are getting ready / to break my heart. . . ." By the end of the poem, where the speaker rushes barefoot to fill her arms with them, what she's really grasping is "their eagerness / to be wild and perfect for a moment, before they are / nothing, forever." Or in "Gannets," where a strikingly visual portrayal of the bird's attack ends with a vision of the prey—either narrowly escaping death in that moment or somehow rising up "from the water inseparable / from the gannets' wings." In depicting the hunt, it's as if you're trying to pry open that narrow border between life and death.

MO: The actual process, the process of what's happening there. Then I blow it apart and see what's inside.

SR: How do you step into that? What is that like when you're writing beyond knowing?

MO: Yes! You're in the realm of the nitty-gritty. I don't know if I could say how I do it except that I have faith that it will happen. That is the vision which must be in the poem somewhere. It's in the thing I've seen somewhere. And it's in the craft.

SR: To do what? To reveal it?

MO: To make the poem transcend from the actual. Almost the best I can say is that I know when I have *not* done it. I know the sag of the unfinished poem. And I know the release of the poem that is finished. I often talk about poems not as perfect, but as working or not working. A poem can always be closed down. It can be a small decorative poem. That's when you know you'd better quit for the day. As for how one does it: with persistence, and certainty.

SR: A certainty?

MO: A certainty that it is there.

SR: Told to you by what?

MO: Perhaps by the instances which have come before? I just know it's there. But whether I can reveal it in language is another thing altogether.

SR: Is there a physical reaction? The certainty you describe almost makes me think of a physicality. Is there something that you're actually feeling inside when you realize "I have taken it one step deeper?"

MO: Satisfaction as a workman. I mean, I worry about the creative arts seeming to be elite. When the poem works, it is like what someone feels when he has done a beautiful job of dovetailing a drawer, and it works. It is almost mechanical insofar as my mind is consciously operating. Whatever else is going on.

SR: But aside from the effort to work this experience into language, at the moment when you're watching the bird, watching the lake, watching the flower opening—and then you suddenly know some deeper level of meaning is working itself out—a message is happening. I just didn't know if there was a sign to you that you've accomplished that leap.

MO: It doesn't happen until I'm working on the poem.

SR: I'm not sure I understand.

MO: Probably it is connected to the dichotomy between life as a felt experience in which we relax and just appreciate, and work—the making of something. I'm forever making statements about the natural world, about its process. Also I could just lie down in a field and do nothing, that would be okay too. I could say nothing forever, and that would be all right. But when I start the process of writing, there's something in it that demands that I try to make a worthwhile statement. . . . It's the process of writing itself.

SR: I was assuming from the poems that the leap occurs when you are out there, stilled by the occurrence. But you're saying it does not really transcend until the pen is in hand and you're actually digging into the poem.

MO: No, no, no. I say, "Oh look, oh look, oh look," to myself all the time. But I don't go through the process, I don't arrive at any emblematic sense then.

SR: Is there a time when you worry about—you mention this in a few of the recent poems—where you worry about the difficult relationship between pure experience and the response of the artist? There's one passage in "Spring" where you are praising the pure presence of the bear: "all day I think of her— / her white teeth, / her wordlessness, / her perfect love."

MO: Yes, and there's another one called "The Notebook" where the speaker is watching a turtle and is so busy writing about it that she or he almost misses the turtle swimming away.

SR: In "The Lilies Break Open," the warning seems even more direct in the lines

> And there you are
> on the shore,
>
> fitful and thoughtful, trying
> to attach them to an idea—
> some news of your own life.

Is there a danger that, in the act of observing and bringing language to an experience, you'll disturb or forfeit the very quality you sought in the first place?

MO: I don't think it violates the moment. We are the "speaking beasts." It is our fate, if you will, to speak about our experience. Still, of course, I'm somewhat in envy of those creatures that do not speak!

SR: Pure experience.

MO: Pure experience! Of the animals. And even the grass and the trees . . . Over and over, what I have scribbled, out in the world, will be the description. The poem then does not continue on into what the poem will become. I don't have the center of it. I have what I saw. That's all I write down in that flavorful first sight of something, and that of course is no more than the easy work, the recording of what I've seen or what I've met up with. Do you know that line of Flaubert's? I love it. "Talent is long patience, and originality an effort of will and of intense observation." Isn't that marvelous? Because we all have those three things. We can all put those three things into our work. I leave the other kind of work for later.

SR: And where will that happen? Will that happen sitting out there by the lake? Or does that happen only back here at the desk?

MO: That will happen when it happens.

SR: Once you've captured that initial description, do you feel more comfortable stopping right there or pressing on into that next stage?

MO: It's not a matter of comfort. It ends. It stops.

SR: Then you can pick it up again . . .

MO: Yes.

SR: . . . and do something with it at another time?

MO: Yes.

SR: "Recollected in tranquillity."

MO: Exactly, yes. And that's the work, that's the making of a poem out of something seen, caught in language.

SR: That's good. I like that—though I must say it's not what I'd have predicted having read your poetry. Let me ask you about the choices and the commitments that you've obviously made to have this practice become a center in your life.

MO: Yes.

SR: And I was thinking about the daily choices and disciplines—everything from where you live and when you get up and how you portion out your time. There are large and small sacrifices required by such a commitment to your art form. Can you tell me a little bit about that?

MO: Yes. It was not a choice of writing or not writing. It was a choice of loving my life or not loving my life. I mean, I wanted to write. To keep writing was always first priority. I worked, probably, twenty-five years by myself.

SR: Twenty-five years?

MO: Just writing, just writing and working, not trying to publish much. Not giving readings. A longer time than people really are willing to commit now before they . . .

SR: Want to be published.

MO: Want to go public or be published, yes. Also, I was very careful never to take an interesting job.

SR: Really? Never?

MO: Not an interesting one. I took lots of jobs. If you have an interesting job, you get interested in it. I also began in those years to keep early hours.

SR: Early like . . . ?

MO: Five. I usually get up at five. Believe me, if anybody has a job and starts at nine, there's no reason why they can't get up at four thirty or five and write for a couple of hours, and give their employers their very best *second best* effort of the day—which is what I did. I mean, there wasn't any question about doing things like that. I don't how to measure the life I lived during those years. I was certainly never in want, and I was never wealthy. I have a notion that if you are going to be spiritually curious, you better not get cluttered up with too many material things. And if you're writing and looking at things all day long, that's your main business. I mean, you don't have time for lots of other things. People I talk to, students and working poets, think they are in a difficult position because there are things they feel they must have. They must have cars and studios and computers. They must travel. There are a lot of things you can't have if you're going to spend an awful lot of time writing poems. You don't make money writing poems. You make money from readings, you make money teaching. You can make some money from books of poetry, not a lot. I think it's sad that so many people who want to write go into teaching, and then the first thing they do is hope and pray that their teaching tasks will be reduced so they have more time to write. And that's an awful way to feel about your profession. Really, I think I've had the best of it. I mean, I have no complaints. I can clam. I'm a good clammer. Yes, yes! I can put together a good simple meal. No restaurant ever got rich from me.

SR: It makes me think of the poem "Spring Azures" where you talk about

> Anyway, Blake the hosier's son stood up
> and turned away from the sooty sill and the dark city—
> turned away forever
> from the factories, the personal strivings,
>
> to a life of the imagination.

MO: To a life of the imagination.

SR: So clearly this is a similar path that you've chosen.

MO: Yes, but you see, it's a commitment but it's also an unstoppable urge toward that life of the imagination. I don't think I have been bored one day in my life, you know, or an hour.

SR: As a writer, it sounds like more than adequate compensation. But do you believe that's an option for any individual?

MO: Oh, yes, oh yes. I think most people really are fairly miserable, and are mostly living for the future. And the future finally must give them a second life if there's going to be [*laughs*] time for them to feel happiness. I do know that there's one life. I am extremely grateful for whatever it was that impelled me to do from the beginning what I wanted to do.

SR: I think you're right—these choices are present for all of us, and our lives take the shape of our choices, the things we are willing to be committed to.

MO: I think I had a sense when I was young that people grew up and entered some other life where they were generally miserable. [*Laughs.*] It may be a good thing that you can take lessons out of a nonperfect childhood. To learn that kind of wisdom is to turn something grievous into a benefit.

SR: I'm curious, what kinds of jobs did you do during those years?

MO: Oh, all kinds. . . . I always had the feeling that certain things were important—and other things were crucial or necessary, but they didn't come up to the category of important. You know, you did things you had to do, but you didn't have to think about them! [*Laughs.*]

SR: In the poem "When Death Comes," you write: "When it's over, I want to say: all my life / I was a bride married to amazement . . . I don't want to end up simply having visited this world." When you say this, is there a specific image that you were dreading? Where did you see the sorts of lives that were "just visitors" to the world?

MO: All over the place. I would say in the world in general pretty much, unfortunately. I don't know of anything particular I had in mind at that time. What I think I had in mind was more my own feeling that if I am at home here, then it's all right to be past and to be dead here, as it were. To be dead is to enter into another state, still being at home, if you will.

SR: And you don't want to be cheated, a mere visitor.

MO: Exactly. If you feel you're a visitor, it's the same thing as feeling, well, you know, "Pretty soon now I'll fix it all. Pretty soon I'll start looking around and being happy and appreciating the fact that I'm alive and not worrying about the big stereo set I want or whatever—the mortgage and all that stuff."

SR: Ours is a culture of want. I think of all the creative energy and technical expertise that the advertising industry, for example, expends in helping to foster that want.

MO: You know, it's true that the life of the creative writer is difficult in this society. It's horribly difficult if yours is a nature that wants things you can't have. If you think you ought to have a fair return for your time. I know people who feel that way. They're good artists, but they resent the fact that somebody else, some lawyer is making the money. If a person can be persuaded from art, let them be persuaded. You know, if there is a question, if it's a battle, then they should not be enlisted. [*Laughs.*]

SR: It's like Rilke in the *Letters to a Young Poet.* The decision about whether to commit your life to poetry should be one about necessity. Only if you must.

MO: Yes.

SR: Let me talk a little bit about what is clearly the primary focus in your poetry, which is nature and your relationship with the natural world. What do you think formed your bond with the natural world? I'm assuming it's something that began when you were very young.

MO: Well, yes, I think it does or does not happen when one is young.

SR: Where did you grow up?

MO: I grew up in a small town in Ohio—at that time it was a small town. It was a pastoral setting rather than a rural or a wilderness setting. It was pastoral; it was nice. I don't know why I felt such affinity with the natural world except that it was available to me, that's the first thing. It was right there. And for whatever reasons, I felt those first important connections, those first experiences being made with the natural world rather than with the social world. I think the first way you do it, the first way you take meaning from the physicality of the world, from your environment, probably never leaves you. It sets a pattern, in a way.

SR: Although there must be a host of reasons why one person would find that special attraction walking in this field; and another person would pass the field by with barely a notice yet might be fascinated by a train going by.

MO: Yes. True. But to figure out the "why" for myself, would be to explore myself. I mean, I simply have never had the time to be interested in that or the nature to be interested in that very much. For me, it was the natural world that was primary. It was not society. It was not family. But very likely if someone does that important work with family or with society, then they don't do it with nature.

SR: There are poets who focus almost exclusively on relationships, for example.

MO: Yes, yes, yes.

SR: But then I was really intrigued by your poem "Picking Blueberries."

MO: Ah!

SR: It's one of those instances in your poetry where nature is clearly a mirror in which we can see our human self from a fresh perspective. Before the deer that found the girl sleeping runs off, you write:

> but the moment before she did that
> was so wide and so deep
> it has lasted to this day;
> I have only to think of her—
>
> . . . .
>
> to be absent again from this world
> and alive, again, in another. . . .

And then it ends with that gentle question, "Beautiful girl, / where are you?" Who is that girl you saw there?

MO: Myself.

SR: But it's not just a memory of your younger self, is it? What else did that contact with the wild deer reveal in your imagination?

MO: Well, I tell you. It's one of those poems you could interpret in a couple of different ways. For example, the writer is saying, where is the girl of thirty years ago? Where is the girl that I was? What has time done? All young girls are beautiful. And especially when you're an old girl [*laughs*], then you remember that you were a beautiful girl once.

SR: But there are other females in the poem.

MO: Yes, the doe is also a girl, and the speaker is a woman—although I almost never give the speaker of the poem a gender so that the poem will fit as an experience to either a male or female reader. Many poets, especially women poets right now, are trying to write poems about their personal lives, to tell or to "share," as they say, with the reader. And I'm trying to write a poem which was not the experience of the reader but might have been. I use present tense a lot for the same reason. Every way that I can, I try to make it a felt experience. And so to use one gender or the other would make all readers of the other gender a little hesitant.

SR: When I read that poem I was reminded of the way we are sometimes only able to discover something beautiful and vital inside ourselves by first seeing it outside us, out in the world.

MO: Yes.

SR: It reminded me of a Kenneth Patchen poem where he says something like: "The beautiful thing—it's not inside, it's out there, dancing." When you were starting out, were there mentors, other poets or writers, who encouraged you and this attraction to the natural world?

MO: I read so, so eclectically and randomly—but ferociously. Whitman always, Whitman was a great companion. Blake, Keats, many contemporary poets later. Almost anyone you could mention, I would have read. I read voraciously. I read with appetite.

SR: What about living poets, or even other adults—were there any figures who spurred you on your way?

MO: Yes, no. I had kindly teachers, but it was the poets that I read. Until I was in my late twenties I didn't publish anything. One quite well-known poet said, "Send me some poems," but I did not. . . . It takes time to go over people's things and, you know, to give criticism kindly can take a heap of time, I'll tell you! [*Laughs.*] And somehow I knew that. So I didn't. It didn't seem the right thing to do. You just worked. You just worked. You read poets and you worked.

SR: I asked only because sometimes in talking to people they remember a pivotal figure. . . .

MO: No, I truly feel that the pivotal moments for me were reading poems. I can remember the original excitement when I read poems and thought, my goodness, these are not chronological—these do not happen on Wednesday and finish on Thursday. These happen over and over and over. This is the most marvelous trick of time unfolding and refolding and unfolding again. And I want to do this too. That, you know, just seemed to me more exciting and more worth investigating than anything that was going on in the world around me.

SR: Let me ask you one or two more things about nature, and then I'd like to examine the opposite side of that coin as well. You mentioned before that if someone talks about a "nature poet," there is usually that strong strain of Romanticism with a capital *R,* and it's used today in an almost pejorative sense. The term compartmentalizes the work and diminishes its importance. But clearly your poetry doesn't offer pretty images and lush landscapes. Your poems open up a marvelous complexity of feeling and get right down to the matter of our living and our dying. You present us with a clear-eyed vision of the circularity in our living and dying. I wonder if you see nature, as the Japanese poets do, as the large text in which we discover human nature?

MO: Emerson said a nice thing. He said, "Every natural fact is an emblem for some spiritual fact." I feel that what I'm looking for are—if not spiritual answers—at least the right spiritual questions. When I was in Japan, in the Far East, in 1984 . . .

SR: Did you live there?

MO: No. I was there on a USIA trip. I was there for only a week or so— rapidly. [*Laughs.*] One day, I talked with some professors. We had a wonderful talk. We talked for two or three hours, which astonished everyone, because the Japanese are apparently very formal, and this doesn't usually—we forgot to eat! We were just very excited. They felt there was a lot of Eastern feeling in my work, and wanted to know why, whether I was interested in the Eastern religions. And I said I was interested, and I knew some things about it, but I was not a scholar. But I had been reading about Buddhism, I was reading about that meditative way of living. I think sometimes my poems have a sort of Eastern circularity—the sense of seeing something, the epiphany, and making something of it which is news for oneself. Yet the Eastern meditative religions seem to me rather self-enclosed and not socially aware. They don't busy themselves about the social ills of the world at all, as Christianity does, which is very different and very busy and very worldly, compared to the Eastern religions. . . . I do think nature is the text of the meditative process. And it has served me all my life and nurtured me all my life. . . . Well, when you use nature as a text, it tells you something about the nature of yourself in relation to the world. It's one-on-one. It's intimate. There is no place in that scenario for the ills of the world. And in that way, it's entirely satisfactory and it transcends and it's radiant and it does all these wonderful things. It's good work. But it's partial.

SR: If it's clear which subjects you gravitate toward, it's curious to me which subjects are wholly absent from your *New and Selected Poems.* In the hundred odd poems here, there are precious few moments where you focus on the personality of Mary Oliver or your family—the polar opposite from the confessional school. But I'm surprised by the degree of distance you maintain in your writing, even, as you said earlier, to the point of removing the gender from the speaker's perspective. Is there a reason why you've closed off that avenue in the poems? Is it simply a matter of privacy?

MO: There might be a couple of reasons. I feel that knowledge about the writer can be invasive. At the time I was growing up, there was a whole twenty-year period when [literature] was involved with the so-called confessional poets. I was not interested in that. I did not think that specific and personal perspective functioned well for the reader at all.

The women's movement—I did not join that, either. I applaud it, and I guess I may even be part of it. I don't see it working very well in poetry. I see good, very good poets just defeating their own poems with polemic. Not always, but too often.

SR: But I have to say that there is a wonderful freshness in those few poems in the collection that do address some social situation or personal dynamic. "Singapore" is one and then the poem sequence about your father.

MO: "Rain."

SR: "Rain," that's right, which is really wonderful. And it seemed to me they wedded the natural observation at the heart of your writing with a more personal landscape. I didn't know if this meant that you have a whole range of poems of this sort that you simply choose not to publish?

MO: No. When I read Whitman as a youngster, I was learning about myself; I wasn't learning about Whitman. I simply don't value or don't find useful or exhilarating sitting down and reading even the most excellent poems which are primarily giving me information about the poet. It just does not work for me.

SR: But with Whitman, though, you're learning about a Whitman who's maybe not equivalent to the poet himself.

MO: Exactly, exactly!

SR: It's a persona he's created for himself.

MO: Of course, that immense ego is just an "I." Anybody can put on that coat and wear it.

SR: But he could do that in a poetry still rooted in his daily experience— and, as a young reader, you learn about Mary Oliver from that. Isn't there a way that I might read about your uncle and your father, events that are clearly not part of my experience but from which I will discover something new about my own family?

MO: That particular passage, about the suicide, is in there for the rain. If that had not happened on a rainy day, it would not be in that poem. [*Laughs.*]

SR: That's fascinating. Such a different way of seeing it.

MO: Yes! I remember once somebody said, what does this poem mean? Not "Rain" but a different poem. I said it was about commas.

[*Both laugh.*]

SR: I loved the fact that, in the individual sections of "Rain," it was that seeing and your awareness of the rain that linked all the individual moments together. But I thought that the idea of being a member of a family and considering your father's life—that gave the power to the rain. But you're saying, no, it was the rain that you were focusing on.

MO: Yes. It was the rain which made that event a part of that poem.

SR: But what about the way you're viewing your father?

MO: He was in the rain; he was in the mud.

SR: He seemed very small . . .

MO: Oh yes.

SR: . . . like a boy or something.

MO: He couldn't fix it.

SR: Was he, in your mind, somehow tied to the rain? When you see a bit of the human world tied to the natural world, does that redeem it, save it in some way?

MO: Oh no, oh no, no. I don't think so. That poem intends in a way to be circular also; it ends on an upbeat.

SR: Circular? Do you mean . . .

MO: Well, a circularity of the influences of the rain. The things that happen. But I don't know; I wasn't looking for redemption.

SR: For me, it cut both ways. I couldn't feel for sure how the girl was seeing her father there. Because the first time I read it, he seemed lonely and too small, too weak. Then, after I read it over again, I thought that maybe you were just feeling his pain or feeling his helplessness.

MO: Oh, exactly, yes. There should be a feeling of compassion at *his* powerlessness. Also, the speaker was in a new place, realizing that the father could not fix it.

SR: So the rain threaded between all those memories, retrieved them for you in some way.

MO: Well, the rain was immovable. The rain just happened. The rain was an influence. And the rain went right on.

SR: A permanence, as opposed to all the other things we do inside of the rain, too. Let me skip ahead then to look at "Alligator Poem," one of my favorites in the *New* section. I have to ask you: is that based on an actual experience?

MO: Oh, yes, yes. I don't make up these inventions. That was entirely true! . . . I was in Florida, and I was in a place called Loxahatchie. There are a couple of poems—two or three are in *New and Selected*—where the speaker is drinking water from some river or pond. I have always done this. I suppose, with pollution, I should stop. I drank from the Mad River, it's in the

Tecumseh poem. And Blackwater Pond. And Concord River, under the bridge. And when . . .

SR: For what reason?

MO: Well, if you take the water into you, you're part of it. I carry away a little mouthful of the Concord River, as it were. And so I did also take away a little mouthful of the Loxahatchie. It was a hot day. It was fall, actually, not summer. But it's hot down there. And I just knelt—this was swamp water or still water, anyway, not a river—and heard this terrible thrashing and crashing. I was with a friend who lives in Florida, but she was off looking at something else and didn't see what I was doing. I was not doing this privately; I was doing it casually. And this alligator made horrible sounds, and I just got up and luckily tipped myself in the right direction, which was away from it, and it just lumbered right past me.

SR: And he made no aggressive move to . . .

MO: It did not attack.

SR: Once you moved aside, he had no business with you.

MO: Exactly. Good fortune.

SR: But then the found emblem arises in that. There you are in the midst of life, taking in the life waters, and death is just a breath away. . . .

MO: Um hm. So close.

SR: But the poem ends with such a wonderful shift in focus.

MO: It's picking the flowers. That happens, you know, if you have a near accident, you blanch and nearly faint. And then you find yourself safe in the world. Things seem so bright.

SR: But I wondered if you're also showing us that unless we feel how close utter loss is, how transient our worlds really are, that we can't hang on to the flowers, as it were. We can't really experience what's beautiful right around us.

MO: When we think of death, or when we're close to death, is when life is the brightest. That's what gives the brightness.

SR: And in one poem you say simply, "of course / loss is the great lesson."

MO: That's "Poppies."

SR: It concludes with the lines:

> But also I say this: that light
> is an invitation
> to happiness,
> and that happiness,
>
> when it's done right,
> is a kind of holiness,
> palpable and redemptive. . . .

Is that the motive behind your forays into the woods and onto the page?

MO: Absolutely. Bull's-eye, to point to those lines. Yes.

SR: Go on with that thought.

MO: Appreciation is a very valuable thing to give to the world. Yes, that's the kind of happiness I mean. And I can't go on with that because there's no language to talk about it. It's very close to the center of whatever I feel spiritually.

SR: There are certain poets that write poems of praise, but they're almost an endangered species. It's almost as if that happiness necessary to write in praise of life is almost considered a weakness in the art world's very definition of modernity. How can you be truly contemporary if you still feel *that!*

MO: To me it's, it's, it is sufficient to have a life and to have these things to go out and look at and praise. We'd all be better off with fewer things. People should not be hungry, no question about that. But when people are assisted by government or whatever—as they should be—then the first thing people want is too much, if you follow. Any possibility of having spiritually interesting lives is gone. I really do think those two things, material involvement and spiritual curiosity, can't go together.

SR: Although this is hardly a prominent line of investigation in the way most people are educated.

MO: Too much of schooling is to prepare students for the making of money.

SR: Instead of what, then? What might it be?

MO: To prepare them for the next sixty or seventy years, so that at the end of that time they feel like they have lived here, in the world, truly.

SR: "The Swan" tackles this idea directly where is says:

> Of course! the path to heaven
>
> doesn't lie down in flat miles.
> It's in the imagination
> with which you perceive
> this world,
>
> and the gestures
> with which you honor it.
> Oh, what will I do, what will I say, when those
> white wings
> touch the shore?

Do you think in some sense that becomes the measure of our lives: how do we honor what we finally discover in this world?

MO: Absolutely. Absolutely and totally. I do believe it. That's a poem in which every person, every reader can take his own measure and decide his response.

SR: And the response doesn't have to be poetry. I assume you think one can honor to the world in a whole variety of expressions.

MO: Yes, indeed. To do honor to the spirit of the world, to the life force of the world. Not to wreck it! Not to wreck one's life, not to wreck the world.

SR: But to do what? To leave it how?

MO: To leave it healthy.

SR: "In Blackwater Woods," which was written over a decade earlier, you distill a simple, austere philosophy from this two-sided mask of life and immanent loss.

> To live in this world
>
> you must be able
> to do three things:
> to love what is mortal;
> to hold it
>
> against your bones knowing
> your own life depends on it;
> and, when the time comes to let it go,
> to let it go.

Since the new collection is so broad a gathering of your poems, it must provide a good vantage point to stop and look back as well as forward. Do these three necessities still govern your living? Is that the "school" you're still studying in?

MO: Oh yes, oh yes, yes. Yes I am. The end of that poem was almost a given. And the beginning of it was almost a given. I was—I could show you the very trees where I was standing. I came home with the description of the trees in my notebook. And then had to work out the significance, if you will, of what I was saying. The poem pleased me in that it ends, in terms of its language, with almost as much simplicity as four lines could stand.

SR: But now you're perceiving a message that seems clearly larger than the conscious mind can normally entertain.

MO: Well, this is what happens. I mean, there's no general unless there's an instance. I don't doubt for a minute that we cannot have a category until we have three things of a kind. And we don't have three things of a kind until we have one thing of a kind. I've always known that you can't write a book of poems. You write a poem. And you don't even write a poem, you write line by line. So, you know, I've always started with the smallest measure and just kept going. And these poems work in the same way. If I find one instance today, and it leads me back to the center, then tomorrow maybe there's another instance and another one.

SR: Has it become easier or harder, though, not only to love what's mortal, but also to be willing to let it go?

MO: Oh, I think it becomes harder.

SR: Then as a last question I'll return to something you touched on at the very beginning when you described your feelings about how important the arts are, how necessary in our lives. Not just for the one who creates it but for the community as well. When a poem has come through your life, I wonder if you can say what's different, somehow altered, by this act? This might clarify why something as simple as words on paper can be important.

MO: Well, I don't think it's important for me.

SR: No? It's not?

MO: The poem lies there and it waits for the somebody for whom it may be momentous. It needs the right person for *its* set of words, for what it is saying. And it can change lives. Art can change lives. Art now has to have more patience because art used to be used so much in our tribal, our community rituals. This is no longer so. The poet is a superfluous person in terms of society now. So you don't go to the church, you don't go to the ceremonies, you don't go to the songfest for your poems. You read them quietly to yourself in a private way, out of books usually, or you hear a poet speak them. But there may come a time when the poem that is the little handle that opens the great door is found—and everything in one's life, thereafter, is different. . . .

I can't define *important.* For the reader? That's one thing. For myself? Not every poem is important. . . . I throw some away. I don't know how to explain it, but if you don't stay tough about that, if you don't stay interested in the process rather than the product, then you're lost. What I'm interested in, vitally interested in, is the poem I haven't written yet, but maybe will tomorrow or the next day. The poems I have written—some of them of course give me satisfaction—various layers of satisfaction. But it's poetry and language and what it can *do* that has been the salvation of my life. And what I think is at the center of human life—we can speak, we can tell each other momentous things to such a fine degree. It's amazing and it's sustaining. We can listen to each other and learn from each other.

Also, there is an absolute joy in being involved in good work, so that you lose yourself. That whole sense of losing yourself, immersing yourself, or whatever you want to call it, vanishing into the work, is sufficient reward for the labor. . . .

SR: But don't you think you, that observing eye, has been somehow altered by such an act?

MO: I suppose it is. I mean, I do suppose one's work is a mirror image of one's life to some extent. But it's almost as if I didn't write them. I feel only the most mild kind of ownership about them.

SR: And then you're out looking for the next one?

MO: Always.

3
John Montague

—POETRY AND THE COMMON WORK

A Grafted Tongue

(Dumb,
bloodied, the severed
head now chokes to
speak another tongue:—

As in
a long suppressed dream,
some stuttering garb-
led ordeal of my own)

An Irish
child weeps at school
repeating its English.
After each mistake

The master
gouges another mark
on the tally stick
hung about its neck

Like a bell
on a cow, a hobble
on a straying goat.
To slur and stumble

In shame
the altered syllables
of your own name:
to stray sadly home

and find
the turf cured width
of your parents' hearth
growing slowly alien:

In cabin
and field, they still
speak the old tongue.
You may greet no one.

To grow
a second tongue, as
harsh a humiliation
as twice to be born.

Decades later
that child's grandchild's
speech stumbles over lost
syllables of an old order.

—from *Selected Poems*

JOHN MONTAGUE IS ONE of the true elder statesman of Irish poetry. Born in Brooklyn, New York, in 1929, he returned at age four to his family's farm in County Tyrone, Northern Ireland. He believes he was destined to have this double perspective on Ireland, both as an outsider with fresh eyes and as a native spirit. "There'd been no Ulster poet of Catholic background since the loss of the Irish language," comments Montague, and so his early books, like *Poisoned Lands* (1961), did much to pioneer a rebirth in Irish poetry. Among his numerous collections are *Mount Eagle, Collected Poems,* and the recent *Smashing the Piano*—all published in the United States by Wake Forest University Press. His work moves easily between the clarity of the natural world and the more tangled paths of human nature; and his subtlety is such that images of modern life and the mythic realm can appear without dissonance in a single text, each serving to revitalize the other.

Along with Seamus Heaney, Montague is responsible for a good deal of the recent popularity Irish writing has achieved in America. He edited

Macmillan's encompassing *Book of Irish Verse* as well as Scribners' *Bitter Harvest,* an anthology of contemporary Irish poetry. For years as a professor at University College, Cork, he nurtured a younger generation of Irish writers. More recently he was made a distinguished visiting professor at the New York State Writers Institute at the University of Albany and, once again, his roots extend to both sides of the Atlantic. In 1998, Montague became the first Ireland Professor of Poetry, an honor akin to the position of poet laureate in the United States.

Shortly after I began my interview series, a special reading tour brought Montague and a handful of the best Irish poets to Boston. I talked with him—after that event and in a later phone interview—about the difference between the climate for poetry in America and in Ireland.

SR: The American audience for poetry has become a good deal smaller in the last few decades and much more centered in academia. Poets write with a curious sense of isolation—from each other as well as the general reader. Do contemporary Irish poets have a different place among their people?

JM: Yes, it's true, especially in the last twenty-five years. There are several reasons for this. One, Ireland is a small country, it's compact. The circle of poets is smaller. We all know each other, and we're very public figures. Our pictures are in the newspapers, and you'll even see poets on the television screen—quite uncommon in the States. Charles Olson argued a long time ago that the great thing in America and American literature is space. While space and your country's size is an awesome thing . . . truly learned people and those who want to practice an art retreat into a sanctuary, and these sanctuaries are spread out across the country. Today poets tend to be isolated inside the universities as if they were medieval monks in time of plague. Perhaps the plague now is American politics and the culture produced by industrial capitalism since the Second World War.

SR: But does that mean the poets have cut themselves off from the people and the daily existence—what Whitman focused on as the wellspring of poetry?

JM: Yes, but Whitman's America was not so vast, not so impersonal. He actually thought the poets could speak to the people on the streets. But which streets? Today, does that mean the streets of Chicago or Cleveland or Detroit or where?

SR: Are you suggesting that America is so large, so diverse, it is impossible for our poets to really speak to a mass audience?

JM: Well, it seems to be hard. In the 1960s you had a drive toward a poetry that broad. You had people like [Alan] Ginsberg and Gary Snyder. Ginsberg for a time had an almost Whitmanian appeal. But of course his America was a very different place, of Moloch, of industrial capitalism and a people who woke up out of Whitman's dream and retreated into drugs and sex— anything to get away from the horror of Moloch. But I don't necessarily think that isolation today is a bad thing. You've got regional [poetries] in America, and they are attached and in tune with their places.

Now, a second difference with Irish poetry is time. Irish poetry is a long tradition that even the young poets can lean on. And a third difference is purpose, which is to recover the English language for ourselves. We've got a long history which has occurred in a small geographical space. And the larger part of that history, from our point of view, was expressed in the Irish language. Yet the majority of our people from the time of the famine only spoke the English language. It's as if the Irish writer—and I think Joyce is a crucial example—had decided that the only victory to which we can aspire is to take over the English language. [Poetry] becomes a turning the tables, an anti-imperial endeavor—to use the language of the conqueror to secretly conquer him.

SR: That's probably not very easy for an American to understand—that when your language is stolen from you, your culture and your power are eventually surrendered. And how successful do you think Irish writers have been in taking back control?

JM: I think it's quite noticeable if you look for the finest poets writing in English. If you look after my generation, which had [Thomas] Kinsella and Richard Murphy and others, you have good poets in America, people like Galway Kinnell, and Ted Hughes in England. But when you come to Seamus Heaney, Seamus is clearly the best poet of his generation writing in the English language—except perhaps for Derek Mahon, who has a pure lyric voice, and Michael Longley . . . In the next generation, you see a poet like Paul Muldoon who is very gifted. Are there any English poets now who are able to write the way he writes? (He has I believe five books now and he's only about forty.)

I think "the Troubles" . . . provides some impetus for these voices. We're like a people who are living inside a Greek tragedy. There is something terrible which is happening to our family and we all try to speak about it in our various ways.

SR: There are few American poets who could claim that with any authenticity—that they are writing as if they are members of a family and they're speaking to this family's joy or pain. It's not often that I read a poet's work and feel I am confronting my own story on the page, my language, real-life, history.

JM: I think that's the reason we get along so well, as you can see by our public performances. We are writing about something that has taken place within our household, so to speak. We are not to blame, but we are compelled to think about it and bring it to the page. We don't think our poems will quickly change the struggle, but we provide clarity to the situation, to edge toward some solution. Poetry focuses the eyes of the world on the problem but from a surprising point of view.

SR: When you read many Irish writers, you can almost hear the voice of history speaking through the contemporary poet. Do you feel that in American poets as well?

JM: Americans seem almost to want to get away from history. You see that idea in William Carlos Williams for example, *In the American Grain,* the desire to do away with European history, to start again in order to create a new American way of looking at the world. In Ireland, it is almost impossible to do this, even if you wanted to. History is everywhere around you—in the streets, the old churches, in the remains of ancient civilization scattered across farmers' fields, in the very place names where you live.

SR: In the poets you've selected for *Bitter Harvest,* I feel they are not only speaking from the personal but also the communal imagination.

JM: I think they do, but they achieve a kind of communal presence by using the old axiom about being true to themselves. If you take a poet like Nuala Ni Dhomhnaill, who writes in the Irish language, a mixture of Kerry Irish and school Irish—she cannot help but incarnate some of the problems of the Irish because she is writing in the language and she is also a woman. So this brings up the long tradition of Irish women in poetry and the subjugation, not only of Ireland but of our language. All these things she has to tackle. She doesn't mean to—they're just *there,* directly in front of her.

I think of somebody like Paul Muldoon who is from Armagh and is not particularly interested in history—or at least, he's very playful about history. He lives up close to the border and his poems contain that sense of menace. For a lot of us, history isn't something separate. It's all around you and it's in your family and it's in your bones. You can't escape it. . . .

I was born in America . . . then sent back from the U.S., so I had a double experience of both places. I felt my heritage even more intensely perhaps than those who grew up inside its borders. I see it with different eyes and it became part of me. In school, we'd take walking trips through the ruins of Ulster history and through the countryside that was rich with stories. But all this is now disappearing from the landscape with the bulldozers and the rush of modern development. So it's all coming out in a last wave into the poetry.

SR: As if to preserve it by words?

JM: Yes, indeed. The place names have been changed, the roads have been driven through them, the quarries are being torn from their sides, the hills and rivers are being polluted . . . The poets of the south are especially involved on the ecological issues. After years of great poverty, the south of Ireland is turning with great speed into submission to the European Community. In striving toward prosperity, in a sudden and drastic way, our whole landscape is threatened, vandalized. There are very few Irish people who still plow the fields—it's all tractors now. The rise of the factory-farm dramatically effects so small a country. Our lakes and rivers are being polluted with slurry from the large farms.

You see this same change in America—the land no longer being valued for its own sake. The land is no longer a sacred trust or a living presence as in the Native American beliefs. It's merely a commodity, real estate, something used to produce wealth.

SR: In the older Irish poetry, the land is revered as a spirit, a presence. Does that tradition reach the younger poets today?

JM: We say that any good Irish poet would have to have what we call *dinn shenchas* or "place wisdom." If he's going to write, he'd need to know the spirit of a place and all that's gone on there, what gives it meaning. The older people would have the same sort of attitude toward the countryside and the landscape as the Indian probably had here in America—that is, to say, reverence. The mountains and rivers were like deities, and that feeling still flows on.

SR: I think in America we are beginning to see once again a poetry that is rooted in the poet's sense of place and community. But the training of future generations of poets is almost exclusively the province of the university and the network of creative writing programs. Do you see that as healthy for younger poets?

JM: A young poet who goes from college into graduate school writing programs and then maybe into a Ph.D. program and then on to teaching creative writing—now where in all this does he gain his experience? There's a danger in this. You have poets writing for other poets.

SR: Poetry about language, not the world. Doesn't that underline one of the differences between the situation of the poet in your country and mine? In America, poets and artists are hardly the predominant makers of images. Television fills that role. My feeling is that in Ireland, perhaps poets play a larger role.

JM: What you are saying is that you're not "the uncreated conscience of your race," as Joyce put it. It sounds like arrogance, but I think the Irish writer feels he is playing a public part—at least partly as a conscience of his people—even if he doesn't set out to be.

SR: I think many poets desire a more public role. It's evidenced by the poetry/performance hybrids springing up in bars. Look at the number of poets who conduct workshops in elementary schools, nursing homes, prisons. But our function outside of academia is still unclear, at least in the public perception. If I'm at a party, for example, and introduce myself as a poet, the reaction is frequently a strange one. People aren't quite sure what to make of you. They want to know what your real job is.

JM: You know, you shouldn't say you're "a poet." You should say "I try to write poetry." "Poet" is a title other people confer on you. And it's very sweet to overhear, when people refer to you as "the poet." They understand what that job entails: saying the things we all want to hear or feel but often fear we cannot put into words—a sweetening of the atmosphere.

SR: And that adds a certain force to the work when you know you are speaking into that listening, instead of into a vacuum.

JM: And you know you're going to be read by the polity . . . the people and the politicians will read you and the newspapers will quote you. It's changed a great deal in Ireland, even from, let's say, the time of Patrick Kavanagh. We've regained a sense of ourselves . . . There was a time when there was a good deal more censorship of the writer and artist, but that has broken down. And the country is quite proud of its literature once again; we realize how central it is to us. I think its good for the poet to be respected in his or her own community as a craftsman. If you spend all day writing in your studio, people approve of this. It is seen as something that should be done and part of the common work.

Cassandra's Answer

1.

All I can do is curse, complain.
I told you the flames would come
and the small towns blaze. Though

Precious little you did about it!
Obdurate. Roots are obstructions
as well as veins of growth.

How my thick tongue longs
for honey's ease, the warm
full syllables of praise

Instead of this gloomy procession
of casualties, clichés of decease;
deaf mutes' clamouring palms.

To have one subject only,
fatal darkness of prophecy,
gaunt features always veiled.

I have forgotten how I sang
as a young girl, before my voice
changed, and I tolled funerals.

I feel my mouth grow heavy again,
a storm cloud is sailing in;
a street will receive its viaticum

in the fierce release of a bomb.
Goodbye, Main Street, Fintona,
goodbye to the old Carney home.

2.

To step inside a childhood home,
tattered rafters that the dawn
leaks through, brings awareness

Bleaker than any you have known.
Whole albums of Births, Marriages,
roomfuls of tears and loving confidences

Gone as if the air has swallowed them:
stairs which climb towards nothing,
walls hosed down to flaking stone:

you were born inside a skeleton.

—from *Mount Eagle*

4
Charles Simic

—THE TOY OF LANGUAGE

WHAT'S MISSING is the laughter.

I can describe the setting for the interview—a small house in a rural New Hampshire town. The pine slope behind us runs down to a quiet lake. I can transcribe the words of the conversation. I can even offer you a glimpse of the poet's face, his dark brooding eyes. But I can't give you the deep Slavic voice, still heavily accented after so many years in America. I can't show you how his hands would spring to life, shaping the air in front of him or punctuating an idea with a quick gesture. And, most crucial of all, I can't include the laughter that boiled up after so many responses. (Occasionally I make note of it here, but only when its presence alters the meaning of his words.)

Sometimes the laughter is dark, ironic, echoing distant memories or nightmares. But often it is the deep throaty unbridled laugh of a grown-up child, savvy to the ways of the world but still delighted by its quirky beauty, its undiminished sense of possibility.

The poetry of Charles Simic has garnered many of the prestigious awards the literary world bestows: the Edgar Allan Poe Award, the P.E.N. Translation Prize, a Guggenheim Foundation Scholarship, and a MacArthur Foundation Fellowship. The author of over sixty books of poetry and prose, his collection, *The World Doesn't End,* was awarded the 1990 Pulitzer Prize. Recently, Braziller brought out *Charles Simic—Selected Early Poems.* His writing combines the surrealist's flare for surprising imagery with the lyric poet's sense of the immensity in the particular, the power of the small well-crafted moment. His imagination bears witness to the awesome effect our century has had on the life of the individual.

Since I first began reading Charles Simic's poems three decades ago, I have always admired the vivid, startling, humane vision of a man who is capable of wringing so much mystery from the mundane. It's clear to me our native tongue has been greatly enriched because of the daring he brings to its exercise. But I'd never really heard how much laughter was simmering behind the sad, absurd, mesmerizing moments of his poetry. Despite the wear and tear of survival, Mr. Simic is still playing with the world and the toy of language. Reading the poems now, I am able to find a measure of redemption in the sound of that laughter.

SR: The sensibility in your writing is so unique, I find myself thinking of your poetry as Eastern European. But you've been in America since you were a boy.

CS: Right, I was fifteen when I came here. I left Yugoslavia in 1953 and spent a year in Paris and then arrived in New York in 1954.

SR: What made you leave your homeland?

CS: Well, my father was already here. He was in Italy during the war. And his options afterward were to return to Yugoslavia, which was Communist, or come here. My father worked for an American company before he left Yugoslavia. So he went essentially to continue working for the same company in Chicago. And we could not join him for a long time because of the so-called Iron Curtain. In 1948, Tito broke with Stalin and eventually by 1953, because of huge American aid to Yugoslavia, they allowed the family of "dependents" to leave.

You see, in the old days, it was unthinkable for anybody to ask to leave one of "the most admired societies in the world." The "Scientific Socialism"— especially the Yugoslav variety—so much admired by French intellectuals, English intellectuals. So if you showed the desire to emigrate, this would be kind of a sign of deep disturbance, possibly being a traitor. So it was impossible to leave until it became an official policy to permit the families of people who were not war criminals, people who were in the U.S. So that's why we left.

SR: Were you already engaged in writing when you were very young?

CS: No, not in those days. I started when I was in high school. I was in a place called Oak Park, Illinois. There's a very nice high school there. And the last year, when I was a senior, I began—simply because I had a couple of friends who were writing. They surprised me one day—they were writing poetry. So I—just to show them I could do it better, I suppose—I wrote some terrible poems, [*laughing*] really bad, awful things. But that's how it started.

SR: When you were first writing poems, were you already attracted to the surrealist style?

CS: I think [my early poems] could best be described as "garbage!" [*A gale of laughter.*] Not any particular style. I became, fairly quickly, enamored with surrealism because my interest in those days was art, painting. I painted before I wrote poetry. And I knew modern art better than modern literature. . . . I used to go to the local library—a beautiful library in Oak Park or to the Chicago Public Library—and I'd bring home these huge books about Braque, Matisse, histories of modern art, . . . and so I began to know something about the artistic avant-garde through art books . . . because nobody was talking about surrealism widely in those days in the U.S.

SR: But there must have been some click of recognition inside—that this was a "language" your thoughts could work inside.

CS: Well, I think it wasn't just me. That was a period when the sense of the avant-garde was much stronger. The sense of breaking rules, being irreverent, of doing something outrageous. That seemed to me the most interesting tradition in art. You know, I was eighteen, nineteen. . . . I always loved that kind of free use of the imagination. And surrealism is an invitation to make up wonderful figures of speech endlessly. The entire movement, the lives of the individual members—it was all fascinating. Eventually I began to discover in libraries in Chicago—this beautiful library called the Newbury Library which had a fantastic collection of small press magazines of this country, early 1930s through the 1940s, some of the surrealist magazines, all the New Directions books. So it was a kind of educating of oneself, and getting very excited about it.

SR: Surrealism seemed to move in and out of fashion in America. Some poets in the 1960s and 1970s used it as a tool to shatter older conventions and revitalize their approach to language, but much of it seems very artificial today, as if they were merely dressing up in someone else's clothes.

CS: Yes, it's true. It's like anything else, it can just become academic—imagine that? An academic surrealism. Many poets of my generation, American poets, were interested in surrealism and were accused later of being "neosurrealists"—always used pejoratively. The feeling was, "Here is a disgusting, meaninglessness poem that is just an accumulation of images." There were other people in Chicago. There was a guy, Franklin Rosemont, who published a magazine called *Arsenal*. They were sort of dogmatic surrealists who wanted to continue to live like André Breton and to stick to the way surrealism was practiced in France in the 1940s.

But my friends and I had absolutely no interest in this because we were very much influenced by Spanish poets, South American poets, some of the Eastern Europeans—and poets who were themselves influenced by surrealism. And we liked the openness, the notion that you didn't have to be a realist; you didn't have to constantly keep your eyes open, looking at the world, which is the realists' view: "Look! See!" Sometimes when you close your eyes, you can really see the world better. . . . There were some attempts even in the early days when James Wright was bringing surrealist images into his work and Robert Bly—there was a kind of programmatic quality. "There's not enough of the unconscious in American poetry, so let's bring in this dark side of the soul!" But I'm thinking of people of my generation like James Tate or Mark Strand or Bill Knott. We really had nothing like that. We liked poems that depended, however, on striking images, metaphors, and so forth.

SR: But do you think there's a reason that strain of writing, the strange juxtapositions and syntactical leaps, thrives in South America or Eastern Europe? Is it more akin to the artistic spirit of those cultures?

CS: I think it's unusual even there. I think in American literature there is a prejudice toward realism. It's everywhere—in fiction, movies, television. But it's a realism of a very pedestrian kind, the most linear: first this happened, then that happened. And this is a fairly primitive way of telling a story. However in surrealism, you throw everything out of poetry except what really makes poetry distinct—which is metaphor, one metaphor after another, wild flights of imagination. It's a risky business. You really have to say to the world, "This is my poetry. I believe in this. You, reader, are not going to get it right away, but you may eventually." That sort of thing. Yes, it's true there have been more surrealists in Eastern Europe, but it really was never a big success even there. That kind of poetry is always something a small minority is interested in. What most people really favor is some version of the Romantic poem.

SR: Yet a lot of the poetry translated from Eastern Europe—

CS: Yes, in translation, you see this—but they are almost atypical. So this gives us the wrong impression, simply because there is no interest in translating poets who sound like so many of our poets already. Translation brings out all the eccentrics, so someone gets the idea that everyone there is "way out!"

SR: I've been asking poets in this series about the relationship in their work between life experience and language. The connections are so subtle in your poetry, it's impossible to tell if the "I" narrator is describing memory or fantasy.

CS: Sure, because I don't make a big fuss over the line between one and the other. There are poets who feel it is important that they say what truly happened. For me, very often I may have started with something that really happened. But then, if a more interesting fictional twist offers itself, I follow it. I'm perfectly willing to leave my dear old grandfather or the dog I love behind, erased, to go off in some more fascinating direction. It's the logic of the words on the page, the situation as one writes the poem—whatever they offer, suggest, I'll take it.

SR: In the opening poem of *The World Doesn't End,* you say, "My mother was a braid of black smoke." The reader's natural impulse is to take this as an image of your real mother, to match our reality against the experience portrayed in that line.

CS: Well, I *was* thinking of my mother there, yes. I think in those poems, I was thinking of her, but perhaps not in the most literal fashion. The word *mother* is a powerful word. . . . Oh, but I've written poems about my "mother" and "father" that were completely fictional.

SR: But when I read a poem like "Celestial Overseers," with the lines:

> That must be our grandmother there
> In the open coffin. Her hands are chapped
> From scrubbing so much
> The floor we walk on in black shoes.

> The three little steps I took then
> So that I might be lifted up to kiss her,
> And the three equally tiny ones to withdraw . . .

—the detail is wholly convincing. It's hard for me not to read that piece as autobiographical.

CS: Yes, that's true. There are certain things that are purely autobiographical like that. My grandmother died—I believe it was 1948, the grandmother on my mother's side—and this funeral was very tense because my grandfather, who comes from a long line of church people, I mean, high figures in the Eastern Orthodox Church—this grandfather hated the church, despised his father, grandfather—and still the family thought that at the last minute he would allow a priest. I think somebody even brought one to stand outside the door, just in case. And grandfather threw a fit: "Get rid of that bum!" And so, walking up to the open coffin was quite memorable. First of all [*laughs*], anytime you kiss someone in an open coffin—I don't think you forget such things. A memorably tense situation. And everybody is going like this— [*makes a stiff face*]—with everything that is going on in the wings.

SR: I wonder what it is about the act of reading that makes us want to look for autobiography in every aspect of a writer's creation? But when you present us with a crucial detail like those "three little steps," we are almost compelled to conceive of you as a young boy again, to see you dressed for the funeral, your tentative approach to the casket. It's in the moment we feel this about the author's voice that our emotional response in unleashed—instead of just imagining any boy, any soul who must pass through such a moment.

CS: Again, that's because I do want to give the impression, create the sense that the "I"'s story is authentic, the first person is an authentic individual. But that "I" is very often a sort of creation somewhere between what really happened and what was invented during the process of making the poem work.

SR: And that authenticity is determined, not by corresponding to some event that happened out in the world, but some inner truth?

CS: The consistency is in the poem. The fact that the reader has a sense that this "seems right," what a human experience truly is like . . . It's not enough for us, when we're reading a story or poem, to believe in this voice, in this individual, this character. Sometimes we want a sort of certificate to go along with it, that this really occurred. Well, sure it occurred—but not that way! But so what? It doesn't matter!

SR: What about the poems "St. Thomas Aquinas" and "Shelley" from your recent book [*The Book of Gods and Devils*], which seem to describe a young immigrant's experience in first coming to America?

CS: Yes, those are very much autobiographical in a more direct way. I always wanted to live in New York. So I left Chicago and came to New York in 1958 . . . and it suddenly hit me: I don't know anybody! So I had crummy jobs and it was hard to make ends meet. I was very lonely, as those poems convey. I never thought much about that period. It's not a heroic period in my life—or interesting even! But then it became interesting *remembering* it. I saw myself as an absurd naïve character. It wasn't even me anymore. It was funny to think of me—the kind of jobs I had, what I did, my gullibility, my total innocence. And there I was! It was a source of great amusement. And those poems were wonderful to write because I could look at this character and describe him in that space without really feeling anything personal—except compassion. Like compassion for a character in a book. I just kept laughing. . . .

SR: But there was also the sense of something redeeming in that experience. In the cold, impersonal city, you take refuge inside of that book of Shelley's poems:

> How strange it all was . . . The world's raffle
> That dark October night . . .
> The yellowed volume of poetry
> With its Splendors and Glooms
> Which I studied by the light of storefronts:
> Drugstores and barbershops,
> Afraid of my small windowless room
> Cold as a tomb of an infant emperor.

CS: Yes, those were the days of glorious enthusiasms, of momentary epiphanies—like when you discover a new author. There were so many books that seemed like they were going to be the keys to all the mysteries, the secrets of the dead Tibetans or something. You go, "My God! Got to get that book! Before somebody snatches it!" And you run out of there into the night: "Oh my God, this will solve all my problems now!" [*Laughter.*] You know, there's a poem in my book called "The Initiate," which is a description of that kind of mood. I really knew a woman, a black woman called Alma who I met like that. I was also fascinated by the occult, voodoo and so forth. It was really a period of innocence; I was still not a cynic. Later on, you realize: "Oh, I'll never become a monk," or "I will never reach some great wisdom" because I'm lazy. One gets a more level-headed view of oneself.

SR: But certainly you do preserve a part of that innocence. Many of the poems seem to imply that without that perpetual freshness in one's vision, then life is hopeless.

CS: I agree, you have to preserve it. For me, the delightful thing about that period—suddenly remembering it—I didn't think about it previously, so it all came with a surprise. It allowed me to write a certain kind of poem which I can't quite write in the same way now. I mean, there's a kind of quote–unquote mysticism in there, almost a religious kind of longing which was true then. I was a very great reader of Christian mystics, of Buddhism, of the Sufis—all sorts of occult things and so forth. And I had a deep longing for some enormous visionary mystical experience. And slowly that left me.

SR: Entirely?

CS: It's not so much that it left me. I think I "understand" my impulses now. I don't have that innocence, that combination of foolishness and purity of heart and a dopiness of youth—it's a wonderful combination.

SR: Like the Fool in the Tarot deck—the pure beginner, so full of life's exhilaration, who, without realizing it, is about to step off the edge of a cliff.

CS: Precisely!

SR: Bill Knott once said he keeps a notebook of images and lines that strike him which, later on, he mixes together into a poem, kind of a mosaic design with a certain randomness built in to it. Are your poems gatherings of random flashes or the product of individual experiences?

CS: Very often, they are done randomly, the way Bill describes. I think that's where Bill, James Tate, and I are very close. I bring these things from notebooks. Then I find a plot, an experience emerging in there. A lot of times, notebook entries over a period of time all circle some unspoken core. And then it takes a while to open it up and see what you've really been after. I have a belief that things that come out of oneself at a given time are all related in some way. The poet is like a fortune-teller who looks into a cup of coffee, the grounds in the bottom of the cup, and sees images, sees through to what he's after, what these things are about. So you discover your subject, your experience—rather than coming at the poem with these things already worked out.

Not always, of course. I would say, in my poems, they are half and half.

SR: Someone like Bill Stafford performs his "listening" as a daily discipline. Every morning, early, he's going to be there at his desk, waiting to see what's happening—in his mind, his dreams. As if somehow, the act of this continual "tuning in" is his way of grounding himself in this world—and perhaps of grounding his readers inside their experience as well.

CS: Makes sense, makes sense. I've done that in some periods of my life. But I think it really depends on the poet, how individuals work best. There are poets who do everything in their heads before they write anything down. I write regularly, but not quite with the regularity that Stafford has.

SR: What I've always admired in your poems is that, even in the most fantastical scenes, the images would be so delicate and so tangible. Clearly the intention was never simply to dazzle or overwhelm the reader. They made you feel as if you were seeing the real world, but through a dreamer's eyes. The image of your mother as "a braid of smoke" conjures up all sorts of connotations—both the pleasurable (braided hair or the sense of lives intertwined) and the horrific, hinting at the crematoriums, war-torn Europe in flames. The ordinary objects of the world are featured in your poems— a rock, a fork, a table, a pair of shoes—as if the simplest experiences have the potential to erupt in your mind if you can only turn a certain attention to them. How does that sense of the world come up in your life?

CS: I think I'm very interested in the world around us. Imagination is simply a way to clear [your] sight, to restore a certain kind of vividness and intensity to the world around you. The visual presences of these simple things have always meant a great deal to me. It's where I begin. In the spirit of William Carlos Williams's famous line, "No ideas but in things." Everything begins with the rock-bottom reality, which is the reality in front of my nose. The table, the teacup—for me, writing always has to begin with something concrete—and ideas come out of that later. I never trust ideas first. I never begin a poem because I have an idea. But it's always some kind of experience—an experience which is tied to a physical place, some object, some image—they're the ones that make the poem begin to be written.

SR: Yet there are many writers today whose work is based on far less involvement in external experiences. I'm thinking of the whole "language" school of poets who seem to have reduced the realm of the poem from the world to the word, the mindscape of language. Or in the case of Bill Knott— I once heard him remark at a reading that the world could disappear and he could still go on writing, as long as he had his notebook and his room.

Though the tone of your poems has some similarities, I don't think you'd make the same statement.

CS: It's a question of different kinds of temperaments—just the way people experience the world. Sometimes you take a walk in the woods with two or three people, and different people see different things, and somebody sees nothing at all. . . . There are people who live inside their heads and their intellects. It's something one is born with and stuck with. It's not something you make a decision about.

I think of my family—my mother, my brother, and I—and our experience during the war. . . . When you're being bombed and you live in a place where there's not much to eat, one lives in a kind of solitary confinement. You run across the street, buy some bread, run back, looking over your shoulder. Inside your room, there's not much. You keep seeing the same things over and over—the same walls, the same chair. It's a kind of minimalist art. In wartime, there is still a further reduction. Everybody sleeps in the same room. It's cold, so you keep your overcoats on all the time. You've got your little corner, your little nook. That's the only explanation that's occurred to me over the years as a cause for my predisposition, my attention to physical objects and space.

SR: Because your entire world is reduced to these primary experiences, then how must your mind respond? Inside that small corner, you've got to create a whole world.

CS: Right, you've got to make life interesting. Like da Vinci's advice to his students to study the cracks in the ceilings and the walls. That's where the imagination gets engaged. You have to reimagine the object daily in order to make life bearable. As far as being a child—a child plays with these objects. You might have a few banged up toys, but nobody's buying you toys in wartime. So whatever is there . . . There's a cup—I remember, as a little kid, going: [*he makes an engine noise as he moves his teacup across the table*]. Turn it on its side, it becomes a tank. The parents are always saying, "Put that back, leave that alone! I can't stand that noise!" It drives them nuts because the *real* [tanks] are on the streets!

SR: And here you are, bringing the war inside.

CS: You're constantly looking for something to play with, an old crack on the table, in the wood, and you say, "It looks like this or that." . . . So everything becomes transformed in your mind into a toy.

SR: Which is wonderful because I think you play with language as an infinite toy—to see what can happen if you turn it on its side.

CS: Exactly! I never thought of this, but one could say, "Simic, all you've done is to continue to play in that room of your childhood!" [*This too is followed by a storm of laughter.*]

SR: That brings to mind a whole slew of quotations, from Mencius to Picasso, that stress the idea that the child's experience is the core of the artist's, and that as adults we expend a great deal of energy in trying to recapture that vivid, surprisingly fluid sense of the world. Your experience seems to reinforce that view of creation—the child's ability to play merged with the adult's expansive vision. But this makes me wonder about the war's impact on you as a boy. Though you don't write specifically about the conflict, its shadow seems to fall over much of what you've written.

CS: Well, there are only a few instances when I remember being really afraid. I must say—especially toward the end of the war, 1944, when I was seven years old . . . when the Russians liberated Belgrade—let's see, the 20th of October. One of the terrific things about the war, if you're a kid: parental supervision is minimal. They leave you alone, because they're busy. If you were a man, you were busy hiding, keeping from being inducted into the army. If you were a woman, you had to go out there and get some food. They all had their worries, so you were left alone with your buddies—so it was a great life. A life of adventure and of constant lying to your parents. Belgrade was bombed—by the Allies who were bombing the Germans, not bombing us because we were allies, but they kept missing Germans! What can you do? Buildings were hit on my street. There were *wonderful* ruins! Terrific for climbing.

SR: What did they look like?

CS: Just the way you've seen in the movies, maybe just the facade was left standing. Just a big pile of bricks. They were dangerous places because occasionally they would collapse, or people would climb and fall off. And I actually knew kids from my street who fell. I knew one kid who fell while jumping over something and got a concussion or something—but he was never the same afterwards, poor guy. The parents would keep warning us, but we'd go anyway. We played war which, many years later, struck me as being absolutely hilarious in a way. I mean, here the war was going on and we were *playing* war! So despite the horror, and dead people in the street, being so young at the time, I thought, "This is great! Wow!"

SR: To a child's limited experience, anything can seem "normal." So if you grow up with bombs falling, buildings in ruin and death close at hand—you have to create a worldview where all this is, if not acceptable, at least comprehensible. I am tempted to say one might almost expect a poetry such as yours to result, one where jarring absurdities and the commonplace combine effortlessly into a dreamlike reality.

CS: Because that's my experience. As a child, you make things normal. I have much more of a sense of tragic times later on in the [1940s], '49, in the dark years of Communist Yugoslavia when there was really nothing to eat. And feeling then the sense of fear on the part of people around you—because everybody was afraid to complain, couldn't complain. The sadness of people, the anger, the difficult lives people had just to make ends meet. But then I was really older, twelve, thirteen. But before, during the war, my relatives (most are dead now), they told me this because I don't really remember it myself—it was the 9th of May when the war ended in 1945, and I came running in from the street. I was always running in, getting something, running out. And they shouted to me, "Come back! The war has ended!" And I replied, "Now there won't be any more fun." They really cracked up about that.

SR: Let me take a look at the ways this may have entered your poetry. Reading through the bulk of your work, I was struck by how often certain images or situations would reappear from book to book. Your very first collection, for example, has the poem "The Stone," and the stone is an icon in your most recent poems as well. From the outside, it feels as if there is something you're reaching for or struggling to reclaim. A memory of home, perhaps? A vision of the past? Are you aware of that sort of reaching?

CS: First of all, this is true of all poets. If you study the works of almost anybody, you will find certain obsessive things: words, images, subject matter. There are obviously things we respond to more than others. For example, when I wrote those "object" poems, many years ago, I looked around my house in New York City and thought, "I should write about this spoon here because I really like this spoon." We have certain things that are almost like amulets, magic objects, that we return to over and over again. We never quite [convey] the fullness of the experience. Or maybe we do, but to our great surprise, we find that it still generates a great deal of mental and imaginative activity. For me, the stone is an example. I love stones, pebbles beautiful to touch.

SR: But there seem to be broader yearnings that reoccur. "To All Hograisers, My Ancestors" begins, "When I eat pork, it's solemn business. / I am eating my ancestors. / I am eating the land they worked on." Two decades later, you're writing, "My ancestors, meanwhile, are eating cabbage. They keep stirring the pot looking for a pigfoot which isn't there." Losing your childhood homeland, being dislocated—is part of your poetry a desire to recapture or recreate your sense of home and personal history?

CS: It's interesting, you saying that. I don't really talk about it that way, but it's true. My early life seems like a dream because I left [Yugoslavia] and all that disappeared. The people who knew me then, for the most part, have died. I don't know what happened to those kids from that street. . . . I went back there twice but I never found anybody. And so there's an element of unreality about it. Well, this is not just my story but many people's story. I came from a family that had considerable roots there in Belgrade. But people scattered all over the world. So there's little left there.

Now, recently for example, even the country where I was born, Yugoslavia, has been erased. So, with my past, the war and everything, there's no place I can really go back to. The first part of my life is like a book, a novel that I read a long time ago. I can't remember parts of it. A sort of long nineteenth-century novel. [*Again, the comment is punctuated by laughter.*]

SR: Yours is not the sort of writing one generally thinks of as "political poetry." Yet throughout your work I can feel the gravity of politics. In a subtle way, you describe the experience of people whose lives have been shaped by history and the affairs of governments.

CS: A "political poet" is one of those labels that is really vague. No, I don't think of myself as a political poet. On the other hand, I do write a great deal about history. Twentieth-century history is a major subject for me, all the wars, atrocities, the horrors of the century—that has always been important to me for the simple reason that, given the casualties of my neighborhood in Belgrade, I could have easily been a casualty of war. Not to mention, later on, all the wonderful opportunities to be in some war for this country. You can't just ignore Vietnam. I was in the army for two years. And then I was on active reserve for two additional years, from 1963 to 1967. I lived in considerable fear I'd be called back. Lately, in the last couple of years, with my son—the Gulf War, he is of that age. And my brother was in Vietnam. A lot of fear has followed me since I was young.

My first memory in my life is when a German bomb hit across the street. It was 1941, I was three years old. And I flew out of bed, the crib, with the impact and my arm broke. [*Laughing.*] Flying in the air! I was asleep. I remember being on the floor and the room being brightly lit from the fire across the way. It was early in the morning. April 6, 1941. So that subject has always been with me.

SR: That's exactly the sort of connection between life and language I mentioned. You have so many poems with characters that rise up and fly through the air. And the images of flying are often wondrous and haunting, at one time. There must be a strong psychic link to these early memories.

CS: [*Laughing, with great pleasure.*] Yes, I started flying!

SR: I remember the poet Richard Hugo, whose war experiences are central in a good deal of his writing, telling a story about being a bombardier in the American air force. His squadron was assigned to destroy certain bridges in Belgrade. And he said that, years later when he met you, the two of you figured out that a young Charles Simic might have been a boy sitting on that very bridge. And Hugo said, "Had I better aim, Simic wouldn't be here! I'd have erased all this wonderful poetry."

CS: Yes, yes! He bombed me! Twice a week! He was actually very horrified when I told him this. This meeting happened in San Francisco and I had just taken my first trip back to Yugoslavia in 1972. There was a poetry/literary magazine conference. I was living in Santa Rosa so I came down to this hotel where this was happening. I walk over to some tables after lunch—all these people I knew, sitting at this huge table—so I sat next to Hugo. He asks me, "Where've you been?, What're you doing?" So I tell him I was just in Europe, in Yugoslavia. He asks me, "Where in Yugoslavia?" I tell him Belgrade. And he says, "Ah, Belgrade! I know Belgrade well." He begins showing me, drawing it out on the table: "Here's the main post office, the parliament, here's the Hotel Moscow, the bridge over the Danube"—almost like a city map. And I say, "Oh you've visited Belgrade, spent time there?" And he says, "No, I just bombed it twice a week!" And so I say, "Jesus Christ, Hugo, I was down there! You son-of-a-bitch, you bombed me!"

And he was really mortified. He had never been back there or met anybody who was on the ground. And he explained to me why they were such terrible marksmen. They used to fly from Southern Italy to Romania—there used to be oil fields in Romania; there still are. These were the last oil reserves that the Nazis had for their tanks, and they were heavily protected. They would lose at least one plane each trip from the flak, really scary stuff. They were supposed to bomb Belgrade on the way back. They'd unload all the bombs as quickly as they could so they could get back to the service club in Italy and get blasted.

SR: You couldn't make a better argument for a contemporary poetry that needs to jar the readers imagination. Because you have warm, jolly, humane individuals like Hugo who find themselves in a situation where they must routinely behave in an inhumane manner. How do you contain all this inside one consciousness without the imagination doing leaps and somersaults?

CS: Yes, and you know Hugo was a very sensitive man, a good man. And he was astonished when I told him we Yugoslavs never blamed the Allies for all this destruction. We sort of felt, these were the fortunes of war—they're trying their best to get the Germans. I'm sure the children—the orphans of the families wiped out by the careless American bombs dropped on a slum— had a different view. They must have been pissed off!

SR: Hugo said if you were sitting on the target bridge, that was probably the safest place to be.

CS: Yes, that's what I told him: the building that was the Gestapo headquarters still stands. The bridges still stand. And the city was not protected very much because, all in all, there were not that many Germans there. There's a big dispute, historically, about why the hell they were even bombing the city. But they did hit mostly slums. In any situation, the poor always get it, no matter what.

SR: It's chilling to think of your story in light of the Gulf War with Iran, and how proud we were of our "precision bombing" and "smart weapons"— only to learn how much that safe, sanitized language masks the horror of war. In fact, as I read your most recent collections, I kept detecting an undercur- rent of criticism, almost a warning about the crossroads we've reached in our history. It's as if the consciousness of the individual and that of our culture have evolved to a point where they are in a dramatic conflict. One of the prose poems from *The World Doesn't End* says, "'Doubt nothing, believe every- thing,' was my friend's idea of metaphysics, although his brother ran away with his wife. He still brought her a rose every day, sat in the empty house for the next twenty years talking to her about the weather."

This character sits in his "empty house with every one of its windows lit" conversing with what's already been lost, while outside the "dark trees [are] multiplying all around it." He seems to me to be an icon for the lost soul of our technological paradise. Has the modern mind swallowed so many thirty- second commercials and prepackaged philosophies, that we have forgotten who we are or what we've surrendered?

CS: You know, I always find it difficult to blame everything on the "modern mind." Sure the modern mind is as you've described it. We have our superstitions, television, and other kinds of nonsense which we believe in. . . . But I have a sneaking suspicion that human beings have really not changed that much over the centuries. "The Modern World" and "modernity," for most human beings, are just another set of superstitions. That's a wonderful thing and a horrible thing about them. It's wonderful in the way they're so sturdy, and it's horrible because they don't learn any lessons from history. They still love violence; they still like to hurt each other. . . . It's essentially what they did hundreds of years ago. I have a friend who constantly talks about "our age" and how full of dopiness it is, prejudice and foolishness, and how we've lost our way. And I don't disagree with this. But I must say that when I read books on, let's say nineteenth-century England, 1850s, 1860s, I'm terrified. That world seems to me equally nasty, narrow-minded, awful, and maybe more so. So I never draw this line—"the modern."'

SR: I know you don't think of your writing as playing a role in some social or cultural development, but do you feel a conscious desire in your poems to sound an alarm so we might be awakened to the dissonance in our lives? So that the poet's language might serve as an antidote to the forces that have lulled us to sleep? One of the prose poems contains the lines: "You apes with heads of Socrates, false priests' altar boys, retired professors of evil! I imagine cities so I can get lost in them. I meet other dogs with souls when I'm not lighting firecrackers in heads that are about to doze off. Blood-and-guts firecrackers. In the dark to see. . . ."

CS: Yes, I think a poem should wake the reader. But I don't think I have a message, that I have a set of beliefs and ideas that I've set out to convey. I think that what happens is that, certain poems, because of the logic of their individual situations, take me in a certain direction. But I don't have a sort of menu of ideas which I'm trying to sell. I do believe that a poem needs to remind the reader of his or her own humanity, of what they are, of what they're capable of. Awaken them, in a sense, to the fact that there's a world in front of their eyes, that they have a body, they're going to die, the sky is beautiful, it's fun to be in a grassy field when the sun is shining—those kinds of things. But I never think of advancing some philosophy.

SR: Perhaps that's the proper response to a contemporary poem: we, the readers, create the philosophy, map the ideas as we travel on the path the poem has opened. The prose poem I quoted earlier contains the lines: "My life was a beautiful mystery on the verge of understanding, always on the verge! Think of it!" And of course we're compelled to think of it, to examine whether we too approach that verge.

CS: That's, I think, the distinction. What poets do is to create. They have a nose for where meanings live. *Meanings,* plural. I want the reader to do this—because I myself am not so sure of all the possibilities. I'm saying, "This is interesting—look over here."

SR: I think that's the area where your strongest poems occur, where some simple instance of our mundane experience suddenly verges on the mysterious. A simple object is enough to carry us over. In the poem, "With Eyes Veiled," there's that marvelous image of "A dusty storefront . . . full of religious paraphernalia / Made by the blind"—and already we're hooked, we're drawing close wanting something to be revealed. But you only present the object, with just that last crucial detail to propel our imaginations. "The blue and gold Madonna in the window / Smiles with her secret knowledge. / Exotic rings on her fat fingers. / A black stain where her child used to be."

CS: Well, that aspect of contemporary society *has* changed, unfortunately. The objects our society produces are not as good or interesting as we used to have. It's a desperate search just to find an object actually manufactured in this country.

SR: And most have little "feeling" about them whatsoever.

CS: Even a souvenir from Strawberry Banke [a simulated American Colonial-era village]—made in Taiwan. Shaker furniture from Korea.

SR: And worse, we've accepted this faux reality. Like Busch Gardens in Florida—why go to the trouble of traveling to Europe when you can visit make-believe Europe right at home? So we can eat the "foreign" foods and take home the international souvenirs, and lose ourselves quite comfortably in an endless series of falsifications. Am I off the mark in saying a good deal of your recent poetry is a response to this process of alienation, dehumanization? The child being carried like a ventriloquist's dummy in "A Bit of Mummery"; the "child's Sunday suit / Pinned to a tailor's dummy," whose pins we will feel on our own backs—is this pain something that operates inside your work, your resistance to the loss of an authentic individuality?

CS: Well, I think it's not so much in my life, I think it's the human predicament. I see these things around me. You mention these two poems and the one about the Madonna. I had always liked scenes which have an intrinsic mystery—where I look and say, "It's almost as if this were staged just for me today." I'm looking at the seashore, nobody around, and see (let's say) at the edge of the surf there's an old-fashioned tripod camera, a black box. That's an image from Thomas Mann's *Death in Venice,* which I've been reading lately. Things like that—those pins, that dummy, that suit—they haunt me because I have a feeling that there's a larger meaning that eludes me. So I grope, I attempt a reading of the situation—but there's always the feeling that no matter how much I read it, it retains its mystery. I can only go so far.

This is my religious life, in a sense. My religious life consists of such icons that I have not been able to solve. I come back to them and say, "How strange! What is this? In this unlikely neighborhood of no stores, no shops, there is this scene—just for me. How is it that I can't get this out of my head, when so many other things that were much more spectacular, I have forgotten?"

SR: I think we all know such moments that feel like they were a lesson, a gift presented to us if only we are wise enough, awake enough to take it in. That is the power of the common language—the tools for this opening are all right there. It made me think of your poem "Le Beau Monde," where some dishwasher climbs a soapbox in the park and begins lecturing, not about politics, but Marcel Proust.

CS: That happens to be a true story.

SR: Really? Proust?

CS: It was so lunatic! It took me years to write that poem. It really occurred exactly as I described it. I knew a little about Proust at the time, maybe I'd read one of the books. Proust is the height of French refinement, decadence, an upper-class Frenchman, a difficult writer who hardly anybody reads. To be spoken of from a soapbox in New York City, what a wonderful thing!

SR: I was sure that was one of your invented moments.

CS: No! You cannot invent things like that!

SR: But the poem concludes,

> Everybody perked up, even the winos.
> The tough guys stopped flexing their muscles.
> It was like being in church
> When the High Mass was said in Latin.
>
> Nobody had a clue, but it made you feel good.

And the crowd is slow to disperse, to relinquish even this odd whiff of mysteriousness. It made me wonder if you had a faith that, despite the marginalized state of poetry in America today, when language conveys even a whiff of such power, people can still be drawn in, awakened?

CS: Sure! That's a good point. It's not even that there was a truth to his words. The crowds in these kinds of places—if somebody got up and made some statement about politics or this or that, people would boo and whistle and tell him, "Beat it, Stupid!" It was a very vocal audience. If it was something very boring, they'd yell, "Shut up! Get lost!" It's the strangeness of the guy's appearance, the subject he addressed—which nobody had a clue about!—people had to watch that and say, amazed, "What!?" It's true, the poet is, in a way, sort of like that guy up on that box. Of course a poem is probably more accessible than this man's mumbling talk. He was somebody who probably didn't get tenure from some college and now haunts the neighborhood. The poet is like that—someone who risks that response. People will say: "What the hell? What's going on here?" And then, kind of reluctantly, sometimes people will—this happens to me—after poetry readings, they'd say: "I understood everything! "—as if it can't be poetry if *they* understood. . . . They see someone who seems to be speaking a foreign language—but who seems dedicated, passionately involved. And then—lo and behold!—after a while, it begins to make sense. Then they're really confused!

SR: If you listen to the continual debate over funding for the National Endowment for the Arts, it's clear that broad sections of our society hardly regard poetry and art as essential to our society's survival. When you're alone at your desk, scratching away on your poems, do you feel this work makes a vital contribution to what goes on in the world?

CS: I think so. I think poets have always been reliable historical witnesses. There's a way in which they take the pulse of the age better than anybody else. I've said this before: future historians, if they want to know the truth of our age, will find it more faithfully rendered in the work of many poets or novelists than in the pages of daily newspapers. . . . Poetry has to be close to daily reality. It's always been about daily reality and individual human beings. Poetry is the place where individuality, an individual's experience is defended, protected. That's why it survives.

5
Seamus Heaney

—THE WORDS WORTH SAYING

THERE ARE FEW POETS OF THIS CENTURY who have received as much critical acclaim and public scrutiny as Ireland's Seamus Heaney. In reviewing his collection *Seeing Things*, the London Times critic compared its arrival with the publication of "Keats's *Odes* and Milton's 1645 collection." Mr. Heaney bristled visibly at the mention of this—not simply because of his inherent modesty; as a professor of literature, he regards the past masters too highly to count himself comfortably in their company. Ironically, the great expectations his work has generated also serve to appropriate some measure of his freedom—something too hard-won and cherished to be easily surrendered.

From his earliest books, he was hailed with the accolade "the new Yeats," an honor that carried with it an enormous burden. A native of County Derry, he felt pressure to write more about "the Troubles" of Northern Ireland. He was virtually accused of abandonment when, seeking the solitude to further his work, he moved his family south to the Irish Republic. Eventually he began to spend a portion of each year teaching at Harvard University, where he is now the Ralph Waldo Emerson Poet in Residence. He is considered today, quite simply, one of the finest writers in the English language. And he has used his prominence to introduce American and European audiences to a whole host of new Irish talents.

Aside from the masterful craftsmanship and utter dignity of his verse, what I find most remarkable about Seamus Heaney is the way, through all the pressures, he has determinedly steered his own intuitive course, creating a body of work that is scholarly enough to include translations from the ancient Irish, Latin, and Greek, and personal enough to offer us lyrics of astonishing beauty about family, friends, the battles of conscience, and the landscape of his homeland.

Many poets in America and around the globe expressed an almost proprietary satisfaction when, in 1995, Seamus Heaney was awarded the Nobel Prize in Literature—as if the selection of this assiduous craftsman, this maker of enduring imagery and veritable music, conferred a certain dignity on the entire guild. *Opened Ground, Selected Poems 1966–1996* brought together the full range of the poet's achievement. His recent translation of *Beowulf* became a bestseller on both sides of the Atlantic, an astonishing achievement, as any classics professor can attest, and one due as much to the regard readers have for Heaney as to the visceral quality he articulates in the text. In his homeland, his work and his spirit are honored as enthusiastically in the public house as in the academic hall. Having passed through one of his verses, the reader is able to feel a bit more human, to sense the resonance in the very word. It is not surprising readers in so many countries think of the poet as "one of us."

SR: Since you spend a portion of each year teaching in America and a part in Ireland, I wondered how you make the transition between the two cultures. From my visits to Ireland, I found the shock of the transition quite dramatic—the difference in landscape, the sense of time, the way people use the daily language. I can't imagine a writer working from two different mind-sets.

SH: Not of two minds—two places. I mean, everybody in the English-speaking world is familiar with America because of the . . . international culture exports everything from Hollywood to Coca-Cola to jazz. It's not a shock. Americans go to other places to get away from all that. . . .

SR: But isn't that jarring to you, as if you have to retune your mind, your inner voice, as you move between the two?

SH: No, no. I don't retune. It would be very disabling if I did. . . . I teach at Harvard for one term a year. I've been here for ten years, so there has been a natural acclimatization to that rhythm. . . . I go home for eight months of the year, so I still think of myself as being at home in Ireland—even though I feel at home here, you know. It's kind of an amphibious life, I guess. And maybe that need to displace oneself from complete at-home-ness anywhere is partly why I do it.

SR: With teaching, lecturing, and international readings, yours is a very public literary life. Does all that help or hinder the writing of the poems?

SH: Well, I think your social self and your writing self form a very puzzling relationship. I mean, what was the relationship between the Shakespeare you met in the tavern and the Shakespeare who wrote? This is the real problem— for a poet especially—to find access to that which is not your usual self, to find access to that which is not codified, to admit up through the organized and efficiency levels, the more free-ranging and sportive impulses. . . .

I have had the belief, just for my own purposes, that the . . . busy life puts the other part on its mettle. . . . I don't know what is the correct proportion between will and waiting in lyric poetry. There is evidence that if you are a Yeats, the will to keep it moving is very important. There's evidence that if you are not a Yeats, the will may just keep cranking out material. Every act of poetry involves some kind of strategic engagement between the passive and the active parts. I do think the older you get, the more the will is important, and the more the capacity to keep going gets developed. But no matter how experienced you are with your own ways and means, there has to be the initial energy. There has to be something, to put it simply, waited for, something that comes and starts the process.

If I were teaching full time all year at the pace I go on during these four months, I would be very anxious. But then you look at a writer like Philip Larkin, who worked full time in a library, and okay—there isn't a voluminous production, but there is a kind of perfected thing, you know. . . . It's so much a matter of temperament. There are no particular rules except not to fake it, and not to think that somebody else's way will necessarily work for you. The constant problem, the constant question, is the relationship between the conscious and unconscious aspects, and the relationship between intention and capacity. If you see too much intention in another person's work, you resist it. [*Laughs.*] If you see too little, if it's not been brought far enough, you regret it. I don't think you ever learn much about it. I think every writer feels they're starting again in innocent conditions.

SR: When I interviewed Bei Dao, the Chinese poet in exile, he talked about a new internationalism in poetry, due to the number of expatriate writers working inside other cultures, the ease of global communications, and so on. Because you travel a good deal, I wondered if you saw that influence within your writing?

SH: I think you're right about this internationalism; in a way it's getting back to Renaissance conditions. In Renaissance Europe, there was something like an international poetry, wasn't there? I mean, there were the classical allusions. There was the Christian mythology. There was a classical mythology. There was a sense of Dante and Latin and so on in the background. So if you get High Renaissance poetry, whether it's English, Spanish, Italian, there are some commonalties. Milton, for example, goes and spends awhile in Italy. He's at home with the humanists there. So what's happening now is not so extraordinary. Poetry has always had an inclination to know it's way around the world and to go its way. And what we have today is a great deal of translation and a new sense of access. And in these conditions some poets have traveled particularly well. I'm thinking of somebody like Zbigniew Herbert in Poland. Or Constantine Cavafy in Greece, who is among the older, so to speak, dead poets society. And I suppose there always has been open access to French poets. A sense of Baudelaire, a sense of Rimbaud, Mallarmé. And of course Rilke and Pasternak. Certainly within the Euro-American nexus, the cultures have become pervious to each other. But that doesn't mean that poetry is international in its origins. Poetry is a local product. It depends upon its first language, its first acoustic, and the delicacies and secrecies and intonations and subtleties of the language. Even though Miroslav Holub translated into English undoubtedly travels well, and even though Czeslaw Milosz seems to travel with full orchestral force, we are still just overhearing them. The international thing doesn't mean that poetry has absconded from being a domestic activity that belongs in its first language. There is a deceptive sense of familiarity because of all the conference-hopping that goes on. But that's more like networking than poetry working.

SR: I'd like to talk a bit about the acoustic qualities within your verse. I think there are few poets writing in English today who have as pronounced a musical charge to their poetry as you do. Clearly the ear is as important as the eye in reading your poems.

SH: I would have to say this: verse is a physical phenomenon. The sound of poetry seems to be preeminent. I mean, if it doesn't have a melody or a rhythm or a meter—some kind of physical emanation—it just becomes a set of semantic signals on the page. It just doesn't hold, so to speak, as verse.

Verse is justified differently from prose. Prose is technically justified by a printer. . . . Each printer can justify a piece of prose in a different way, and the rhythm won't be affected. Whereas verse is justified by the line ending of each line; it has to be printed like that every time. That is why the medium of verse means something. The word *versus* actually means "the turning." So verse means the turn at the end of the line, and the turn *into* the next line. And therefore, whether it's traditional verse in couplets or tetrameters . . . or [more open] forms of free verse, that turn is still a physical torsion. And I can't imagine any poet not feeling it within the body.

And that inner sensation is a slightly different thing from the actual voicing. I can only say that my sense of poetry is based, as most people's is, on reading the traditional canon. When I read Shakespeare or Marlowe or Hopkins or Keats or Eliot or Yeats, the extra voltage in the language, the intensity, the self-consciousness of the language is what I associate with its "poetriness." Even if you pretend, like William Carlos Williams, that it's "speech," there's still the turn in the line, you know. It's not an unbroken "So much depends upon a red wheelbarrow. . . ." It's "So much *depends* / . . . ," and once again, the deliberate articulation makes the language self-conscious. It may not be a rich diction, but it's still a matter of overlanguaging the language. I mean, poetry is born out of the superfluity of language's own resources and energy. It's a kind of overdoing it. Enough is not enough when it comes to poetry. . . . This extraness may be subtle and reticent. Or it may be scandalous and overdone. But it is extra. . . . In my own case, the early poetry is much in love with the richness of language itself, and at the start I consciously sought for physical density. But I don't do that so much now. I'm sort of inclined to play it down a bit.

SR: Reading even the new poems aloud gives you the sense of almost chewing on the rich syllables. "Hazel stealth. A trickle in the culvert. / Athletic sea-light on the doorstep slab, / On the sea itself, on silent roofs and gables." The music of each line is an ideal accompaniment to the images the words conjure.

SH: But this isn't peculiar to me. This belongs to the language. I think everybody, whether or not they're conscious of it, responds to these things, you know. I once taught in a teacher training college. And I used to ask my students about a nursery rhyme like

> Ding dong bell,
> pussy's in the well.
> Who put her in?
> Little Tommy Thin.
> Who pulled her out?
> Little Tommy Stout.

Is there not something meaningful in the very vowel sounds here: *thin*—
"little Tommy *thin* put her *in?*" Is there not a kind of Cassius-like lean and
hungry feeling? Isn't it almost a moral judgment? This is overstating it, but
we do have certain associations with certain sounds. And what a poet is doing
is unconsciously working with that.

I am very devoted to T. S. Eliot's notion of the "auditory imagination."
. . . Eliot talks about the feeling for syllable and rhythm reaching below the
conscious levels. Uniting the most ancient and most civilized mentality. I
feel that about the word "culvert." It's got a kind of *dark hole under the ground*
within it. And stored in the system, in the big archive of every ear, there is
a memory of hearing a very thin trickle of water in a big, echoey underplace.
As Keats says, "It strikes you as a remembrance." The collusion between the
verbal thing and the human store in the ear, I mean, that's the mysterious
nub of the matter.

SR: Today, though, a much plainer diction seems to be the fashion. And it
seems to matter less whether you confront the poem aloud at a reading or
silent on the page.

SH: Well, Robert Frost is a plain poet, yet there is a superfluity there too.
You take one of my favorite Frost lines, the first line of "Home Burial," which
is a set of monosyllables. "He saw her from the top of the stairs before she
saw him." Plain as they may be, it does have a kind of electricity. Immediately
there is a sense of a hunt and of entrapment, one person being furtively in
pursuit of the other. I think the point is that in poetry, one way or another,
the language has to be working. There's no point in it's being there just for
richness of effect, you know. Or plainness of effect, for that matter. You have
to be going on about something, actively after something.

SR: You make me think of all the ways you parallel intellectual and even
spiritual work with that of physical labor. The image of digging, for example,
of using language as a tool, reappears in the new poems. It begins with your
first book, *Death of a Naturalist*, where your father is at work with a shovel,
your grandfather with the turf cutting implements, and it runs through most
of your collections—the thatcher's knives, the plow, and now the pitchfork

poem in *Seeing Things*. In "The Pitchfork," you lavish praise on the physical object, but seem to be digging at a deeper purpose, at the way a man makes a life from his labor.

SH: I've used the digging metaphor once in my life and it has followed me ever since. The pitchfork one was done for sheer pleasure, written when I was back at home a few years ago, in the house where I grew up. It was about the sensation of holding the fork again. But it's also about changing, that poem. . . . I hoped the poem would carry beyond the pitchfork as a thing in itself. At the end, it says that the pitchfork wants to go to another side where perfection isn't in the perfect *toolness* of the thing, but in the way it can go beyond efficiency into a kind of opulent weightless elsewhere. Where it's not weaponly or forceful, but where it is generous, where it's the opening hand rather than the shut hand. One thing I've been harping on over the last few years . . . is this notion of the poem as a piece of work, taking "work" in its definition as "moving something through a distance." And the pitchfork has to move across a middle ground, become a little bit of a something else, you know.

SR: It seems to me you make the association between the tools—"The thing used well"—and your father. And I couldn't help but feel this is emblematic of the spirit you attempt to shape inside your poems.

SH: Well, yes. But that is your own observation, and I am pleased to hear you make it. There is no conscious rubric in my mind saying, "this is a tool image." Those things come up habitually and, I suppose, temperamentally, rather than deliberately. They aren't pulled out of the store. And, of course, I agree: the sense of language effecting its purposes efficiently, without any kind of swank but with a kind of artisan's unself-conscious assuredness— that would certainly be an ideal I have.

SR: In rereading *Seeing Things*, I was astonished by the wholeness of the material, from the section of individual poems to the forty-eight–poem sequence called "Squarings." It seemed to me that each piece serves to amplify the vision of the others.

SH: Well, I'm glad you felt that. There is a lot of interweaving. . . . I had a year to myself when I was doing those things, and I just let them swim around. . . . I gave myself over to impulse, but there was this set of, I suppose, metaphorical predispositions which were habitual with me when the work was being done—images of "the light," of "crossings," little boats, and so on. It was the first time I had ever surrendered so freely to a whimsicality, almost, of invention. And that had to do with the arbitrariness of the twelve-line form. I wrote the first one in 1988, at the end of August. I was in the National Library in Dublin. For six weeks I had been battened down, working with my nose to the grindstone. And then the weight lifted, I had a sense of coming through, and I wrote this poem which is the first one in the sequence. I don't know where it came from. But it arrived with a terrific sense of surety and it was a different idiom for me. . . . So I thought, "I'll do another. I'll make it a diptych." And after that, one thing led to another. And then the word "squarings" came up in one of them and I got the idea of twelve poems of twelve lines. But these things always involve discovery, energy, a delight factor, a surprise factor. And then the will can work and the things that have been waiting to get said, get said.

SR: Did you sense something bigger in the task when you began to put them together? There are two large formulations you appear to be working on: One is the building of a house, the way you move back to the cottage in "Glanmore Revisited." The "Squarings" sequence also begins with the images of building, and you even talk about the sort of house your father would have made. The second task seems to be some sort of reconciliation with the loss of your father. It felt to me as if you were building a place for his memory and from which you could go on with your life.

SH: That's very well said, I think. There is indeed a very important house underneath the poems—it may not be specifically a theme in them, but it's very important as a resource out of which they came—a particular house, where we lived for four years in the early '70s in County Wicklow. . . . I was finally able to buy it. It's outside Dublin. It's kind of an "extra," a house in the country. It's in effect a studio, you know. It's really the place of writing for me. My life changed and was invested in this house in the early '70s, and I feel completely enabled by having got back to it. It's a still point which withdraws me from the amphibiousness, you know, between the two places. It's a lay by, but it's also a center. So you're quite right: a lot of the poems were written there. And I feel that's the Archimedean point, the place from which the world can be moved. That sounds very grandiloquent and boastful. It's just that it feels like the right place, the *locus amoenus.*

SR: In the "Glanmore" poems, you reluctantly let your wife put a skylight in the cottage. And all through the "Squarings," you are breaking down physical barriers and constructing openings to the light. It's like a new receptivity to a new sort of experience, perhaps one of enhanced wonder, mystery.

SH: You're right. I mean, that's an ideal reading. And then there's the image of roofs coming off and light coming in. And there is one of my favorite poems in the sequence, the one of the boat in the sky, the apparition, which is described in the annals.

But this sky-place is a kind of mind-place. There's a poem about a harbor that says, "Sky and ocean known as antecedents of each other." So that kind of grammatical sense, of having an antecedent, is at work in the background. I think of the poems as having antecedents, a kind of spirit-life. The second half of the book is more volatile and fluent, I think, than the first half. The first ones are more like the traditionally articulated poems that are in the other books.

SR: Did you get the sense by the end of the series that you had carved out a new room, a place for yourself to grow?

SH: Yes, indeed. I had a notion of printing them as a book, just the forty-eight of them, a thing on their own. But then I had these other ones that I wanted to print anyway.

SR: Perhaps this is merely the complexity of the unconscious, but I was struck by the foreshadowing hinted at in the preamble poems—"The Golden Bough," your translation from book six of the *Aeneid,* and then "The Journey Back" where you meet Philip Larkin's ghost spouting Dante. Almost all the major symbols and themes are present there, sort of a road map through the forty-eight–poem sequence.

SH: A lot of them are, yeah.

SR: As if the "Squarings" poems are what would naturally spring from such ground.

SH: That's right. You know, there's the Larkin and crossing over. And there's the crossing in the boat in "Seeing Things."

SR: And the skylight . . .

SH: And the skylight, and then the crediting marvels in "Fosterling." Yeah, one would have to say they are arranged in that way. But once again, to go back to the caveat I was making earlier on—before the book was in existence, I didn't know things were going to work out like that. I mean, they [the twelve-line poems] tended to give themselves up as one-offs, to grow out of a bed of preoccupations, okay? There are two poems in the beginning of the book, for example, "The Pitchfork" and "The Ash Plant." They were both written during the summer when my father was, I knew, dying. I had not yet translated "The Golden Bough," but I called the ash plant—which was so much a characteristic part of my father's life—his silver bough. And since I always had a desire to translate something from book six, I eventually did the Vergil when I was invited to contribute to an Irish issue of the magazine *Translation*. I already had the first three cantos of the *Divine Comedy* done. So, as you say, the connections began to multiply.

SR: To me, this is where your poetry creates a crucial awakening for readers. You open a place where we are able to experience the material world and, at the same time, question the nature of that experience. In one of the "Squarings" poems [number xxii], you begin,

> Where does the spirit live? Inside or outside
> Things remembered, made things, things unmade?
> What came first, the seabird's cry or the soul
>
> Imagined in the dawn cold when it cried?
> Where does it roost at last? . . .

SH: Oh, yeah, the Yeats one? This is a kind of hermetic event. It's a set of questions I wrote for Yeats's shade as the fiftieth anniversary of his death approached. In his autobiography somewhere Yeats talks about going out on a boat with a fisherman to hear the bird cries at dawn because he was writing his play, *The Shadowy Waters,* and wanted to know about the bird cries. And then in *The Shadowy Waters,* the spirits of the dead perch upon the masts of the ship as seabirds. Then too there is the wonderful poem by Yeats called "The Cold Heaven," where he conveys a sense of the world suddenly opening above his head—he says the poem is about the experience of seeing the sky in winter. And there is still another image from Yeats's *Tower,* of a bird nesting on sticks. It's a kind of dirty, old, wet refuge at the top of the stairs, something I actually saw in the tower fifty years after Yeats lived there. There is a whole set of these images. And fundamentally the poem is asking, "What's the use of something formal that cannot be assailed for reassurance?" I think one of the justifications for established form, whether it's poetical or sculptural, is that we can rebel against it; but we still want it to be there. This particular Yeats poem is linked to another one about being in the Roman Forum at night and seeing the marble forms, and then the person says, "down with those stone-cut faces, down with the"—I've forgotten what it says—"the autocracy of pure form. We attend again the return of pure water and the prayer wheel." That section is about Yeats too. Yeats, for all the immense physicality and finish and materiality of his verses, Yeats credits the immaterial also.

SR: I feel the same tension of forces in your work as well. Again and again it seems to result in an uncovering of the marvelous amid the mundane. There was one poem about St. Brigid's Day where, by custom, the people step through a hoop, a straw rope, in order to enter the new life. It seemed as if this was a perfect description of what poets offer to society. We take a nothing, the stuff of common language, and make it into a something. And the people as a whole can then make use of this insubstantial something. We can step into its ring, and come through into a life somehow renewed.

SH: Aye, aye. I agree there's a sense of refreshment; . . . that would be my sense of it, a sense of the world "glamorized" by language. . . . The first meaning of *glamour* is "to be snatched into the world of the fairies." And returned. So if somebody has glamour on them, they have that radiance. As in the *Odyssey* when Odysseus comes from the bath, sometimes he's shining with an extra light; or when Athena appears in the figure of a young warrior or something, there's a sheen. . . . So if somebody has glamour on them, they have that radiance . . . And I guess [Czeslaw] Milosz is getting at this when he talks somewhere about the idea that "to be is to be perceived," you know, the old Latin, *esse est percipi.* So, in a sense, the being of the world, the fullness of it, is realized and emphasized and confirmed by being seen in language.

SR: I know it is a danger to equate Seamus with the speaker in the poems, but it feels as if this book navigates you through a spiritual crisis. It's as if, in losing your mother and father, you were compelled to question your whole belief-system and to redefine your own spiritual place.

SH: I agree. I mean, there is that is the sense of the roof coming off. This is a book by somebody who has been at two deathbeds, and who remains both unchanged and changed completely by that. Because it's at once immensely mysterious and mercilessly ordinary. Now there is life, now there is no life. And what has departed? It gives you a lack of shyness in the face of words like *spirit, soul, life,* whatever. So that is the turn, the crisis and the emboldening of language towards the ineffable areas.

SR: But you know, most individuals remain mute through these sorts of experiences because we fear we don't have the language to attend to such feelings. I keep thinking that when an artist or a poet creates something like this, in a sense you do it for the whole human community, the whole circle. You create a hoop that we may step through, so we too may be confirmed by that experience.

SH: Well, that is deeply gratifying to hear. And that is, of course, what I believe the function of art to be. . . . But I'm very shy of saying what I think has happened there. I trust these poems. And then it's up to them. [*Laughs.*]

SR: I have to say that, even as your work has matured, you've managed to retain a certain boyishness in your poetry. *Seeing Things* is especially filled with children, games, early experiences. There's the actual boy that we see playing soccer games and marbles. There's the girl I took to be your daughter at the Giant's Causeway. It's as if much of the impulse inside the poems is aimed at reclaiming that child's perspective.

SH: Yes. That's fair enough. It's taking possession again. But on the other hand, unless you make the move out, you don't make the move back, you know. I had a very deliberate desire when I did *Station Island* to absolutely not write, as it were, "poetry." I mean, those recent poems are lyric poems. They listen in to their own impulses and fly with them. But for a few years I refused to do that and wrote a verse that was blank verse and discursive, and set the plow almost against the grain, you know. I intended to put in subject matter and prose content and social data and documentary rubbish of all sorts. And, okay, you can say that takes you away from some wonder-source. On the other hand, it seems to me necessary to try to encompass the full range, you know. I'm very happy to live within the gravitational pull of the actual as well as to get out of it now and again. It's a kind of seesaw. And when I listen to people who move me in the way they write, I find myself attracted to those who—once again, like my hero Milosz . . .

SR: He's your hero?

SH: Yes. He's among the great ones. But in his Nobel Prize lecture, he talked about a story he had read when he was a child about someone traveling all over Europe on a bird's back, looking down at the earth from a great height. And he said this represents one of the big poetic impulses and desires—this airy whole, a vision in the sense that you see the whole thing and you feel it buoyantly and with delight and you're above it. On the other hand, he says, we also feel that if we fly too far, we've betrayed Earth and the cries of the earth. And so the difficulty always is that if you fly, you break solidarity with the people on Earth. Auden puts it in a different way. He says there is a mixture of Prospero and Ariel in every poet—Prospero representing poetry's impulse to wisdom and Ariel representing the impulse to pure song. So Auden says: when an Ariel poet is writing badly, as it were, all you can say is, what's the point of this? This is beautiful, but what's the point? Whereas when the Prospero poet who's writing badly you say, "God, this man can't write! You know, this woman can't write! This is just roughage."

So, while I was doing *Station Island,* I was going towards the kind of a Prospero solidarity with the usual. But then there's a dialectic in you. Up and away in a different direction.

SR: You've spoken of the sorts of "gifts" you feel you've received from the work of other writers, poets like Milosz. What's the gift you'd hope is offered within your poems?

SH: My friend, Derek Mahon, has the following couplet: "The ideal future / Shines out of our better nature." And that better-naturedness and assent and jubilation—if not jubilation, adequacy to the difficult things, a sense that there should be something fortifying—I would like that to be present in the work. On the one hand, to give delight. And on the other hand, to help survive the test, you know. When I read poetry, I like to feel that the writer is clued in, so to speak, knows the score, has encountered the negative . . . has taken the measure of it and said, "Okay, we know all that . . . But granted that, *this* is still worth saying."

6
Donald Hall

—THE WORK THAT MAKES A HOME

Donald Hall greeted me at the screen door, his dog Gussie cautiously inspecting the visitor. Like a boy enthusiastically sharing his box of treasures, he guided me through the rooms of Eagle Pond Farm, showing off the artifacts of his family's long generations in this countryside. Wicker prams, bed quilts patched from still-older dresses, a bone ring from a Civil War soldier, a box of carded wool from his great-grandfather's first season of shearing. There is the shelf of photographs featuring the grandparents he so lovingly immortalized in books like *String Too Short To Be Saved* and *Here at Eagle Pond*. In stories, plays, essays, memoirs, children's books, and over a dozen volumes of poetry, this award-winning writer has excavated and explored the very idea of what it means to be part of a family and to feel at home.

Hall's own recent history makes such a compelling myth, it's easy to understand why book reviewers so frequently offer it as pure fact: Donald

Hall, poet, professor, gives up tenure at a major university to return to the familial farmhouse; inspired by this homecoming, he is transformed as a poet and begins to write masterfully about family history and bucolic New Hampshire.

This is closer to the truth: For a well-educated suburban boy from Connecticut, the summers spent working with his grandfather in the fields and hills around Eagle Pond helped give birth to a second self. Poetry and the life of the spirit were cultivated in this green territory. And for decades he has labored determinedly and lovingly to explore that emotional land-scape, to preserve the people and memories he—even at a distance—called home. In 1975, exchanging the staid security of academia for the invigorating riskiness of the freelance writer, Hall and his wife, the poet Jane Kenyon, transplanted their daily existence to the terrain he'd been homing in on for decades. It has been a bargain neither have ever regretted.

Today Donald Hall writes in the room he once slept in as a boy. The physical presence of Eagle Pond has only magnified and accelerated the ripening of his talent. As one reads through the selection in *Old and New Poems,* it is clear that his gift is more than the colorful family roots and vanishing rural culture. It is a musicality of language wedded to an uncompromising vision of how an individual explores, savors, and passes on the sense of being home. Within his poems, we begin to discover where we too are lovingly tied to the people, places, and tasks of our lives.

SR: Were you fearful when you decided to move to rural New Hamp-shire—away from a tenured position in academia, far removed from the literary scene?

DH: I wasn't fearful about moving away from the culture I had known. You know, I had very good students at the University of Michigan where I was teaching. It was a pleasure, but I didn't really like the way we all lived together at the university. I grew up in the suburbs, and the university town is like the suburbs. . . . People of the same economic class lived near each other, and they drove the same cars. I went to school with kids who tended to be like each other, wanted to be like each other. This place [Eagle Pond] was an alternative—my mother's people's place, my grandparents' place. I came up here where there was such a diversity. And I was met at the depot by an old man driving a horse and buggy. What could be more different? In 1975 I came to a different culture, one that resembled the old one. Things had changed less than I expected and I really admired it. I was frightened of making a living, quitting tenure, quitting regular income for the rest of my life—but with the support of my wife, who was very brave, I had the courage to do it. And it's worked out very well.

The one thing I feared or really gave up on—it is curious to think of this now—is that I had always written in the absence of this place, about this place. I had written a prose book, beginning it in England and finishing it in England, writing some of it in the Midwest, about New Hampshire. I had written poems all my life about this place. But I had written them mostly in the absence of this place in order to restore it. So I assumed—and it made perfect sense—that if I came back and lived here, I'd never write about it again. I was willing to take that chance. I thought, "I like Eagle Pond so much, I'll give up writing about it."

Of course it didn't work out that way. I came back here and I was full of it. I write about all sorts of different things, but writing about this place has been a sort of center for me. It's given me a place to come back to. And the culture—or maybe the feelings I had toward the culture and the old people when I was a kid—have made a sort of platform for me from which to view the rest of the world. Remember the poem by Yeats, "Lapis Lazuli," in which he looks at a piece of sculpture on which three Chinamen climb away from the world and look back down on it? . . . It's a way, not to separate themselves from the world, but to gain enough distance on it to see it clearly and to comment about it. It's a vantage point. And I think that, in terms of my writing as a whole, this landscape, these people, this place has been a vantage point from which to look at the place itself and at the rest of the world that I have known.

SR: Aside from the financial insecurity, the new home must have involved a deeper emotional, even spiritual shift. In your long poem *The One Day,* there's a passage that reads

> The One Day recalls us to hills and meadows, to moss,
> roses, dirt, apples, and the breathing of timothy—
> away from the yellow chair, from blue smoke and daydream.
> Leave behind appointments listed on the printout!
> Leave behind manila envelopes! Leave dark suits behind,
> boarding passes, and soufflés at the chancellor's house!

Tell me about this sort of interior change. You must have felt its influence immediately on your work as well as your daily experience.

DH: Absolutely. I needed to marry Jane first. Obviously I did not know what I was doing. Make sure that's clear. I had a previous marriage and a divorce. Five years of . . . being not married in Ann Arbor. And then—it's a long story which I will not tell. Jane and I got to know each other, got to be friends, and then more than friends. And then were married. She loved it here at Eagle Pond and wanted to come here. She also was brave and was also writing poems herself. She loved the solitude and fell in love with the landscape.

When I lived in Ann Arbor, my sense of time was so different from what it became here. . . . I was never content in the present that I lived in. Most of the time I remember thinking, "Well, in just another year an a half, maybe I can take a year off and go to England," or I can do this and that. You know, there are so many people who live for retirement—"Five years from now . . . only ten more years of working, then I can retire and go where I want"—and I did not want to be like those people. One of the most important things of my life was the early death of my father, who had worked at a job that he did not love, and who had planned to retire—and then died at fifty-two. This is a common American story, probably a common human story, but I was determined it should not happen to me.

When I had lived here less than a year, I realized suddenly that I was living in the present for the first time of my life, . . . that I got up in the morning and I sniffed the wind and I saw where the sun was and I looked at things and I got to work—and I lived in that moment. And if I looked forward, it was looking forward to waking up to the next day. It wasn't looking forward to some trip I was going to make six months from now or some career change ten years from now. I was where I wanted to be. This was an extraordinary change. This was the biggest change in my life. It led to the biggest inward change. It was that sense of time. And of course, that's another way of speaking of happiness. Curiously, or frustratingly, the greatest happiness is not to know you are happy, is not to know what time it is, is to be lost in the hour.

Sometimes at the desk I will sit down to work at 6:00 A.M. or so, and all of a sudden I'm exhausted and it's 9:30, 10:00 A.M., and I have been working steadily and I haven't known the time. This is bliss. It's absolutely wonderful. To be lost inside your task. You don't know where you are. You're certainly not aware you are somebody who wants to win the Nobel Prize or get a MacArthur [Fellowship] or be terribly rich. You're just into your task. It's not that you're modest; it's not that you're beyond these desires—for heavens sake, you have all the desires anybody has—but it is wonderful to be free of them. This is not the Nirvana of nothingness, the freedom from desire in the Buddhist notion—but the reloosening of yourself, into work that you love.

I saw Henry Moore—he was a man quite important to me, you know; I hung around him quite a bit—I saw Henry Moore absolutely lost in the love of what his hands could do, fiddling around with clay or with wax. I heard him talk dreamily as his hands were shaping a wax derived from a plaster. Just before the wax would go to the founder he would spend a few hours, patting it and so on—and it made me think of the pleasure that I had at the desk. Which is not a pleasure of my fingers. It is not a pleasure of a discernible sense organ, exactly.

You were talking earlier about poetry not being just a matter of the brain and so on. I've just been writing something that makes me think of this. To me the brain is involved, is part of the wholeness of it, but poetry is a very bodily thing. There's just no discernible sense organ, but I think maybe the tongue and the lips are tremendously involved in the writing of poetry— certainly in the reading of it, when it is well done. And also the limbs, because it's the dance, the rhythm. When you talk about the sound of poetry, you are talking about two things, at least two things, that are enormously different. Sort of taste and chewing and lips and tongue-rubbing of vowel sounds, adjacent sounds—and then the *boom, boom,* cadence of the marching line. So at my desk, I can keep time, I can feel my throat muscles working. My body is involved in it to some degree, though not to the extent that a painter or sculptor has. All the writers I know who ever hang around painters and sculptors envy them in getting their bodies more directly into the work. You too, I can see.

SR: Yes, I've worked with some dance companies, combining poetry, music, and movement. And in rehearsals as I watch the dancers, I just ache with envy because I don't have anything that approaches that bodily freedom.

DH: But, you know, in one way I feel more fortunate than them. I've got pain in my shoulder now. I've got calcium deposits there. I'm sixty-three at the end of this week, Friday. A friend, an old athlete, was up to see me the other day. He's thirty-seven years old, formerly a baseball player. Even if we [writers] can never dance—yet we can keep on dancing [inside the poems] until we are old, if we're lucky.

SR: Let me ask you about your grandfather and great-grandfather. In many of your books you talk about the way that they invested their lives in this place. You came here as a boy to help with farming—working the land, working inside the community. Now, in your return to Eagle Pond, do you see this new life as word-farming? You may not farm the fields, but you write books and essays and letters; as your livelihood, you cultivate a vision of life from this same landscape. Do you see your word-farming in relationship to the work of your ancestors?

DH: Well, I really find it more continuous with their lives than I did for awhile. Wendell Berry is a dear friend of mine now, but it's been mostly by letter in the years since we've moved here that we've become close. When I first moved here, Wendell Berry wrote me a letter and he said, "Don, don't put in too many acres at once." I answered, "Wendell, don't you worry about it. It's going to be all right." At the time, actually, I thought that I might have a big vegetable garden that I would work in. I daydreamed about it a lot and I started one, but I would not work on it so much. I wanted to work at the desk so much that I would neglect it. I'd forget to weed. Jane grows flowers and some vegetables, but I don't. It turned out I wanted to farm when I was a kid, not so much because I loved that work but because I wanted to do something with my grandfather. I loved my time here, but it wasn't the farming I loved. I can remember that a rainy day would come so that we couldn't go haying, and I would say, "Terrific, I can work on my poems." No, I'm not a physical laborer; I've got to admit it. I've felt guilty about that; I probably still do.

But I also think that I have another function, and I know I work very hard. I grew up in a culture—this is true of my family in Connecticut as well as the family up here—where work was very important, where your sense of your place is the universe is dependent on doing a good job, doing it well, working hard, all that stuff. I have no skepticism about that whatsoever. I have no irony. I may be smiling as I speak to you, but I believe every word of it. Honest to goodness. I love to work. It's important to work, and I respect other people who work hard.

So, I put in the hours that a farmer does. Perhaps not coincidentally, I live a farmer's hours. I get up—this morning it was 4:45, lately it's mostly before 5:00 A.M., but sometimes in the winter when it's cold, it's after 5:00. Say, 5:00 A.M. is probably a year around average. At night I stay up later than the farmers, but I take a nap in the middle of the day. I get to bed around 10:30 or 11:00, now. When you get older, you don't need so much sleep. Put it together, I get five or six hours a day and that's fine. Every now and then I do need more.

There are several ways in which, amusingly and possibly seriously, my work parallels that of my ancestors. One way is that I work on many different things during the course of a day and during the course of a year. I don't have one single product. And these were farms that were mixed farms. I can't remember what the phrase in agricultural history is for this kind of farm; it's a common expression at any rate. Cows may have been at the center of things, but there were always other animals. There were always chickens and sheep, as well as the cattle. Often a farmer had some sideline by which he made a little cash, too. Somebody was a blacksmith fifty percent of the time and a farmer the other half. People grew wood and sold it, maybe chopped and delivered cords of wood for people. It's freelancing. It's freelancing, in many different things.

I write children's books. I write textbooks. I write short stories. I write book reviews. I write essays and articles. I write book-length essays called biographies or whatever. I write everything except novels. I write plays. Of course poems are the center of things, but I'm talking about the crops that I eat by. Actually, I do eat by poems more and more, I think, because of the poetry readings. Poetry readings are where the poet gets a little financial reward for his work. Very little from the sales of books, very little from anthologies, reprinting, but some. Very little from magazines, but some. But the poetry reading is considerably more; it accounts for most of the money that comes in for most poets, if any money comes in at all.

So I'm a multiple conglomerate, horizontal rather that vertical. It's all the same product, which is language. It's not that I sell my trees for pulp and make paper. That's what I would have to do to be a vertical conglomerate. The farmers were all making food, maple syrup, honey. How many products did my grandfather, my great-grandfather sell? At least maple syrup, maple sugar, honey, board timber, cordwood for fires. He might sell hay. Mostly, they grew hay and grew corn in order to feed their own animals. They sold, of course, bull calves for meat and male lambs for meat and male chickens for meat and eggs and wool and milk and, some people, apples as well. In the winter they had to chop ice from the pond and to keep it under sawdust for the whole summer—you see, that's refrigeration. In the winter they were taking the cold for the next summer. But they were also cutting the wood which is the heat for the winter after next, and so on. Well, in my work as a freelancer, I have to work now for the income that [will be] coming in three years from now.

I do work on many different things on a given day. I always begin the day by working on poems. I would very often, say, begin by working on eight or ten poems. And probably the average length of time, from the beginning of a poem to the publication of it, is four or five years. You can imagine that some of my poems, almost all, spend a lot of time stuck away in drawers. So I'll work on eight or ten for a few months and then put them away and then work on another eight or ten. But then I will be working on an article for

Yankee, or a book review for some other place or a preface for a book, short pieces of prose and maybe some ongoing big piece of prose, or maybe some children's books. It's wonderful for me because all these things have different audiences, which means they have different tongues, different characteristic vocabularies and syntaxes. If you are writing a book for a four-year-old, which I am working on right now, the eyes you are imagining are enormously different from the eyes you are thinking of [when] writing a book-length poem called *The Museum of Clear Ideas,* which I'm also doing at the moment. Or, say, writing a book review for the *Times Literary Supplement.* I write for highbrow places and lowbrow places, for three-year-olds and for old people.

Every time you change your audience, you change the kind of sentence you write and the kind of vocabulary pool you work out of. I don't do this super-consciously, you understand. I don't assemble myself, saying, "Now, reorient yourself to a different kind of sentence." I just imagine the whole ambience and it brings a different kind of tone to my voice. It's as if you walk though the streets of the city and you meet one person after another whom you have known in different places—and without thinking about it, you adjust the way you talk according to the people you meet. This is what I do, and there's tremendous variety.

SR: And I imagine they probably open up different rooms inside of you, inside your memory or imagination.

DH: Absolutely. One of the things you may have noticed, I work with the same material in different genres. I love doing this. I wrote a poem called "Ox Cart Man." But then I told it as a story for a six-year-old, telling a story with lines jagged on the right hand side of the page. I also wrote about the Ox Cart Man in an essay. If you read *Here at Eagle Pond,* I use that story as an analogy in an essay. Every time I use it, the language is a little different. The story is the same, as it were, but it's different.

SR: I want to ask you a question about the way you "fit in" here in New Hampshire. I'm curious because, in several places in your writing—and notably in the new book of essays, *Seasons at Eagle Pond*—it seems like being accepted, becoming a part of this place, is very important to you. You mention a good deal about "the outsider"—whether it's the New Yorker who attempts to spend a hundred dollar bill at the garage sale, or just the unspoken ways that the distinction between the insider and the outsider is marked. It made me think of my visits to Ireland; they use a term, "blow-ins," to mark people who are recent arrivals in the town.

DH: A blow-in, just like leaves—very good.

SR: But one man from Sligo told me, "I'm a blow-in, because I was actually born about seven miles down the road and I've only lived here since I was about ten. Maybe my kids, who were born here, will not be considered blow-ins. If they stay, their children will certainly be considered natives."

DH: Certainly my position has always been anomalous—I'm not sure that's the right word; *ambiguous,* perhaps. You know, I wasn't born here and I'm perfectly aware that I'm not a country person. Two reviews I got lately—one of *Here at Eagle Pond* and one of *Old and New Poems*—both sort of accused me of being a fake farmer. It pisses me off because I don't think I'm a fake about it and I think I've made it clear.

SR: It's certainly clear in the essays.

DH: I'm a suburbanite, but also Harvard and Oxford and all that stuff. This house has got a lot more books than it has, say, cans of apple sauce. We all know that. And the way I fit in here—as I believe I do—I fit in here because I love it so much. . . . I published a piece in *Yankee* about thriftiness, stinginess; people here pride themselves on thrift and giggle at themselves, and I included a lot of things that neighbors told me and now they are telling me more. I am like an ombudsman . . . or a spokesman. I feel I can do that as long as I don't take myself too solemnly, too seriously.

In another way, I take it very seriously, because I remember the old people who are gone, and whose type isn't entirely gone but is attenuated from generation to generation. I say, "Man, I want to preserve this. I want to keep it." Certainly, that's one of the motives for literature, always. You look at Homer, and epic writers, saying the heroes are wonderful but it's we—the poets—who preserve them, who make them live. Shakespeare would say in his sonnets, "It's by me that you will be remembered." This is your pride, but this is also your duty. There is something fundamentally conservative in a great deal of literature—the desire to preserve things, if not conserve things, and it's a strong motive for much if not all of my writing.

SR: Indeed Wesley, your grandfather, is so alive in *String Too Short.*

DH: I wanted him to be. I couldn't quite keep him alive, literally, but I try to do it on pages.

SR: I feel it. My dad also died when I was young and I believe that early experience of loss spurs that desire to embody and preserve experience inside something more permanent.

DH: I think that desire began for me, or the potential for it, before any of these people died.

SR: So it makes sense that, through writing, you've reinvested yourself in this place. Although there's always the small telltale signs of strain, of distance. I'm thinking of a passage in one of your poems ["Speeches"] where you meet someone from this area, and they say, "Saw a piece about you; you're everywhere these days," and you respond—

DH: "Just like horseshit." That was Les Ford who lives down in Potter Place. He's an ironmonger, or blacksmith; he does all sorts of great things with iron. He's wonderful. He's so funny, and he really did say that.

SR: There is another one concerning the stories about your family you've recorded from the locals, and one of them comments—

DH: "Told you a lot a lies."

SR: I think that voice contains both the desire to mock you, in a friendly way, but also the intimacy of acceptance.

DH: Absolutely. It's both. . . . My cousin Clyde Currier—when you come through Andover, you go by a gas station on the right hand side, Currier and Phelps, that's his place. He is my age and my second cousin; we share John and Martha Wells. Clyde's been working at that station since he was fourteen. People like Clyde or like Les never sit still more than five minutes. . . . I've heard this tease again and again, "How in the hell do sit still all day?" But here, more than in other cultures I've been around, it's okay to be different. You may wonder at somebody else, but you don't put them down. So that I get referred to like this: "Fella over there in that house, he writes books all the time." . . . It's not awe and it's not contempt. It's more like, "Imagine that!"

SR: Each might be a hindrance to an artist—to be regarded with awe or to be looked down upon with contempt. Both, I think, would make unhealthy climates for creative work.

DH: Awe and contempt are the same thing, in a way. They are the one side of the coin or the other. Here I'm essentially free of all that. When I go to Old Home Day—every town has its ceremonies, you know; the one up in Danbury is the Harvest Festival Grange Parade—somebody will come up to me and say, "You're Donald Hall, aren't you?" and say, "I really like what you write." For the most part, it doesn't have any edge to it. It's just plain and it doesn't have any exaggerated deference. I get a lot of deference when

I go around reading my poems in English departments. Some of it is straight and honest and touching, but it's hard to deal with. . . . This place and this culture is something that just allows me to get on with the work.

SR: Reading your memoir, *String Too Short To Be Saved,* about your summers at Eagle Pond as a boy, it struck me that you had somehow acquired an almost Confucian regard for age and for the wisdom that is passed on from one generation to the next. It's remarkable in someone so young. Where do you think that feeling came from?

DH: I was the only grandchild of two sets of grandparents. The young people I met up here [in New Hampshire], the middle-aged people, were pretty quiet, rather dour. The old people were the wonderful storytellers and the repositories of so much that fascinated me. I listened to the old and I loved to hear them talk. When I was away from those old people, I dreamed up questions to ask them to prompt new stories.

My grandfather was at the center of it, probably at the center of my life— my New Hampshire grandfather, the old farmer Wesley Wells. He was a great storyteller as well as a reciter of poems. Most of the stories he told were reminiscence, anecdote. He told them with a wonderful sense of narrative, a wonderful sense of shapeliness. He loved language—not poetic language, but the good comeback, the witty turn of phrase. That really tends to be true in New Hampshire or maybe in rural places in general. The storyteller is valued. He loved it that he had someone who was a good audience for his stories. So he set a kind of pattern in me, the love for old people, which I think has gone through the rest of my life.

SR: Listening to his stories and recitations when you were working together—do you think that created a rhythmical sense that affects the way you work inside your own poetry?

DH: I'm almost sure it does. I don't write with the rhythms of the poems that he said to me. But still, the love of rhythm and the . . . sense of closure that rhythm can give all come through.

SR: I have a writer friend who says he remembers his grandfather reading the Bible to him when he was an infant. He understood nothing of the meaning but the forcefulness of the cadence and his grandfather's tone of voice still remain with him today.

DH: Well, I heard a good bit of that in church, too, read by a great-uncle of mine who was a minister. He had quite a sense of rhythm and was a good storyteller. He was very old, born in 1856. I remember sitting on the porch with him and asking him stories about the end of the Civil War. He was nine years old when the war ended and he could remember the soldier boys coming back.

SR: Because of your attachment to your grandfather and this place, I suppose it's somewhat painful for you to see the remnants of that old life slowly being erased as New Hampshire becomes more developed, modernized, yuppified.

DH: Yes, it does. I resist a lot, as I make obvious in some of the things I write. But I'll tell you one thing that interests me and that also makes it more poignant. At the time when I was writing *String Too Short to be Saved,* thirty odd years ago, I thought the New Hampshire of my grandfather was all gone. In a way it was like the fox and the grapes: because I could not live there, I needed to say, "It no longer exists." But when I came back, some of the young or middle-aged people whom I had known as a kid were now old people; and now they opened their mouths and told stories. The rural culture lives—and I think this is common all over the world in rural countries. The old people are the repositories of wisdom, and people learn by listening to them. "The repository of wisdom" is too pompous. They are good talkers and people listen to them. Some of these people shut up and listened for forty years, and when I came back, now they were there, talking! . . . But if these folk are outnumbered fifty to one by people moving up from the south, they are going to be just trace elements, and the culture will not survive. It will die, not of television and not of the automobile, but of outnumbering.

SR: That's sad, because it's a process you see in so many aspects of our culture. Our cities have become so homogenized, you find carbon-copy malls and main streets wherever you go in America. And since television truly has become "the great modern storyteller," our voices and imaginations are becoming equally homogenized. It makes me think of a question I've asked several of the poets in this series. Do you know the book by Wendell Berry, *Standing by Words?*

DH: Oh, yes.

SR: I think he even cites your work as an example of the sort of language and poetry he advocates—a poetry grounded in knowledge of place. He talks about poets being cut off from the lived experience that necessarily informs language, and he argues against the poets of pure imagination, the writers whose work is so self-referential, it is almost a closed system. Clearly what we've been talking about is the way your lived experiences have infused the landscape of your poetry. I was talking to Bill Stafford, and he surprised me by disagreeing with that premise. He says that wherever he is or however he is living, it is the blank page and fresh view his mind confronts that grounds the voice of his writing. Do you feel your lived experience at Eagle Pond gives power to the language you shape here?

DH: I think when Bill Stafford writes, there is a lot of Kansas in him, wherever he may be. I doubt that he'd deny that. I think that the first twenty to thirty years of his life are a very strong presence in his work, though he's lived away from it so long. In my own poetry, there are some that are surely detached from the land in any obvious way—the poetry of the oasis or the imagined place. Often I love that poetry in other writers. But I feel that if I don't have this land to touch down or go back to—even in the midst of writing something that is highly imaginary—I end up lost. Within the imagery of the fantasy, there will be lived experience. It won't be obviously about it, the subject matter won't be clearly there, but there is something loved and lived with—that is there at the core of the experience out of which the language makes itself. So, I write more variously than Wendell does, I think, but I value what he does enormously. But I do think that the basis of my love of place comes into the poetry even when the subject is, in an obvious way, continents or oceans apart.

SR: I can see the imprint of that idea at the heart of *The One Day*. In this long poem, you present us with a single day that somehow contains all days. And the one individual consciousness becomes a repository for a multiplicity of minds and experiences. And what does the speaker do? He builds a house there, a place to anchor and explore the divergent forces. How does that sense of multiplicity come from your life?

DH: It comes from a lot of lived experience, of chaos and variety—too much variety—and an attempt to hold on to something through it all. There is an epigraph to that book—or maybe it's a quote within the poem, I can't remember—about something someone once said to me, that "I'm not a person; I run a boardinghouse." Everybody feels like that. . . . I want to name and shape the boardinghouse and the inhabitants of it and do it in such a way that other people can understand their membership in this community. Everything *is*—multiplicity is singular, singularity is multiple—and this is the vision the poem tries to embody.

SR: Are we all those voices or is there some core voice that holds them all together?

DH: I think, finally, there is a core. At our most fundamental, we're most like each other. And there are enormous differences of tissue, flesh. But at the skeleton we resemble each other more. This is a premise of my poetry.

SR: I don't think it would be too much of an exaggeration to say that, in your boyhood, you touched something—in this house, with these people—and it has been the blueprint of your poetry ever since. You've been building in words a reflection of what you uncovered on this land. In rereading *String Too Short,* I came across a passage that said,

> The farm had an order to it, for the animals had to be fed and the vegetables had to be weeded, and the hay had to be cut for winter. Everything done was part of a motion we didn't control but chose to implement—a process of eating, mating, and dying. I liked the sense of necessary motion. The farm was a form: not like a set of rules on a wall, but like the symmetry of winter and summer, or like the balance of day and night over the year, June against December. My grandfather lived by the form all his life, and my summers on the farm were my glimpse of it.

That's Don Hall speaking thirty years back, and look at the life that's followed from it.

DH: I don't reread *String,* and I'm glad to have you remind me of that passage because it seems to me in so many strange ways that's it's true—what I wrote then, having no notion what I was going to live through, the distancing and the misery of many middle years, coming back to this farm-form—that I predicted it or asked for it when I wrote that book, without knowing what I was doing. I am amazed to hear it and to understand and to be able to give assent to it from the point of view of sixty-three years as opposed to the point of view of thirty-one or thirty-two when I wrote it not knowing, as it now seems, what I said. . . . That's the form that my life has followed and my work imitated, by a series of what seem to be accidents and impulses—but one tends to doubt that anything is so accidental or merely impulsive.

SR: So much of your writing is about "home-making"—in both the literal sense of "one's daily labors" and in the mythical dimension of human culture. Robert Frost certainly had his say about the idea of "home" in his New Hampshire poems. How does it shape your work and language?

DH: I don't know if I can answer that. Home is a comfort. Home is where you want to stay, where you can imagine yourself living in the present moment, continuously canceling out time. When I was away from here, when I was in bad times, I had an image in my head—a physical image, the topographical landscape of this place with all the associations of family, of history, of the ghosts of the dead. It invited me and comforted me. I came back here and it was all enormously welcoming. This is a center that I've filled with the ghosts and the spirits of place in order to make it as dense as possible with human contacts in time. . . . The way of the moment is the result of everything that happened in the past. The thicker you can construe the ways leading up to this present moment, the more thoroughly you live in the moment itself.

I'm not sure I've spoken to you about home. . . . I think I have "home" in a sense more than most people are able to—and maybe sometimes I am shy of speaking about it. There was an old cartoon when Goldwater was running for the presidency in which HerBlock [Herb Block] had Goldwater saying to a beggar woman, "Why don't you go inherit a department store?" I feel that way about my connectedness here. I have this, and I can't tell other people, "Why don't you go have it?" I'm just the lucky one . . . and you can't brag about luck.

SR: Yes, but in reading the poems, don't you think a reader is pressed to look at his own home in a different way, maybe with a more open and attentive eye?

DH: That's what I would hope. And I can try to make models of fitting into where you are, and leave it there for people in the future to take a look: this is how it was possible to live.

SR: In all your books since *Kicking the Leaves,* the landscape is treated as a presence, a voice that speaks of the tension between home and time. The larger cycles of time both enrich the moments of our lives even as they're carrying the experiences away from us. The poem "Great Day in the Cows' House" is a perfect example where the sense of celebration and loss are inextricably coupled.

DH: In that poem, I talk about the experience of canceling out time. That turns up in poem after poem. Part of that notion I took from the mystic and theologian Meister Eckhart, who had the phrase, "God cancels the successiveness of men." Now the "Great Day"—which is my own phrase for this—cancels the successiveness of creatures, because I wanted to include not just men and women, but also Holsteins as well, and trees—so that the trees of the tie up are both ancient timbers and saplings that are still damp.

At moments, I can feel the coexistence, the copresence of everything—and I desire this sensation. It's a little frightening, but it seems to me a portion of reality, something to be seen, to be discovered . . . I don't mean it as something coming from the outside in a supernatural way but as a function of inwardness. It's a soul thing. I think of the world as existing laterally at any given moment of time in its multiplicity, and its many nations and its many sorts and its many conditions of life. I also think of the vertical line which goes back to the Egyptians and the Babylonians and our first literature. They're all focused on the sense of human endeavor.

This sense of the depth of time surrounds me here. I could show you photographs going back a number of generations of people who I know are connected, whose lives are tied here. I don't know a whole lot about some of them but there are others, like Ben, about whom I know a great deal. Obviously the thickness of the association gets greater the closer you come. But then I think of all the people I know, friends of mine, who don't know their grandmothers' maiden names. This is more typically American; it's probably the predicament of the modern world, always changing, moving. Americans are people who typically said, "Good-bye to all that,"—and that too is a wonderful thing about us. . . . Our ancestors had to say, "To hell with that." Cutting off the past, cutting it off in order to get on with life.

But I regret the losses a lot and mean to make a connection to this possible for myself and for my descendants. The fact that I now have granddaughters does not diminish this sense of desire. I'm giving you the cross motion, the horizontal and vertical, but the past implies the future. If there is no past, it seems to me, the future is much less implied.

SR: There are several passages from "Kicking the Leaves" where you convey this sense of being both rooted inside your life and also propelled by this curious sense of time.

> This year the poems came back, when the leaves fell.
> Kicking the leaves, I heard the leaves tell stories,
> remembering, and therefore looking ahead, and building
> the house of dying. I looked up into the maples
> and found them, the vowels of bright desire.
> I thought they had gone forever . . .

By way of contrast, there's a line, I believe, in *The One Day* about "the businessmen who don't know the names of their grandmothers." It's as if we're being reminded that to be without history is to be cut off, in a sense, from yourself; it's the means by which we steer to the future.

DH: Good, good. . . . The people who like my work seem to like it post-New Hampshire more than the earlier poems. But the breakthrough began with that poem, "Kicking the Leaves," which started in Ann Arbor. But I knew I was coming here and it was perhaps that looking forward that started things. I thought at first I was just coming for that one year, but you know what happened.

SR: I was struck by that phrase, "building the house of dying," as if you were preparing yourself for a greater acceptance of your life, both the light and dark natures.

DH: The "house" is such an important word, isn't it? I was sitting in this chair in Ann Arbor when I wrote those lines. But it was this house I was envisioning, not the one in Michigan.

SR: The poem closes with a set of lines that almost sums up the new home you'd begun creating inside your life.

> Now I leap and fall, exultant, recovering
> from death, on account of death, in accord with the dead,
> the smell and taste of leaves again,
> and the pleasure, the only long pleasure, of taking a place
> in the story of leaves.

DH: When you acknowledge your own dying and your connection with the past, and the fact that in your future you will go into the cycle of leaf mold and new leaves—only then are you truly connected. That's true, that's real. That's the only big truth. Accept that and take your place and be content. This is a vision. It's nothing where you can reside for twenty-four hours a day, your whole life, but it's something. Now I'm talking about the poem that I wrote so long ago. There I say, "and in six years I will be fifty-two." I'm now sixty-three, so that's seventeen years ago.

SR: There's something a little frightening, but at the same time *good,* secure in that idea.

DH: It's supposed to be frightening but good. What I mean to do, even consciously, is to embrace the frightening and cuddle it, and therefore make it less frightening. That's probably true of a lot of my work.

SR: I've heard a phrase, derived I believe from Native American culture: *ceremonial time.* It refers to the *now* in which we stand, which is somehow simultaneously giving birth to the great stretches of time. Time, not as simple measure, but as a way of ordering the world, making sense of our limited experience.

I've been reading through all your poems in preparation for our talk, and I can't escape the feeling that there is a simple constellation of themes, three prominent stars, by which all your work is guided. There's this overarching sense of time, time that orders our human existence even as it is expunging it. And this is set against the stillness, the rootedness involved in making a home, in committing your energy to knowing one small portion of the earth, making it your own. And how do you cope with the ever-present sense of loss? How do you, as an artist, move your mind from the mundane ticking of the clock's minutes into the arc of ceremonial time? The answer is always work. Through all your books, and especially in the recent poems, work is both the refuge, the solace, and the bridge out of the quotidian and into some other awareness. There's the good work of haying and blueberry picking with your grandfather; of your early morning rendezvous with the poems at your desk; and the daylong word-farming of the freelancer. But in *The One Day,* you also have some horrific descriptions of the bad work, the sort that drains the life out of people while offering only a salary in return.

DH: There's bad work and good work, absolutely. . . . In *The One Day,* I collected all those quotes from the painters, one after the other, amazing. Rodin's "To work is to live without dying." Maybe I found Georgia O'Keefe. . . . Did I quote her?

SR: I think there was one from her: "The days you work are the best days." You have Flaubert and Henry Moore.

DH: Matisse, too. He said, "Work is paradise."

SR: The first section of *The One Day* has us stare into the abyss of time and loss. But by the final section, we experience the ways work is able to redeem this moment, to make a home inside time. It's there in the voice of the sculptor saying

> and by these hands I join
> the day that will never return. This is the single
> day that extends itself, intent as an animal listening
> for food, while I chisel at alabaster. All day I know
> where the sun is. To seize the hour, I must cast myself
> into work that I love . . .

Work is the one agency that binds us to this cycle and yet has the redemptive power of carrying us beyond it. And in that gem of a poem, "Ox Cart Man," the whole of the man's existence is encapsulated by the seasonal cycle of labor.

DH: Work, work, work! And the exhaustion of everything he does. And you know, when I first published that poem or read it at poetry readings, I was astonished to hear many people say, "Ohhh, how sad! He does all that work and then he's got to do it over again." Well, I never had that idea. It is not a misreading of the poem, of course; . . . it's a response to the poem. But I had never thought of it.

SR: It's a measure of where the readers stand in relation to their own work and the cycles of their lives.

DH: I thought of that sort of total disbursement of everything. Everything that you have done goes out, gets changed into something else. Then you come back and start all over again. That always exhilarated me. It was as if the human life was a perennial plant. You die down into the ground and come up again and blossom. I can say that every day is like that year, that cycle of years, from the getting up in the morning all excited to get to work, till you're going to bed at night sleepy, in order to get up again, get going. And I only resent the fact that this will have to end when I die.

SR: So you aren't one of those writers who will complain about the pain and the anxiety of writing. In the early mornings, when you wake to another day's work, the feeling for you is . . . ?

DH: It's bliss. I don't apologize. It's bliss. I get frustrated at my inabilities, like anybody, no more than anybody. I get stuck or sidetracked and don't know what to do next. But let me not exaggerate that. That is simply part of the context. It's part of the work.

SR: And that pleasure comes across in the reading of the poems as well, along with a challenge: to look around at your own day and your own labor and see whether you are fed by the experience.

DH: Indeed. I can't tell people to go and have grandparents like mine, go and have a farmhouse to move into like me. . . . But I can say, "Find what you love, and do it." I'm happy to say that.

7

Maxine Kumin

—NEW LIFE IN THE BARN

I*T IS A FALSE-SPRING DAY* in late February, and so my car fishtails lazily, hauling itself up the once-frozen, now mud-slushed road. The first thing my eye catches when I arrive at Maxine Kumin's home is the sign high on the barn wall: Pobiz Farm—a bit of humor twice compounded, just what one would expect from a crafter of language. This modest horse farm survives (the sign implies) only through the auspices of that other business Ms. Kumin is engaged in: poetry. And, of course, only another poet would grasp what a tenuous and absurd occupation it is—selling words: practicing the art of making language and images sing themselves alive so that a reader's mind might join them.

Maxine Kumin has long survived in the "pobiz" precisely because of her unreasonable and passionate commitment to the life of language. Never one to be steered by literary fashion or academic orthodoxy, she has cultivated her clear, intimate, irrepressible poems in the same determined manner she's used to nurture family, farm animals, her small corner of the earth. A Pulitzer Prize winner and Poetry Consultant for the Library of Congress, Ms. Kumin is the author of novels, short stories, essays, over twenty children's books, and twelve volumes of poetry including *Selected Poems, 1960–1990. Inside the Halo: The Anatomy of a Recovery* is a recent memoir detailing her devastating accident at a horse show and her struggle to recover.

Quickly checking my shoe size, Ms. Kumin scrounges up a pair of Wellingtons that will fit me and we head straight for the barn, accompanied by a complement of cats and dogs. Work takes on a dreamlike rightness when it is rooted in daily practice and profound pleasure. I watch her and her husband Victor make their rounds, ministering to each stall, each creature in turn—the ritual of their husbandry that is set down so faithfully in her poem, "Feeding Time" (from *Selected Poems*). I begin to feel how the simple moments resonate inside her imagination. The literature of our time is richer and more humane for the caretaking of poets like Maxine Kumin.

❖ ❖ ❖

SR: Would it be fair to say that in your poems, nature and the natural world come in for more consistent praise than human nature and the society we've made?

MK: I think that's fair, yes.

SR: Where does that feeling come from?

MK: I guess out of my own observations. I don't see the kind and degree of depravity in the natural world that I see in the human world.

SR: But how did that bond with nature come about in your life?

MK: I think it was through the good fortune of my childhood. I grew up in suburban Philadelphia—in Germantown, virtually on the edge of Fairmount Park, a huge park complex that runs from center city well out into the suburbs, about twenty miles' worth. And as kids we had an enormous amount of freedom. That was before anybody worried about children being abducted, sexually abused, or whatever. As long as you got home in time for supper with your hands and face washed, you could be gone all day in the woods. My cousins and I would go off to collect polliwogs and salamanders or watch the park guard—mounted troops that patrolled. We spent endless hours lying in wait for our favorite park guard, who might just let us sit on his horse. So really early I think I cultivated this kind of bond with the natural world.

SR: In the poem "Credo" that opens your book *Looking for Luck*, the relationship you describe with your horses is astonishingly intimate, almost a mystical bond.

> I trust them to run from me, necks arched in a full
> swan's *S*, tails cocked up over their backs
> like plumes on a Cavalier's hat. I trust them
> to gallop back, skid to a stop, their nostrils
>
> level with my mouth, asking for my human breath
> that they may test its intent, taste the smell of it.

MK: Well, I'm afraid of words like "mystical" and "spiritual" since I'm neither, I think. But I'm not sure how to characterize what it is. There's some kind of nonverbal communication that takes place between humans and animals. . . . I'm fascinated just exploring that interrelationship.

SR: But the poem goes on to say,

> I believe in myself as their sanctuary
> and the earth with its summer plumes of carrots,
> its clamber of peas, beans, masses of tendrils
> as mine.

MK: That's certainly true for my horses. I am their sanctuary. We've done this to them. We've taken them out of their wild state. It's pitiful to see this out West. The cattlemen have driven the horses—or what's left of them, the tattered remnants of the wild horse bands—up into the mountains, practically above the tree line where there's virtually nothing to eat, where it's very difficult for them to find enough water to stay alive. And it's all in the name of the almighty steer that we eat. I mean, the West belongs to the cattlemen. This, of course, I find quite upsetting, especially since I don't eat meat.

What I'm saying is we took the horse out of its wild state. We made it into this, you know, beast of burden and draft. We turned it to our own uses. And having done that, we have a moral responsibility to take care of what we've taken on. So, in that sense, I'm feeding them, I'm housing them, I'm cleaning up after them. I am indeed their sanctuary.

SR: I know you've taken in abused animals, horses who would have no chance of surviving without your care. But the implication in the poem is much broader. As a people, are we caretakers of the natural world?

MK: Well, it is to be wished. What can I say? Clearly we're not.

SR: The poem "Hay" has a line that says, "Allegiance to the land is tenderness." But it's not easy to feel such tenderness if you live in the middle of New York City or Los Angeles. You might not even feel any loss in the matter.

MK: I feel great compassion and sorrow for people who have to live in high rises. It would be the death of me, I know. If I couldn't open the door and put my feet on earth, I think I would languish and just fade away.

SR: What would you be missing? Or maybe I should get at it from the opposite direction: How are you enriched by the experience of walking on your hillside, of feeding the animals each day?

MK: I don't know if I can express it. It's very hard to express what I receive from it. But it completes me, makes me feel whole, makes me feel an integral part of the world that I live in. That I'm one more healthy organism in this little microcosm here on the earth . . . It's very much a part of the New England consciousness, I think. The fact that we have four well-defined seasons. This has been a grim year in terms of winter, because we've had no snow, and we really depend on snow. We call it the "poor man's fertilizer" for one thing; and for another, it keeps the ground from freezing so deeply that people's wells freeze. This year the ground is frozen four feet down. The thaw is going to be a long, terrible mud season. . . .

But because we've toughed-out winter, we've earned our spring. Then we go through the season of dreadful black flies, followed by mosquitoes. And you have to be of stern stuff to put up with all that to get those few good months. Usually April is beautiful here, and August, September, and October. Those are probably our best months. In all four seasons, though, we're in touch with the natural world out of necessity.

But to have to live—it would seem to me—in the terrible sameness of the concrete canyons of the city, never to see 360 degrees of the sky, never to see the changing skyscape as the seasons turn: this, to me, is to be deprived.

SR: I lived for a few years in California. And when I packed up to move back, I told my friends how much I was missing the seasons. People thought I'd gone crazy. "What could you possibly be going back for—digging your car out of snow drifts?"

MK: We have a daughter who lives in San Francisco. She's a lawyer, and she has become the total California chauvinist. So that when she comes back here to visit, we have these long serious telephone conversations about, you know, "How cold is it, and do I need long underwear?" Ridiculous! I mean, she grew up here, for God's sake. She can't totally have forgotten.

SR: Had I remained a few more years, I might have been won over by the freedom of such beautiful weather. I probably left in the nick of time.

MK: Well, I think we do need to retain people here in New England. If too many people move to California, it's going to tilt right into the ocean.

SR: But, in seriousness, isn't that one of the traditional roles of the poet— to cultivate, if you will, the spirit of the tribe; to honor nature and remind the community of their place in the broader cycles of life? The opening of "Hay" describes the feeling we've come to have about a life tied to the land, to the seasons.

> Above the river I hear
> the loud fields giving up their gold,
> the giant scissors-clack of Ruddy and Ned's
> antique machine laying the timothy
> and brome in windrows to be tedded,
> this fierce anthood that persists
> in taking from and giving back to the land,
> defying the chrome millennium
> that has contempt for smallscale backbreak.

That's a great little social history of contemporary American society in those last four lines.

MK: [*Laughs.*] Yeah. See, I'm describing the old-fashioned way of putting up hay, piece by piece, as it were, with fields that haven't been drenched with nitrates. Fields that have just had the cow manure put back on them and then they've been carefully brushed-out—which means to remove all the weed trees that have crept in, all the brambles and such. Agribusiness has no time for this uneconomical process and would have enormous contempt for it. But it's quite a beautiful scene, to see everybody who has two cows or a couple of horses and a pony, and they've made prior arrangements with this farmer so they come in with big pick-ups when he calls. You know, he'll call and say, "Well, I'm gonna start balin' around toward three o'clock." And everybody gathers and they load up their hay out in the field, and you pay the farmer per bale. It's much cheaper that way. And there's a kind of sanctity to that relationship—buyer to farmer, farmer to land—that we've lost, that we're in danger of losing forever. But these few entrepreneurs are there still—particularly, I think, here in New England, where people are so crustily individualistic. I mean, tinkering all winter long to get this equipment to run. If you could see the equipment—it's amazing! These guys are running trucks that date back to the 1930s—and they keep'em going.

SR: And by the "chrome millennium" you've conjured a picture of our crowded highways lined with bright little cars that are built to self-destruct after forty thousand miles.

MK: Right, right.

SR: This is why, to my mind, yours is a lived vision, one where the words and deeds are intertwined. The sweat of the day is mixed in with the adjectives. You don't just advocate that we ought to take care of an idealized natural world. You muck out the stables and ride your horses, feed and groom them, and either save or lose the foal through your efforts. Is that part of the responsibility you've taken on as a poet?

MK: Yes, certainly. I think it's the reason for writing the poems. Again, *responsibility* might not be the word I'd use. Maybe I come at it a little bit sideways. I don't think of it as a job to do. I think of it as an obsession. It's something I can't do without. I mean, who would in his right mind choose to be a poet in this culture? There's no glory in it, there's no money in it [*laughs*]. People look at you strangely. For example, I have this experience all the time on airplanes. The guy next to me wants to buy me a drink, wants to chat me up, and so he wants to know what my business is. And I always duck and I either say I'm a teacher, or usually I say I raise horses. That is respectable almost anywhere. But if you say you're a poet, the next question will be, "Oh, have you ever published anything?" And what are you going to say to this guy? What kind of a question is that? If I said I were a lawyer, would you say, [*laughing*] "Gee, have you passed the bar?"

SR: That's right!

MK: A self-proclaimed poet, you see, fits in with the general stereotyped notion of the poet as a kind of fop or fool, a comic figure, very self-important, a sort of inflated dummy.

SR: As a poet, do you see yourself as a vital figure? Are poets essential to society?

MK: Oh, absolutely. And you know, this is the one thing I feel truly evangelical about, spreading the word. In the course of these Woodrow

Wilson Fellowships and the year that I was in Washington as consultant [to the Library of Congress], I did a tremendous amount of outreach with high school English teachers. And I always said to them, "As far as I'm concerned, you folks are on the front line." I feel they are. The fate of poetry really rises and falls with them. So that anything we practicing poets can do to reinforce the teacher's role—as he or she for the first time faces a class of squirmy adolescents and has to try to stimulate them to read a poem, with feeling— we need to do that.

SR: I began about fifteen years ago working in the schools in the artists-in-residence programs. I thought I would only do it for a year or two because it might burn out my own hunger to write. But the opposite has been true. And I still find few experiences more delightful than when a student or a teacher really discovers what a poem can do, discovers they can make a poem themselves, out of their own life experience, that says something truly. They get so wildly excited, I feel I'm reconfirming what is at the source of language.

MK: Well, of course, it's true that of all the art forms, poetry is the most difficult. I mean, you can go to symphony or you can go to an opening at an art gallery or go to ballet—and you get from it as little or as much as you wish to invest your attention. But you can't go to the poem or the page that way. You have to go with all your defenses down, and you have to work at it. You have to bring to it these special tools of prosody. You know, it's not something that you can be a dilettante about.

SR: Although I do use some of your poems, for example, with very young students. Clearly you're writing for an adult audience, but some of the poems a third-grader or fifth-grader intuitively understands and responds to. . . . Maybe it's because, whether you're writing about animal or human families, we are compelled to notice, to savor what is fragile and finite? Our "ground time is not going to be long," as you say, and that's a realization just on the periphery of our attentions—young people or old.

MK: I guess so. I guess you could say I'm a little preoccupied with my own mortality [*laughs*]. . . . I think the early poems almost lugubriously dwell on impending death. Maybe once you're over sixty, you become more accepting of the whole natural process. I don't think about it all that much now. I mean, pragmatically, I do say, "Well, you know, it's time to stop breeding horses," because I don't want to go through this process of bringing them up and selling them. Now we have four that can be in our family for as long as we last. And I'm sure they will all outlast us. I've already written down who

I want to have first choice when we're no longer here. I want to be sure they've got a good home.

SR: You spoke to them before as if they were children in a way, a second set of children?

MK: I think they are. Certainly some of this must be empty-nest syndrome after our last kid left. With horses, you could develop a new family. Just as it says in "Nurture," "I suffer, the critic proclaims, from an overabundance of maternal genes." And Victor's a great nurturer, too. Between the two of us, it seems to be our fate.

SR: It reminds me of the poem "Rejoicing with Henry," where you show your neighbor your new foal.

> Next year, if I live that long,
> she'll stand in the shafts. Come Christmas Day
> we'll drive that filly straight to town.
> Worth waiting for, that filly. Nobody says
> the word aloud: *Rejoice.*"

That's life's prize, isn't it?

MK: Oh, yes! Absolutely. To have, as we say, "a foal in the oven," shortens the winter remarkably. I mean, not expecting one this spring is my great sorrow, because all winter long, through thick and thin, through thirty below, you can console yourself with the thought that come May, come June, you're going to have new life in the barn. And the filly in that poem is Boomer, now twenty-one. whom you met earlier.

SR: But why is the word *Rejoice* left unspoken? Is it forbidden? Have we forgotten the language to express feelings of that sort?

MK: No, I think what I meant was, we are all feeling it in our hearts, but none of us says it. Accepted, but unspoken somehow. It might be bad luck to say it.

SR: I wanted to ask you a few questions about a subject that might be a bit touchy. But reading through your books, I was confronted again with the idea of a "women's poetry." At one time, feminist writers felt this classification marginalized their work, diminished its importance. But more and more now, there are such dramatic differences between men and women poets—not just in styles and subjects but in the sense of purpose that's embedded in the vision. Do you see yourself as a "women's writer"?

MK: Yes, I do. I mean, I write from a woman's perspective because I am a woman. It's as simple as that. I'm attracted to certain subjects because of my gender, and there are certain subjects I clearly can write about that perhaps a man can't write about, just as the converse would also be true. . . . No, I wouldn't bristle at that at all.

SR: A pair of poems from the new collection come to mind: "Falling Asleep to the Sound of Waves" and "Noah, at Six Months"—these just couldn't come from a man's sensibility. The first depicts the time in the womb and the second, the way the world is changed by a single newborn. Your work shows a constant awareness of life's comings and goings, with the image of family as the one steady presence.

MK: Certainly those tribal poems about children are quintessentially female, I think. Our older grandchild is in Yugoslavia with his mother. She went from rescuing animals to rescuing people. She's in charge of the Belgrade office for the U.N. High Commission on Refugees. Her son was here over Christmas for two weeks, and they were supposed to come next week for a week, the two of them.

SR: They're not?

MK: No, because the peacekeeping troops went in today. She can't be spared. We have just the two grandchildren. Our son's son, Noah, is now two years and two months old, and he was just here yesterday. In this sense of family there's this wonderful completion. This little kid sits at the table and counts [us] to see how many we make. Then he counts Josh and Rilke [the Kumins' dogs] because they're family. Then he counts the horses because they're family, too. It's marvelous to see this continuum.

SR: If you look at a poem like "Longing to Be Saved," you see a very different dimension of experience but one that also strikes me as being essentially feminine. It's the nightmare about all the loved ones, all the animals in a burning barn—and the speaker tries to rescue each in turn before she returns to the fire to await her own chance at being rescued.

MK: [*Laughs.*]

SR: Isn't that, in a nutshell, a mother's point of view?

MK: I don't know. That's a very peculiar poem. It's one of my dream poems, and I just feel I'm not responsible for the poems that come up out of dreams. I was away from home, in Fayetteville, Arkansas, for a week doing one of these writers' conferences, and this was just sort of a continual nightmare. Every night I dreamt a different frame. Somebody else was in dire danger, and I just sort of put it all together.

SR: I have to say, I see a lot of my wife and my mother, too, in that poem.

MK: It's the same phenomenon as the mother who always eats the neck of the chicken or the wing of the chicken, meanwhile serving the better parts to all of these other family members.

SR: Taken together, poems like "Praise Be" and "The Green Well" create an astonishingly intimate portrayal of the life-and-death continuum. "The Green Well" begins stoically about the daily losses in the natural world— "else why would He / have made so many?" Then it crosses to the opposite end of the emotional scale when you mention

> . . . Gone
> now to tankage my first saved starveling mare
> and the filly we tore from her in the rain.
>
> After the lethal phenobarb, the vet
> exchanged my check for his handkerchief.
> Nine live foals since and I'm still pocked with grief,
> with how they lay on their sides, half dry, half wet . . .

But from this experience of the natural order, you surprise us with the memory of

> *Grief, Sir, is a species of idleness,*
> a line we treasured out of Bellow, my
> suicided long-term friend and I.
> All these years I've fought somehow to bless
>
> her drinking in of the killer car exhaust
> but a coal of anger sat and winked its live
> orange eye undimmed in my chest
> while the world buzzed gossiping in the hive.

You don't mention Anne Sexton by name. . . .

MK: But it's obvious.

SR: What is it you find yourself struggling to affirm?

MK: That she had the right to take her own life. I mean, I felt that I had to defend her right to take her own life when she did so. I do strongly feel that on a conscious level.

SR: That it was her life to take?

MK: That it was her life, and, if you know her history, you know how hard she fought to stay alive. It was a constant struggle. I feel that when she reached the end of her rope, which she clearly had, she had the right to make that decision. But of course the other part of me is very angry.

SR: I love the image of that "coal of anger" winking "undimmed" inside you. Is that just the insistence that life go on? What is that "orange eye"?

MK: It's the everlasting ember, the eternal flame, I guess. It's hard to say.

SR: But that countervailing force is woven all through your poetry. Close by "The Green Well," you have "Praise Be," which vividly depicts the birth of a foal. It is a refreshing affirmation when you see how dark the landscape of contemporary poetry tends to be. Nature reveals life and death, each in its place.

MK: You know, I almost didn't print that poem.

SR: Why is that?

MK: Because I thought it was sentimental. But I was persuaded by two poets who said it's "full of sentiment, but it's not sentimental." I didn't know. I didn't think it would be well received, quite frankly, but it's the poem that everybody points to. It astonishes me.

SR: It's easier, in contemporary writing, to focus on the slipping under than the rising up. Isn't this too a hallmark of women's poetry? First there was a sort of aggressive push toward life's extremes. Women were going to be more daring, to push themselves to the edge.

MK: Yeah.

SR: As if somehow—if not suicide itself—the willingness to risk everything somehow proved that you had honesty and integrity in your poetry.

MK: Yes. Well, I think it's a very common phenomenon. First you had the poetry of black rage, which certainly had to rush to the edge of the precipice in order to be taken seriously. Then you had women poets who were all fighting the fight against critics like Jim Dickey who said, "If I have to read about one more woman's uterus, I'll throw up." Or close to that—I've paraphrased. Of course, he then went on to write a [*laughs*] graphic homosexual rape scene in *Deliverance.* That apparently was okay.

So I think women poets did feel a kind of compulsion to make a clean breast of it—to write about the unspeakable, the things that have never been said, that were taboo. You get poems like "In Celebration of My Uterus" and "Menstruation at Forty." Of course, Anne was probably the foremother of all of that. But I think we've passed that now—don't you think we've moved beyond that point? Maybe that's what you're getting at. Now women can write about the entire spectrum of life. There's more one needs to experience.

SR: There are also a large number of poems about women in your books. In the new collection [*Looking for Luck*], you mention famous names like Beatrix Potter, Louisa May Alcott, Flannery O'Connor. But more poems focus on ordinary individuals struggling with the burdens of daily existence, like "The Chambermaids in the Marriott."

MK: Well, that's a "pobiz" poem. . . . When I go out to give readings, I try to piggyback them so I don't go just for one overnight. I can do two or three—three is my limit, because I'm no good after that. And hopping across the country you do see scenes like this. . . . They are the unheralded ones who, "with Rabelaisian vigor," are out there living their lives. That was what was so heartening about them, I think—to see that they had so much zest. Even imprisoned in what must look to you and me like terrible dead-end jobs. But to them, there is the camaraderie of cleaning together on the fourteenth floor, and the camaraderie of knowing they're going to plug into the same soaps as they work, and the camaraderie of being able to share even the horrors, the events of their lives—which are more soap opera than the soap operas.

SR: Even though many of your recent poems aren't focused on political subjects, the whole of the work becomes something of a political commentary because it portrays a view on America that stands in opposition to the way we generally see ourselves. An obvious example is the piece called "FAT PETS ON," the palindrome you make from the "NO STEP AFT" warning you notice on the wing of the jet, returning from visiting your daughter in Europe. There's the feel of a nineties version of *Innocents Abroad* when you say

> Long ago, before plexiglass,
> before terrorists, each time we parted
> at the international gate we could
> still touch fingers, talk across
> the token lattice that divided
> ARRIVAL from IN TRANSIT . . .

MK: Yes.

SR: You put your condition in contrast to that of the "twenty refugees in orbit" imprisoned in Abu Dhabi.

> Meanwhile, I ride the current
> of time backward, FAT PETS ON,
> suspended in a calm cocoon
> with Nanny-brisk attendants
> to pamper the paid-up overfed.

MK: That's all of us. We're riding SwissAir, Zurich to Boston. But we are "the paid-up overfed," aren't we? By contrast. Of course my consciousness has been raised by having this daughter, and having pursued her in her area. She was four years in Thailand, in Bangkok, and she was three years back in Geneva at headquarters. And now she's in her third year in Belgrade. So, it's certainly an interesting life for her, a fascinating and heartbreaking life. But to be with her and her colleagues is really like entering another world, one that's totally fascinating to me. They're all trilingual at least. They change languages as casually as you and I might pour a cup of tea. When somebody else walks into the room, they switch from French to German to accommodate the newcomer—that sort of thing. So I've learned a lot.

SR: It highlights the way we live in America; we're hardly fluent in any other language, any other life than our own—though we have a privileged access to the entire globe.

MK: Right. I think it makes me feel very sad. I also feel quite helpless in that I'm not contributing to the betterment of a lot of these people as she is. Although she and I have this argument quite often about the nature of caring. I've always maintained that saving animals and saving people is a sort of seamless process, one is really no different from the other. She has quite definitively turned her back on rescuing street dogs and horses to rescue street people. And of course, hers is the larger and more prominent and obviously more important task.

SR: That's where your poetry takes on a decidedly political edge. You carry your readers into points-of-view that we might normally struggle to avoid. But we risk a certain sort of dangerous isolation if we cannot even imagine how other Americans live—let alone peoples from around the world.

MK: Well, I think we're seeing the danger it puts us in. Look at this recent [presidential] campaign here in New Hampshire. You know, it's just come down to slogans, nothing but a sound bite here, a sound bite there. Everything is reduced to the lowest common denominator. And it just makes people more and more solipsistic than they naturally are. So, in a sense then, it becomes the mission of the poet and any writer to alert people to the danger.

SR: When your poems tackle this experience of isolation, very often they center on language and relationship. There is that painful awareness that sometimes language binds us together and other times it becomes the barrier. There's the section in "Telling the Barn Swallow" about your daughter moving to Europe. "Now she will raise her children / in a language that rusts in my mouth, / in a language that locks up my jaw." What do you fear will be lost between you and your grandchildren?

MK: Well, that I wouldn't be able to communicate with her children if their mother tongue were French or German or Spanish. My mother tongue is English. We're never going to have quite the comfortable commonality of a shared tongue. And no matter how hard I try to improve, for example, my French—which I've labored long and hard over—it's not going to match their French.

SR: But then the poem goes on to warn the swallow:

> to cover well her hatch.
> I tell her that this hour
> must outlast the pies and the jellies,
> must stick in my head like a burdock bur.

Why? What can words and images contain that will penetrate this barrier of time and distance?

MK: Love. What else can I call it?

SR: But the image of "a bur" makes me think of a painful persistence.

MK: No, burdock burs aren't painful. I'm picking then out of the dogs' fur all the time after they go through the underbrush. A bur is merely a seed, a way of moving from point A to point B where it can finally drop to the ground and sprout. . . . Noah, for example, was fascinated with burs because he could stick one on his shirt and it would stay. He was just hysterical with glee. And then he'd pick it off and put it down here and it would stick again. It was sort of, you know, nature's Velcro.

SR: So is that the task that falls to the poet: to preserve your family stories, your family loves, its history and beliefs?

MK: For me, yes.

SR: Even though you describe your brother's reaction to your work:

> . . . his none
> too secret mortification,
> a writer, a species of liar
> thinly disguising the whereabouts,
> squabbles, sexual habits
> of people we lived with, namely
> those voices and mirrors, our family.

MK: [*Laughs.*] Yeah.

SR: But if you're willing to put up with the pain that goes with being a poet, what good comes of it? For your family or for ours?

MK: You collect the saga and you hand it on.

SR: You hand it on? What do we do with it then?

MK: Well, then they, the next generation, will keep it and they'll hand it on. That's the kind of continuity which is our only immortality.

SR: I'm curious. Was this something that was bequeathed to you when you were very young? When did you first begin writing?

MK: Oh, as soon as I could read I was writing. "Can it be that Spring is here," and that kind of thing.

SR: Do you know what prompted that first impulse? I was thinking about the talk I had with Don Hall about his earliest writing. He talked about getting away from his life in Connecticut and spending his summers here in New Hampshire, to live with his grandparents and work on their farm. The poetry was, in part, an escape from his suburban life into something that more closely suited his character.

MK: By the time I was an adolescent, poetry was the salvation for me as well because I was sort of a, you know, an odd stick. I was a very introverted adolescent, not socially adept, and took refuge in books, and particularly in poetry. So then it did become a saving grace for me. But the love of poetry, I think, must have been almost inherent in me because from a very early age,

I'm sure I was read to. I mean, I still have all of Robert Louis Stevenson's *Child's Garden of Verses* by heart. I haven't been able to shed them. [*Laughs.*] I think, for me, it began very early.

SR: I heard one poet comment that, if the world were to suddenly disappear, he'd still be able to write if he were left alone with his notebook. There are many poets who have exchanged, in a way, the word for the world. That's not at all the case with you, is it? What does the word accomplish for you in your relationship to the natural world?

MK: It makes a coherence for me. Poetry distills experience. I say to students all the time, life is not art. Art is something that takes a step beyond. It transmutes what you take out of a life experience and enables you to build on it. But you have to begin with something. . . . I'm constantly counseling students not to go right into an MFA program. I'll say, "Go work as an orderly in a metropolitan hospital for a year." Go teach in a rural school, go do something. Immerse yourself in the culture. Listen to people, and relate to people. Then see what you have to say.

SR: It's clear to me that you have a gift for skirting the fashionable literary trends and simply following your own impulses.

MK: I haven't made any conscious effort, you know, to ride a particular stream or theme. I've just lived my life and written my poems. And I've been very fortunate in my life, too, that I can use it as a metaphor for my art, and that I have this place to keep me sane, for me to go forth from and to come back to.

SR: But if you've not been driven by the choruses of critics or the sway of academia . . .

MK: No, I went out of the academy, thank God. I couldn't live that way. I've turned down offers from a couple of places where I've been invited to stay on as a tenured professor, just because I didn't want to be beholden and I didn't want the responsibility. I wanted to continue to lead this particular kind of life.

SR: Then what steers your poetry? How can you know where the writing should take you or what must be preserved?

MK: That's probably the single hardest question to answer. . . . Just that inner compass that you're probably not conscious of. You know, I don't really see the direction that something has taken until it takes it. You just have to be open. Rilke says, "Await the birth-hour of a new clarity, keeping holy all that befalls, even disappointment, even desertion."

SR: And this farm, this experience helps you to maintain that openness?

MK: Oh yes. This is where you do "keep holy all that has befallen." I know that.

8

Carolyn Forché

—THE POETRY OF WITNESS

ALL JOURNEYS ARE WISE—when viewed with enough time and distance. Looking back on life's passages, the wrong turns, chance meetings, even dead end streets can assume a place in a clear and purposeful progression. It's in the day-to-day navigation that an individual's inner compass and determination are tested. And for an artist, the sum of those daily choices, both mundane and monumental, leaves an indelible mark on the character of the individual and the content of the creation.

Entering the middle passage of her life, poet Carolyn Forché has received more acclaim and notoriety, witnessed more instances of cold brutality and generosity of spirit than one might expect in several lifetimes. In March of 1994, *The Angel of History* was published, the first new collection of her work after thirteen years of silence. Shortly before that time, I met with the poet and her husband, the photojournalist Harry Mattison, at their Maryland home. The two-hour interview I'd arranged somehow expanded into an eight-hour marathon conversation. And the lasting impression I came away with centers on the tangled, dangerous, utterly guileless path she has traveled in her life. Early on, her literary career could certainly stand as proof of the axiom that the angels side with the innocent; time and again, buffered by little more than her naïveté, she plowed headlong through what could only be seen as dangerous waters. But as she matured, both as an individual and as an artist, hers certainly has been a triumph of the honest choice over the expedient, the strength of personal commitment over the tidal sway of public opinion. Along the way, and very likely because of it, she has created a body of work that addresses the terror and inhumanity that have become standard elements in the twentieth-century political landscape—and yet affirms as well the even greater reservoir of the human spirit that persists within our dreams and our voices.

Going back over the tape recordings of our talk, I think what we are presented with is a detailed portrait of three poetry manuscripts, and a unique subjective description of the circumstances and influences that shaped each. At times, the astonishing coincidences and strokes of luck take on the feel of a Hollywood screenplay. I asked her one time whether she believed there was something like "destiny" moving inside her life; she answered with her characteristic honesty: "I don't know. The idea that there isn't horrifies me, and the possibility that there is horrifies me. I do perceive patterns and forces at work—but it's fairly easy for someone who is as inclined toward narrative as I am to construct a narrative that will expose coincidences in such a way as to present a pattern. You have to keep that in mind." That caveat notwithstanding, it is nevertheless quite enthralling to be caught up in the momentum of Forché's storytelling, to question whether you would have dared the same choice had you been faced with similar circumstances, and to examine the vibrant poetry that resulted from her journey.

One of my first questions concerned her reputation as a "political poet," a category generally disparaged in American letters and viewed as a hybrid of the partisan polemicist and the benighted idealist. Her response enveloped the better part of the day and, in the process, provided powerful insights into the politics of language and the education of a young woman writer in the realpolitik of the literary world.

"I started writing when I was nine years old. I don't know why. I started writing obsessively the way some children draw obsessively. I was the eldest of seven children. We lived in Michigan. My father was a tool-and-die maker. My mother, a mother. Ours was a very large Catholic family. An exuberant, crowded, noisy household. Writing was my refuge. My mother also wrote, before she bore all of those children. She published little things in newspapers and I think she published a few poems—but she has always kept them in a silver Christmas box. I'd love to get my hands on that box again. She showed it to me when I was little and too dumb to know that I should pay attention to it. But I wrote, and she encouraged me to write—and taught me rhyme and meter, and took out old books and showed me what poetry was.

Because of what she termed "the largess of the Johnson administration," Forché became the first person in her family to attend college. With an Equal Opportunity Grant and a National Defense Loan, she enrolled at Michigan State University, "and while I was in college," she quickly adds, "I changed my major five times because I was looking for something compatible with writing—there weren't any writing majors then. I finally wound up in an international-relations school, an experimental residential college called Justin Morrell there at Michigan State."

With her degree, she moved from Michigan in search of work. Detroit was in the midst of what amounted to a depression as the American automobile industry was being toppled from its position of dominance. The closest city that presented an active job market was Washington, D.C., where she took a secretarial job for the Epilepsy Foundation of America. "But they discovered within about a month that I could actually write sentences with verbs in them. So they promoted me and gave me my own secretary, and I was suddenly charged with doing all of their writing—brochures and reports and studies, and so on."

It was no driving academic ambition that spurred Forché onward, but the simple lure of the "G-ratings," the government classifications for jobs. "I became aware that if I had a master's degree, I could get the equivalent of a higher G-rating and a better job. . . . Around that time, a professor from my undergraduate days told me about an M.F.A.—a master of fine arts program. There were only a handful of them at the time. What was stunning to me was to think I could actually be given credit for writing poetry!" She received a full teaching scholarship to Bowling Green State University in Ohio. "It was the first time I entered the classroom as a teacher. I was given a remedial composition course to teach. My first assignment was a classroom of impoverished open-admission students who hadn't learned standard English yet. And they made me a teacher, made me fall in love with teaching"—a career choice that had never crossed her mind before this but which forms a central part of her life even today.

"I was writing and writing and writing my poems. And I wrote about my grandmother Anna who was from Czechoslovakia, and I wrote about the wilderness and the forests and mountains—most of the poems of *Gathering the Tribes* [her first book] were written in Ohio. . . . My poems were characterized as sort of nature poems or spiritual poems. I wrote about my life as it had been up until then." She put together a manuscript of poems, completed her degree, and considered the next step.

Upon graduation, she secured what must have been—she says now with laughter in her voice—"one of the last university teaching jobs given to a poet or a writer who hasn't gotten a book published yet. San Diego State hired me and gave me the assignment of teaching four composition courses a semester." It was a sufficiently heavy work load to keep her eyes fixed on the path before her and away from the dreaminess of the far horizon. That is, until she returned one evening to her tiny office and found a note on her door asking her to call a certain Connecticut phone number. "I didn't know anyone in Connecticut. It made me a little nervous. I mean, what's in Connecticut? Insurance companies? Credit agencies?" When she finally summoned the courage to call, she found herself speaking with officials at Yale University informing her she had been selected to receive the 1976 Yale Series of Younger Poets Award—one of the most prestigious prizes for poets at the onset of their careers.

"I had forgotten I had even entered it. Truthfully! I never dreamed I would be chosen. I only entered because people at Bowling Green told me that's what a poet is supposed to do. I didn't know anyone in San Diego at the time; I had just arrived, really. So I went out into the parking lot, and I was dancing around and I told all the parked cars at the top of my lungs that I'd won the prize!" It was then that she noticed a man in the empty parking lot watching her celebration, falling into an embarrassed silence as she imagined what her rantings must look like. And the man was coming toward her. When he was close, he said, "You must be Carolyn Forché. I've overheard you saying you won the Yale Prize—congratulations." He introduced himself as a fellow instructor at the university. (She found out later that he too had entered the Yale contest—perhaps the reason he already knew her name.) They talked for a while and then, Forché recounted, "He said, 'Are you doing anything right now? My wife and I would be delighted to have you over, because we used to live in Spain and whenever any of our group of friends published a book, we always got together and opened champagne.' And I was so lonely, I was happy to be invited. I went with him and met his wife who was a lovely young woman named Maya Flacol. And Maya was the daughter of Claribel Alegría. I really liked her and we became friends. And repeatedly in those days she told me her mother was a poet, but I sort of dismissed it because I was nervous about the prospect of reading anyone's mother's poetry and having to comment on it."

Once the force of reminiscence was upon Ms. Forché, my job as an interviewer became simplified. The story seemed to just tumble forth, gaining momentum like a river coming down from high ground. Occasionally I'd request clarification or ask a question to prompt her in a new direction but the narrative strains braided themselves in and out with their own inner logic. And I must admit, it was easy to be captivated by the prospect of a lovely, bright, inexperienced twenty-five year old woman suddenly poised on the verge of literary fame—or that modest version of fame which may be accorded to young poets. But what Forché chose to do with this opening—this is where (as the dramatist would say) the plot thickens and the complexity increases exponentially.

"One day it was raining and we were trapped in Maya's kitchen, drinking coffee, and she asked, 'What languages do you read?' I said only English really; I studied Spanish in college though. And she brought out a stack of hardcover books, and they were in many different languages except English. They were all by her mother, all translations of her mother's poetry into various languages. And so I read the Spanish and I said astonished, 'Maya, your mother's a poet!' And she said, 'I've been telling you!' And I said, 'But your mother's a *real* poet!' And I asked why she isn't translated into English, but Maya couldn't say. Well, in fact there weren't many women poets being translated into English from any language." You only have to think of the case of Gabriela Mistral to see the truth of this matter; when she became the first Latin American to be awarded the Nobel Prize for Literature, she was completely unavailable in English—much to the embarrassment of the American literary community.

By this time, *Gathering the Tribes* had been published and Forché found herself unable to write, suffering from the self-consciousness and emotional letdown quite common for authors after the publication of a book. She agreed to Maya's request to attempt translations of her mother's poetry. "I thought translating might get me writing again—or, at least, would give me something to do while I couldn't write. And I also thought translation would be easy: all I'd have to do was get a very fat Spanish-English dictionary and look up all the words I didn't know." The statement is punctuated by laughter, somewhat astonished by the combination of confidence and sheer foolishness with which her young self proceeded.

"I started to read the poems and I realized my difficulty was not going to be acquisition of vocabulary or verb tenses. I went to Maya and told her I was having a terrible time with the poems, and that I believed I didn't even understand many of them. Alegría was born in Nicaragua but left there when she was a one-year-old and [was taken] to El Salvador where she grew up. What I subsequently realized is that [her poems] had arisen out of conditions I was completely unfamiliar with, which were the conditions of extremity and life under military dictatorship—the torture and mutilation, incarceration and disappearance of friends."

Forché confessed she couldn't always tell whether an image in a poem was intended to be literal or figurative. "For example, there was an allusion to a guitarist whose hands had been mutilated. And I thought, 'This must be a guitar player who is in emotional pain and can't play his guitar any more because of it.' Because I didn't know about Victor Jara, the Chilean folksinger whose hands had been mutilated with an ax in front of thousands of prisoners in a stadium in Santiago after the coup in Chile. I didn't know I was supposed to render this in English as an actual *chopping of the hands*. And so Maya said, 'Don't worry. I'm going home for the summer to Spain to stay with my mother. Why don't you come with me. And if you don't understand the poem, mother can explain it to you and answer all your questions. Besides, my mother will be heartbroken if the translations don't happen now because she really wants the poems to be read in America.

"Well, I'm from an environment where people come *from* Europe, they don't go *to* Europe. I mean, 'junior year abroad' was not in the vocabulary when I was growing up. But Maya said, 'It'll be fine. Just save up the money for your ticket and for some spending money, and you can stay with me.' Forché set her fears aside and began making arrangements for her first trip outside of the United States.

Once again Forché diverts the flow of her narrative with a small detour, another strand to be woven into the braid. Around this time, she had become friends with Terrence Des Pres, the author of *The Survivor* and *Anatomy of Life in the Death Camps*. In describing her plans for her trip, she explained to her friend that she'd secured the cheapest airfare possible by flying, not directly to Spain, but to Paris; then she would proceed the next day by train to Barcelona and by ferry to Alegría's home in Majorca. Des Pres elicited a promise from her: "Terrence said, 'When you get to Paris, go to Notre Dame Cathedral. Go behind the cathedral and walk across the quay and look for a black iron gate and a white stairwell. Try to go when there are few people around. I'm not going to tell you what you're going to find there, but you'll understand when you get there.'"

In the summer of 1977, Forché flew to Paris, took the bus into the heart of the city and, rather than go hunting for a hotel room for the night, decided to follow up on her friend's mysterious instruction. Dragging her huge suitcase down the shadowy steps, she found herself in "the memorial to the 200,000 people who were deported from France during the *shoah*. There were white rooms with stone walls, poetry carved into the walls, different poets who had been in the camps. And there was a tunnel with 200,000 tiny beads of light embedded in its walls, one for each of the lives . . . And you could hear the river rushing past the windows. I stayed there for a long time." Forché copied down some of the poems in her journal, though she had only the barest understanding of French at the time. Later in Majorca, the notebook was left out in the rain. The lines of poetry remained but the name of the French author was washed away. For a decade she kept an eye out, but never came across the poet's identity. Still, when a puzzle piece presents itself, you have to be patient awaiting an opening in the design.

She spent three months in Deya on the island of Majorca working with Alegría, dazzled by the international coterie of authors and artists who would congregate daily at Algería's house. They seemed so engaged by the business of the world. "There were Latin American writers like Julio Cortázar, Mario Bennedetti, Augusto Robusto. She was close friends with Gabriel García Márquez. And Robert Graves would come down the hill from the house where he lived, with his hat and his cane, and his wife Beryl on his arm. Everyday I'm listening on the edge of these conversations and it was the beginning of my education concerning Latin America. Here I was on this beautiful international jet-set island and I was getting more and more depressed because I was spending my days translating Alegría's poetry and my afternoons in these gatherings and my nights wondering what I was doing with my life." Unmistakable in Forché's voice is the yearning that epitomized young people in the 1960s and 70s: "I wanted to do more. I wanted to do *something*—and didn't know what it was. But it began to be quite apparent to me that—and I want to choose my words carefully here— in the Latin American view, the United States was intricately implicated in their circumstances. The visitors at Deya certainly agreed that if North American attitudes could be changed, a great deal of the hardship would be relieved."

After the summer, she returned to San Diego, taught her writing courses, completed the manuscript of her translations and felt largely uninspired. She did little more writing than the letters she wrote for Amnesty International's Urgent Action Network. It's as if she were unconsciously waiting for another door to open. Once again, at the prompting of her friends, she attempted to spur her literary career onward and applied for a Guggenheim Fellowship "because they told me you had to apply three or four times before you're really even considered. But I was shocked that I was granted a fellowship on my first try." She hoped this might be the stimulus that would convey her over her writers' block. Indeed, the door was opening, but not the one she'd envisioned.

"One day I was home alone and I heard a truck pull up in the driveway. I wasn't expecting anyone so I was a little nervous. I looked outside and there was a white Toyota Hiace in my driveway. It had Salvadoran license plates and was covered with dust. I knew a lot about El Salvador now—through the memories of Claribel Alegría—and much of it was horrifying. I suppose I briefly indulged that kind of youthful sense of self-importance to actually believe I was in some sort of danger. But two little girls jumped out of this vehicle, and I decided [the driver] couldn't be an ax murderer because ax murderers wouldn't travel with two happy little girls." A man emerged from the truck carrying a roll of white paper, a fistful of pencils and a black-and-white Guatemalan woven bag full of books and papers. "He came up to my front steps, rang the doorbell, and I opened it with the chain on. And he said, 'You are Carolyn Forché? I am Leonel Gomez Vides.' And I thought for a minute and remembered that I'd heard the name before. And I thought, 'This man was either someone impersonating Leonel Gomez Vides or he *really was* Leonel Gomez Vides—and in either case I was in trouble.'" Because Gomez Vides was the "crazy nephew" of Claribel Alegría, the one they all told stories about at those gatherings in Deya, the one who gave away his land to various *campesino* projects, who slept on the ground with his motorcycle in his arms—a character that combined equal parts of Robin Hood, Don Quixote, and your garden variety lunatic.

Forché ran upstairs and brought down photographs from her Spanish visit. "I made him identify Claribel and her husband before I would let him in. He even complimented me on my precautions—he said, 'Very good! I like that.' The two little girls ran out back to play with the rabbits I had at the time, twenty-three little rabbits. They were so excited because they had never seen so many. As for Leonel, he walked into my house like he owned the place and asked me to clear off my dining room table and announced, 'We have work to do.' He covered the table with the white paper he had, taped it all down. He put his books and papers down and asked me to make coffee. Then he sat down and talked for seventy-two hours! He didn't leave my house for three days and three nights, and he hardly slept and he didn't eat very much. . . . After a few hours of sleep, he would wake me early saying, 'Come, we have to begin again.'"

He became her self-appointed teacher conducting a crash course in Central-American history, from the conquest through the cultivation of indigo and coffee, and up to the current political climate, all the while drawing little cartoon illustrations and diagrams on the paper as his discussions progressed. Puzzled now, I asked, "Weren't you suspicious about where all this was leading?" At first, Forché explained, she was simply fascinated by his intensity; she thought of his stories as background for her translations and possible introductions to other Latin American poets. And after all, he was the relative of a woman who had just been her host for a three-month stay. "But by the end of the third day, he was giving me these little exam questions. He'd say, 'Now, let's make a coup.' And he'd move objects from the kitchen across the table—'The salt shaker is the American embassy, and this is the army headquarters'—and he'd make a whole battle plan. He'd say, 'Suppose you were this colonel, and this and that happens, now what are you going to do?' And I'd try to answer the question, and he'd say, 'No, no, no! Think like a colonel!' And I'd try to give a better answer. In the end, he said, "Okay. I give you a Ph.D. in El Salvador studies.'"

By this time, Forché was nearing the limits of her patience. "I'd filled up a whole salad bowl with cigarette butts and I'd drunk a gallon of coffee and I was very tired." But his final challenge arrested her attention: "He said, 'Claribel tells me you've won a Guggenheim Fellowship. Congratulations! So what are you going to do with your fellowship year?'" The Guggenheim provides writers with the funding to travel and work exclusively on their writing, without teaching responsibilities of any kind. "Leonel asked me if I'd understood the Vietnam War when it was going on? Now, given that he'd just instructed me in this three-day, intensive course in the intricacies of Salvadoran politics, I had to say, no, I couldn't have explained Vietnam in the detail which he'd just offered. 'Would you like to see one from the beginning? ... My country is going to be at war in three to five years and your country is going to be involved. ... I want to invite a poet to come down there now so that when all of this happens, this person can inform people here about what's going on.'"

Forché explained to him that, unlike some other countries, poets lack a compelling credibility in the United States and suggested that it might be more useful to invite a journalist instead. But Leonel was adamant, insisting that "he needed a peculiar kind of sensitivity" for this task. She demurred, saying that she believed he was either exaggerating or just plain wrong when it came to his vision of American entanglement in another Third World conflict. But Leonel upped the emotional intensity of the challenge. "He said, 'What are you going to do, write poetry about yourself the rest of your life?' ... I was really insulted, hurt by this remark, because I had never considered that my poetry had been about myself. I had drawn from my life as I was educated to do. This is how poets of my time were formed—we were told to write about what we knew. I had not yet realized that there was, buried within that idea, an injunction: not to know too much, to limit what we know to a certain sphere . . . But even in the face of my own defensiveness, he just remained silent. And I realized there was something to what he said. And I think—I'm reconstructing now—I remembered all the conversations the writers had in Spain, and my own desire to *do* something, and my own guilt in a way that I never joined the Peace Corps, had never really given myself over to this year or two of service. And he assured me I would be in the company of women friends there, that it would all be set up properly."

By the time Gomez Vides had packed the truck and gathered up his two little girls, Forché was still unconvinced. "As he was going, he rolls down the window and says, 'I'll send you a ticket in January!' And I yelled back, 'I haven't said I'm coming yet!' I remember standing in the street, screaming after this departing vehicle that I'd made no promises." When she related the details of this strange invitation to her friends, they were unanimously against accepting it, citing all the expected safety and health reasons about a woman traveling alone in Central America. Certainly, Paris or Rome might have been the more romantic choice for a poet on a fellowship seeking a situation conducive to the muse. Despite all her apprehensions, at the start of 1978 Forché journeyed, not east toward the City of Lights but south to San Salvador.

In the end, her mentor was not wrong in the details of his predictions, only in the timing. By the autumn of 1979, the first of several coups had toppled the government, a civil war was erupting, and Forché found herself in the very eye of the storm.

Over a two-year period, she met with people from all around El Salvador and began working with Monsignor Oscar Romero's radio station, YSAX, and other church projects. "We were doing everything from writing reports about abuses for human rights organizations, to looking for bodies on the beach . . . when we heard rumors that people were dumped there, to visiting morgues to match the faces with high-school photographs of missing persons." Not coincidentally, she began to take her first tentative steps back toward poetry. "By 1980, it had become apparent to me that many Salvadorans had invested their time and even risked their lives to educate me about the situation in their country. And their hope, finally, was that I would come back to the U.S. and talk about it here. They didn't realize that . . . discussing the circumstances that gave rise to the Salvadoran war wasn't something expected of poets in my country and we wouldn't be considered a viable source of information. I tried to explain, but because Latin Americans esteem poets so highly, they didn't understand."

The fighting had escalated dramatically and, one week before he was assassinated, Monsignor Romero took Forché aside and persuaded her to return to the United States. "I'd already had some close calls by then. The monsignor told me it was dangerous and best if I left now. 'Talk to the American people,' he told me. 'Tell them what is happening to us. Convince them to stop the military aid.' He had this whole program of things he wanted me to do. And I nodded, because it was obvious this man was a saint. He sat with his white cassock on in the little kitchen of the nuns' Divine Providence Hospital. We were having snacks with the nuns in the late afternoon. This was twenty feet from the chapel where, one week later, he would be killed. It was the last time I saw him."

Back in the United States, Forché struggled to justify Romero's faith in her. "I came home thinking: I have *no idea* how I will speak to Americans." She wrote long articles, but few were published; she was called on to come to Washington, D.C., and testify before the House Subcommittee on Western Hemispheric Affairs. "They were holding hearings to approve or disapprove the first 5.5 million dollars in military aid to the new regime and the first twelve military personnel—rather than 'advisors,' they called them 'trainers.' I don't think they really wanted to remind anyone of some earlier event." There was dramatic testimony from Amnesty International, the Council on Churches—"and then I watched the committee overwhelmingly approve the aid and the advisors." Shortly after, she recalled sitting at a huge memorial service for Monsignor Romero at a Washington cathedral, "and I remember praying, 'Monsignor, help me! I don't know how to fulfill my promise.'"

Forché submitted her El Salvador poems to a literary publisher she trusted. He told her the work was too political, too disturbing. But he proposed a compromise: "He said to me, 'Would you be willing to write twelve briefer poems, tonally very quiet, about things like the light falling on a bowl of fruit, sort of domestic scenes.' And then he would place these between the Salvador poems to—and I remember his words—'modulate the tone of the book.' For some reason—don't ask me why—I went home and actually attempted to write these poems. Of course I failed. Because one can't sit down with an intention and write any particular kind of poems. Such things won't be poems at all. So I put the manuscript away in a drawer for eighteen months, believing it unpublishable."

But she did continue to present her Salvadoran poems at readings. The pieces both startled and galvanized audiences with their depiction of the pervasive brutality the government of El Salvador was employing against its own people." And the audiences got larger and larger, and after the readings, [the people] would ask if they could stay and ask questions—and the questions were always about El Salvador . . . I remember several times when the audiences were large enough to make me nervous, I would talk to Monsignor Romero before I walked out on stage—the way you'd pray to a saint when you were a little Catholic girl—which I was once—and I'd say, 'Monsignor, help! What if I don't know what to say? What if I lose my train of thought?' I would take a deep breath and go out to the audience, and everything would be all right. I was convinced that Monsignor Romero was making it all right!"

Forché was invited to perform at the Portland Poetry Festival, "and they said I would be reading with Margaret Atwood. I was terrified to meet Margaret Atwood. She was someone I esteemed so highly that I couldn't bear the thought of actually speaking with her in person. . . . But she was wonderfully warm with me and very interested in my views on Central America." The reading coincided with the eruption of Mount St. Helens, and Portland lay in the path of the smoky trails of ash. The airports were closed all along the Northwest but, at Atwood's prompting, the two poets made their escape, renting a car for the all-night drive south to San Francisco, the nearest airport still open for departures. "Ten hours in the car," Forché recalls with a mixture of anguish and delight, "talking nonstop to keep awake." Atwood was shocked to learn that the manuscript containing the El Salvador poems, whose emotional impact she had just witnessed on the festival audience, lay hidden in Forché's desk drawer. "She was furious when I said I thought the manuscript was unpublishable. I told her about the comments of the small press publisher, and she said: 'No, no, no! You must take them out of the drawer immediately when you get home.' She gave me the address of a woman in New York to send them to. I did just that and within a few days, the book had a publisher."

The Country Between Us appeared in 1981 and quickly generated a torrent of critical attention, both praising and damning the collection. "Its publication was concurrent with El Salvador becoming the hot spot of the moment in the media—this little country the size of Massachusetts that no one could locate on a map in 1978 . . . Two newspaper columnists—Nicholas von Hoffman and Pete Hammill—must have really wanted to write about what was developing in El Salvador early on, but they didn't have what journalists call 'a hook,' a way in. And they came across my book and they wrote columns—both of them, within weeks of each other, I believe. And both mentioned the oddity of having to receive news of the conflict in El Salvador from a poet rather than the usual journalistic sources. These columns were syndicated, and as a result, *The Country Between Us* was born in a flood of notoriety that was very uncommon for poetry books."

The accolades came in the form of the prestigious Lamont Poetry Award, a prize from the Poetry Society of America, and a growing and enthusiastic readership for her work. But the critical barrage was formidable as well and arose, not only from conservative elements of the media, but several unexpected sources as well. "The criticism has never been easy for me. But the criticism from the Right I could at least anticipate. They were very predictable. One could read their ideology quite clearly behind their words. . . . After all, I was writing about the formation of death squads and widespread violence against a people by their own government—a government supported by American funding—and some publications believed I was inventing everything. Or that I was just an hysterical young woman who had simply been overwhelmed by her first experience in the Third World. Or that I didn't have enough perspective to interpret very astutely what I had seen."

But Forché found herself assailed as well by several Left-leaning constituencies and even other literary figures. Their criticism, she felt, was based "on erroneous assumptions that people had made: first, that I would—anyone would—be harebrained enough to have risked their life intentionally, simply to have a poetry career. This sort of comment can only come from someone who wished deeply to be a recognized poet. Maybe the writers in this country are so frustrated that they become somewhat emotionally crippled by their desire or hunger for an illusory notoriety that they think is somehow going to improve their sense of well-being."

And indeed, there was more than a hint of jealousy in some of the commentary. "Mostly these accusations came from men. At the time, some women said this to me: 'Well, Carolyn, it's your gender that's the problem—because maybe they feel this quest—the young writer going off to experience danger and difficulty, coming back to write about it—that's not a female venture.' . . . Interestingly enough, these attacks never came from anyone who had actually been in a war zone. I was very much comforted by poets who, for example, were veterans of Vietnam and Korea and the Second World War. I would have taken these accusations far more seriously had they been leveled by someone who had actually experienced something like this. War does something to human beings that cannot be undone.

"Some poets even went so far as to suggest . . . I had never even *been* to El Salvador!" Forché explained, astonished at the very thought of such a deception. [The mention of this brought an ironic smile to her husband's face; Mattison first met his future wife in El Salvador while covering the war for *Time* magazine.] But the poems of *Gathering the Tribes* had borrowed heavily from Native American and Latino cultures and, so her critics extrapolated, it would not be beyond this poet to appropriate an entire experience.

The sadness for Forché was that all this sound and fury focused primarily on the personality and politics of the writer, almost obscuring the poems themselves—a mere eight of which were explicitly focused on the Salvadoran conflict. Even today, a decade and a half later, it is easy to see how much these circumstances trouble the poet as she tries to piece together her feelings about the matter.

"As I said, I didn't go off into danger. El Salvador was a country 'at peace' (in quotes). I thought I had good reasons for going: I wanted to improve my Spanish, to learn about the culture of the poet I had just translated and perhaps translate other Central American poets. So I was not traveling to a country at war nor was I seeking out a war . . . While there, I became very deeply involved and circumstances changed very quickly. . . . I really believe that the person I was who got on that plane to go to El Salvador the first time was not a person who would have done so had she known what she was about to enter. I became that person, later—the way you become someone when a house is on fire. You become a person who will stay and try to help or who will run. One becomes things by one's surroundings and circumstances and, yes, inclinations."

Because One Is Always Forgotten
In memoriam, José Rudolfo Viera
1939–1981: El Salvador

When Viera was buried we knew it had come to an end,
his coffin rocking into the ground like a boat or a cradle.

I could take my heart, he said, and give it to a *campesino*
and he would cut it up and give it back:

you can't eat heart in those four dark
chambers where a man can be kept years.

A boy soldier in the bone-hot sun works his knife
to peel the face from a dead man

and hang it from the branch of a tree
flowering with such faces.

The heart is the toughest part of the body.
Tenderness is in the hands.

—from *The Country Between Us*

Following the assassination of Monsignor Romero and the murder of six American church women, the conflict in El Salvador was rapidly thrust into the American consciousness and Forché's book became a part of the national debate on Central American policy. The brand "political poet" was used to both damn and lionize her work. She found herself mired in what she now sees is "the cyclic debate peculiar to the United States concerning the relationship between poetry and politics, or the writer and the state. . . . And I felt that the debate wasn't a useful one, that the grounds were reductive and simplistic and unhelpful to anyone who wanted to think about the responsibility of citizens, much less writers. . . . There was no notion that language might be inherently political or perhaps ideologically charged whatever the subject matter and even when the person isn't aware of [it]."

Perhaps, in the cynicism that had taken hold of post-Vietnam, post-Watergate American culture, a new character was being forged in contemporary poetry. The focus was shifting away from the communal world onto the inner workings of language and imagination. A poet rooted in prewar ideals such as Nobel Laureate Czeslaw Milosz could speak of "Literature as a passionate pursuit of the Real." But Terrence Des Pres decries the postmodern sensibility's tendency to abandon poetry's broader concerns for "the further adventures of the self-delighted self." Forché was coming of age as a writer just as the agenda was being redefined, and her clear political stance made her an easy target.

Still, Forché used the platform that had been thrust upon her to carry on the work she had been charged to do by Monsignor Romero. She found herself reading and teaching all around the country. Most writers would thrive on the prospect of a national readership; it had the opposite effect on Carolyn Forché. Between the hectic travel schedule, the absence of any solitude, the anguish over the deaths of Salvadoran friends and the weight of responsibility she'd taken on, she felt something of her self was being obliterated in the process. She was learning that this was the price of her desire to "*do* something." In the following years, she taught, traveled with her husband, reported for National Public Radio from war-torn Beirut and South Africa, and worked for Amnesty International. But the inner voice that had brought her the poetry was gone.

Or, if not gone, altered. "At this time," Forché remembers, "I was writing something that was unrecognizable to me and it was strange, so I thought I wasn't writing. The work on the page was rather fragmented and unusual looking. And so I thought these must constitute notes *toward* poems. Because I was still laboring under the assumption . . . that a poem was a first-person lyric narrative free-verse construct. That it had a voice which was governed by an authoritative subjectivity that could experience the world and express that experience with all its truth claims. . . . And what I was doing was not that at all. . . . I was very frustrated and I put it all in boxes and didn't know what to do. And seven years passed."

In 1986, while pregnant with her first child, Forché was working in South Africa with her husband, covering the antiapartheid campaign. As the time of the birth approached, and determined not to bring this child into life on South African soil, Forché and Mattison moved to Paris to live in a borrowed apartment. To ease the physical discomfort and the lonely hours, she embarked on a new project. "There was a book in the cupboard of French poetry. I went and got a very large French-English dictionary . . . because I decided that if I was going to have a baby in France, I should learn some French! And I had this romantic notion that I was going to learn French by translating poetry." Her husband warned her that she'd never capture the real music of the language but, as time went on, even he grudgingly admitted that some of her versions had accomplished that linguistic alchemy. "I had almost worked my way through the French text. And what was on the last page? [" . . . dans ta vie ensoleillée"—"into your sun-blessed life"]. The lines I had copied from the Holocaust memorial! I had found him—it was the poet Robert Desnos who died in the concentration camps."

The discovery not only led her to publish a translation of Desnos's work, it inspired an even larger undertaking. "I was having difficulty writing at all, much less writing politically or nonpolitically. . . . I felt there was something broken within me and that brokenness manifested itself in the language on the page. And so I began to read the works of other poets who had endured warfare or . . . had been imprisoned or forced into exile, or had endured conditions of extremity of a social or political nature. I read these works the way that someone who has a disease might go to a medical library to do research. I didn't know what I was looking for. I think I do now."

Forché began obsessively collecting these poems from writers representing numerous national and ethnic groups, many of which weren't readily available, especially in English translation—because if poetry as a whole is marginalized in the publishing world, poetry with overt political content is even more so. "I was interested in the impress of extremity on the poetic imagination. I wanted to know what these conditions and circumstances did to the mind of the artist, to the poet. And even if a work was not explicitly about war, would you be able to tell that the poet had been through this? I wanted to know whether there was an indelible mark left by the experience, and whether that mark was 'readable' in the work."

After a decade of gathering poems, her efforts would culminate in the 1992 publication of *Against Forgetting,* a giant compendium of what she calls "the poetry of witness." Forché sees this anthology as "a symphony of utterance, a living memorial to those who had died and those who survived the horrors of the twentieth century. I wanted something that wasn't a statue that pigeons could defecate on. I wanted something that would stay alive like language stays alive." And indeed, her reading of this literature convinced her that "if, for example, a poet is a survivor of the camps during the *shoah,* and the poet chooses to write about snow falling, one can discern the camps in the snow falling. The camps are *in* the falling snow. This is true of all the work of Paul Celan, all of the work of Primo Levi, and all of the work of other poets who have been afflicted by such conditions, yet lived to write about them.

"I started thinking about this notion of 'witness,' because I had some of the same difficulties with so-called political poetry that many of its critics had. And my difficulty had to do with the way such works are produced. I believe that poetry is made by going to the page and retrieving, through the hands, something within the consciousness that is irretrievable by any other means than this physical act. Writing yields a kind of knowledge that one can't talk one's way to or think one's way to. What I felt about political poems which, for me, failed as poems was that the poets were approaching the page knowing what they wanted to say. They weren't allowing them-selves . . . that meditative expectancy, that resonant free play of mind. You have to approach the page with open hands if you're going to carry back something not previously in conscious awareness." Perhaps without realiz-ing it, she had also opened the next path on her own journey.

There are times when the child seems delicate, as if he had not yet
 crossed into the world.
When French was the secret music of the street, the café, the train,
 my own receded and became intimacy and sleep.
In the world it was the language of propaganda, the agreed-upon lie,
 and it bound me to itself, demanding of my life an explanation.
When my son was born I became mortal.

    —from "The Angel of History"

Forché moved back to the United States in 1987, still carrying with her "these strange cryptic notes" that had been accumulating in her notebooks. "We were floating around. We had no home, no full-time job between us. Harry had left *Time* magazine by then. We had a one-year-old baby to care for. It was a very hard time." While her husband had to be away on business, she and her young son Sean took a small apartment for the winter in Provincetown, on Massachusetts's Cape Cod, an affordable retreat once the summer tourist season was over. A friend, Daniel Simko, lived nearby—a Czech poet who fled to the United States following the 1969 Warsaw Pact invasion of his country. He could easily empathize with the distress that had blocked Forché's poetry. "He was upset that I wasn't writing. I told him, 'I have this baby and we live in this tiny place—it's just not possible. I'm too tired, too distracted.' And he said, 'I'll take Sean for two hours every afternoon. I'll bring him to my home, I'll take him out in the carriage, we'll go for walks . . . but you have to promise to write poetry while I'm gone.'" And knowing she might succumb to the motherly impulse to clean or shop during these respites, he added, "And I want to see the pages when I get back here with him."

The gift of time was precisely what Forché needed. The same strange multivoiced lines began appearing in her mind, but now she had the means to receive them, to pursue their leads, to shape them on the page. The work began to mount quickly. "And I realized that now it was emerging as something intact in and of itself. And yes, there were absences in it and disruptions in it, and there was not this discernible first-person voice sustaining itself and gathering momentum through a certain rhythmic pattern that would finally allow for a resolution, that would connect this whole personal experience to the outer world and wrap things up and be finished. No, this was something ongoing and building, interrupting itself and shifting course. In places, it was almost like a mosaic. It was something broken—and I started thinking perhaps I had broken. Sometimes I thought the cause was Salvador or Beirut or South Africa. But I thought that this thing within me that makes language had somehow been smashed and what I was attempting was to put it back together again.

"I found echoes of that idea in other writers. I found it in Celan; I found it in Walter Benjamin in his essay 'The Task of the Translator' where he talks about the translation of a literary work as being akin to reassembling a broken vase. You can remake it, but the cracks show and the new vase doesn't hold water. But it will look like the original vase, the way a translated poem will look something like the original piece—but won't hold the same water as the original. . . . So I was thinking that this was what I was involved in—and I kept doing the work. That was 1987 and that was when *The Angel of History* was started, and those earliest pieces of language are in the first poem of the book, the title poem."

What emerged after seven years as *The Angel of History* is a collage of voices in three long poem sequences; the book creates the feel of an overarching human memory in which the people and events of our century hover. Despite a pervasive sense of alienation and despair, at the same time the poems are structured around a feeling of connectedness, the interpenetration of experiences and lives. The lines tend to be long colloquial utterances, dreamlike and strangely calm; often the poem's narrator or perspective would shift midstream. Yet so transparent and unaffected is the writing, we find ourselves offering our own memories, our personal voices into the gathering presence. I asked Forché about the source of those voices, those memories clearly not her own. "I have thought about them a great deal. I had this idea that language, human spoken language, might be like radio waves in the universe, always intact as they move onward. Everything that's ever been said stays in the universe in some way—that the earth is somehow wrapped in the poem. There's a line in [the book] that says: 'The earth is wrapped in weather, and the weather in risen voices.' And all I could feel when I was writing was that I was somehow pulling at these pieces, these fragments, these swatches of human language. Some of the work obviously issues from my own circumstances, but I don't know where the others come from."

Though the book has sold well, it's created none of the stir of her second collection—and Forché was greatly relieved. Even before the book appeared, Forché herself admitted "this is not, I suppose, what people will expect of me," referring to both the paucity of material over the years and the shift from her more intimate lyric style. "But the expectations have nothing to do with it. This is what I had to do, what I had to write. And that's how long it took. I really didn't have any choice in the matter." And after so long a silence, how did she hope her readers would react? "The process of making this book was mysterious to me and I hope that reading it is mysterious. And since it's so brief a book really, I'm hoping people will read it all at once, in one evening. It seems to do something all at once that doesn't occur if you read it piecemeal." Indeed, Forché has taken the step from writing poems to writing poetry; like the experience of reading a novel, this material grows inside a reader and the rewards are not a series of discreet climaxes but a slow symphonic unfolding. In a comment referring to the *Against Forgetting* anthology—but which seems to me equally applicable to *Angel*—Forché says, "If I could make a hope for my book, the way you could make a hope for your child—I hoped it would haunt the future."

> Smoke wrote from its fire something brief
> in the city of what could be said.
> As if a cemetery were a field of doors. *Requia* crying against the walls.
> Little roofs of moonlight.
> The ecstasy of standing outside oneself—
>
> Anna said "carry this" and "follow behind me."
> The earth is tired and marked, human after human.
>
> "The Notebook of Uprising," section III
> —from *The Angel of History*

When she talks about poetry—her own and that of writers she admires—Carolyn Forché points out that it is "the one art that's really resisted commodification." Its creation is steered by something greater than fashion and market forces. And perhaps the most powerful writing is one where its author is able to restrain the demands of the ego, to intuit the presence of that vitalizing force and allow it to propel the development of the work. I was reminded of the Zen koan concerning the leaf and the river: humans are like leaves that land in the river and think they ought to decide which direction to travel in. We expend a great deal of energy in our lives just paddling against the current, all the while being swept along. But the real grace and momentum in life is derived from allowing the river to determine the course while we simply try to steer with the current. Forché seemed quite pleased with this formulation, laughingly adding that "the river won't let you steer unless you follow her. Even when you *think* you're the one in charge! In that way, art's more like prayer—you can't dictate the terms."

9
Martín Espada

—POETRY AND THE BURDEN OF HISTORY

Hunched over the podium, Martín Espada is an imposing presence, a grizzly bear of a man with dark eyes that devour the page. His poems are, by turns, ferocious, tender, ardently political or touchingly biographical. But in between the poems, when he tells stories about his writing and his life, the audience is caught off guard by his playful and self-deprecating humor. There is a largeness of feeling in the man, and we are willingly snared in the net of his words.

His first two volumes of poetry—*The Immigrant Iceboy's Bolero* (with photographs by his father), and *Trumpets from the Islands of Their Eviction*—made him a rising star in contemporary Latino writing. But it was with his third collection, *Rebellion Is the Circle of a Lover's Hands*, that his work began to be widely recognized. The book was awarded the first PEN/Revson Foundation Fellowship and gained him a national audience. The judges' citation praised the intensity of his writing: "The greatness of Espada's art, like all great arts, is that it gives dignity to the insulted and the injured of the earth."

When I interviewed him, shortly after the publication of *Rebellion,* Martín Espada was still a full-time tenant lawyer and supervisor of a legal services program. Today he is a professor at the University of Massachusetts and his recent collections, *Imagine the Angels of Bread* and *A Mayan Astronomer in Hell's Kitchen,* reveal a deepening of his vision and a still-pungent sense of the political ironies in American life. His social commitment continues to energize his writing, "a poetry of advocacy." In our conversations, we discussed three of the larger themes that seem to run through all his work.   .

❖   ❖   ❖

SR: So much of our poetry revolves around the personal experience of the individual. But yours has a broader, more communal focus. I'm impressed by the way history seems to be one of the large concerns in your writing.

ME: First of all, I think that a poet can be a historian, just as a poet can be a sociologist or journalist or teacher or organizer. I see no contradiction there at all. Secondly, my undergraduate degree was in history, with a focus on U.S. foreign policy in Latin America. I'm also very aware of a tradition that I come out of, which is the tradition of Latin American poets writing in historical terms. If you look at Ernesto Cardenal's *Zero Hour,* for example, that is a history of Nicaragua under Somosa. If you look at many of the poems of Pablo Neruda, likewise you see him writing with his country's history as a focus.

I begin my book [*Rebellion Is the Circle of a Lover's Hands*] with a series of historical poems concerning the island of Puerto Rico—for two basic reasons. First, the need. My sense of the educational system of this country—having been through it myself and also having taught in that system—is that it has in general no sense of history beyond "souvenir history," the kind of history that is commemorated every Fourth of July. A very superficial understanding of history. And that furthermore, there is no sense of the history of Puerto Rico whatsoever—which is not a coincidence. Anytime a country is a colony of another . . . you can expect that the history of that people will be conveniently forgotten at best, and suppressed at worst. So that is the context in which I operate.

But beyond that, beyond the fact that I'm trying to counteract the historical amnesia upon which most political analysis in this country seems to be based—but particularly the analysis of the island—there's also the fact that I really believe that the best stories come out of history. Either the history of . . . great events, great people, or the history of one's own community, one's own family.

SR: It's interesting that in your writing—whether you're talking about large events or small—you focus on history in human terms, putting a human face to history.

ME: That's exactly the phrase that I use. And there are several examples in that series in the beginning of this book. If I were to talk in general terms about the Ponce Massacre, where all those [Puerto Rican] pro-independence marchers were killed in that town in 1937 by the police, it would be a mere footnote which would not be retained by the listener or the reader. I think we are in an age when we have to be conscious as artists that our audience is bombarded—that there is a sensory bombardment going on at all times—and that [they] are going to be desensitized to information. And there has to be a way of presenting information that will reopen the eyes and ears, make it fresh.

SR: You certainly do that in a shocking way when you open with an image like

> The marchers gathered, Nationalists
> massed beneath the delicate white balconies
> of Marina street,
> and the colonial governor
> pronounced the order with patrician calm:
> fifty years of family history
> says it was Pellín
> who dipped a finger
> into the bloody soup of his own body
> and scratched defiance
> in jagged wet letters on the sidewalk.

ME: Exactly. So in the case of the Ponce Massacre, what I do in the title poem of the book is to focus on the real human impact of that historical tragedy. What does it mean that there was a Ponce Massacre? Well, one of the things that it means is that a woman named Nina lost a lover named Pellín she was about to marry. And yet because our struggle as a people has not abated but simply shifted—so that now we also have a political battle to wage in the streets of Boston or New York, just as we did in the streets of Ponce—what she has to contend with in the later part of the poem is that her son is now out in the street the way Pellín was, exposed to the same dangers, and she may lose him also.

And yet, the point of that connection is to say that for these individuals, there is an understanding that the struggle is necessary, that the sacrifice is necessary, that resisting what is put upon us is essential to maintaining our humanity. And so the image of the hands in that poem refers both to Nina's hands, which weave, and to Pellín's hands, which write in blood. But both sets of hands are essential for our resistance and our survival.

SR: Do you think people are aware that their lives move through history? Can we consciously remain focused on the present moment and, at the same time, on the overarching currents moving around us?

ME: I think people are not as aware as they should be—in this country, certainly. There are other places in the world where people are much more aware of historical continuity. If your family has lived in a place for five hundred or a thousand years, you have a stronger understanding of that. But even if we can't name it as history, I think there's a sense that people have that certain things "have always been this way and must always continue this way." In this particular poem, Nina does understand what has to be done and she also is a part of it.

SR: In the poem, she understands that her lover has died before she is even told, as if some deeper voice inside her is narrating events. So if poetry such as this provides the individual with some sense of the motion of history, how does that change the way they will behave tomorrow? The poem ends:

> Years later, with another family
> in a country of freezing spring rain
> called Nueva York,
> Nina is quietly nervous
> when her son speaks of rifles
> in a bullhorn shout,
> when coffins are again bobbing
> on the furious swell of hands and shoulders,
> and the whip of nightsticks
> brings fresh blood
> stinging from the scalp.
>
> But rebellion
> is the circle of a lover's hands,
> that must keep moving,
> always weaving.

ME: I think having this historical sense makes it a little easier to get through the day. One of the most painful aspects of being human is when you don't understand what's happening to you—when you lack the ability to analyze the forces that are shaping your life or destroying it.

SR: That's certainly what the historian's perspective provides. What more than that does a poet/historian offer?

ME: Language. A unique way of expressing the history outside the fairly narrow academic confines in which you normally find it. I think what a poet can do is make history real, make it live, make it accessible, make it human— in a way most historians do not.

SR: And maybe the reader can make choices in a new way as a result.

ME: People already know what it is I'm describing. I have the opportunity, the forum, to express what they already know. And if I've done it right, they may then recognize themselves in the poem.

SR: Poets today so often claim to be only writing for themselves. There is an artificial barrier erected that implies: "Poetry is purely a private act, created out of an individual need. If readers, afterward, find the words useful, so be it." But it sounds to me as if you are consciously speaking to a certain audience, a certain type of reader.

ME: I am conscious of an audience beyond myself. Obviously I'm the first audience, and if I don't like it, no one else gets to see it. But if I put a poem out into the world, it's for a number of different audiences. But suffice it to say it is more than simply the Puerto Rico or Latino community, that they are a starting point but not a finishing point. Ultimately my audience is anyone who is willing to listen. . . .

SR: I've heard you say that "one of a poet's duties is to challenge the official history." You do this in your poetry when you proclaim new heroes, ones we may not be aware of, while you also struggle to tear down some old icons we probably take for granted. I'm thinking specifically of "Clemente's Bullets" versus the poem "Bully."

ME: That's a very perceptive observation. The fact of the matter is that one of the duties a poet must assume, I think, is to challenge the "official" history—the history found in middle school textbooks or in tourist brochures. In the first of the poems you mentioned, you have the case of Clemente Soto Vélez. Here is an individual who is unknown in this country for very deliberate reasons. If you consider what the poem tells you about

him, that he was thrown in jail, spent six years in various federal penitentia-
ries—for what he spoke and wrote. He was convicted of seditious con-
spiracy. He was convicted of thinking, speaking, and writing about indepen-
dence for Puerto Rico.

This is the sort of circumstance when the First Amendment becomes the
last amendment. So Clemente went to prison, an experience which would
destroy most of us, which would turn most of us into bitter self-destructive
human beings. Instead, Clemente came out of prison and went on to become
the founder of the Puerto Rican literary community in New York. He was
an organizer, a journalist, and someone who at the age of eighty-six is still
fighting. An extraordinary person. [Note: Clemente Soto Vélez died in 1993,
at the age of eighty-eight.]

So, yes, I am trying to redefine heroes and heroism when I write about
Clemente. I am also doing the same when I write "Bully" [about the Boston
school that changed its name from Roosevelt to Hernández]. It amazes me,
but maybe fifty years from now, society will remember Richard Nixon as a
great man. That is distinctly possible if Theodore Roosevelt can be seen as
a great man. Here's a man who not only was one of the architects of U.S.
imperialism at the turn of the century, not only made his political reputation
in the Spanish-American War, which was as imperialist a landgrab as was
ever orchestrated by the U.S. in recent history—but here was a profoundly
racist individual, who believed in social Darwinism, believed in biological
determinism, was very up front about it as people were during that period
in history. Yet there is this cult of sentimentality that has grown up around
him, largely because of his support of environmentalism, which has sanitized
some deeply obnoxious traits. Walking into that school auditorium, seeing
his statue and seeing all these kids who he would have been appalled by—
all I could think of was that it was a fitting revenge. The school no longer bore
his name because he was no longer a hero to that community.

SR: Yours is a strongly political viewpoint. But what I love in your work is
the effort you make to avoid purely political rhetoric and the strident voice
of the partisan. Take a poem like "Two Mexicanos Lynched in Santa Cruz,
California, May 3, 1877," written about an old photograph. It doesn't even
overtly criticize; it only seems to describe, to present the cold fact of
experience to the reader.

ME: First of all, it's the basic writer's distinction between showing and
telling. If my work is based on the image, the image will show and that should
be enough. Certainly when you get to the end of that poem and I am
describing the faces of the lynching party, how different they all seem to be

from one another—there is an explicit condemnation there of the one feature they have in common:

> [the faces]
> faded as pennies from 1877, a few stunned
> in the blur of execution,
> a high-collar boy smirking, some peering
> from the shade of bowler hats, but all
> crowding into the photograph.

I am aware of the pitfalls of political poetry, which include the possibility of polemic or didactic results. But what I am striving for is to tell the story as a journalist would, and that involves a multiple series of choices including choice of story, choice of sources, choice of images and language. . . . But this is not a history that gets told. People are not usually aware that, not only Blacks, but Chicanos were lynched in the American Southwest in appalling numbers, and this was a major way of consolidating power over land. When you talk about how the West was won, you have to talk about that too.

SR: What I find so powerful in the poem is the way they are *trying* to fit into the photo, to assume a place in a historical moment that, ultimately, they cannot understand. At our distance, we can see what they cannot. And we see them as being, not only terrible, but pitiful and profoundly human in their weakness. But it's the framework of the poem that does that, that shifts our perspective—and perhaps makes us even rethink our confident understanding of our own present situations.

ME: This, of course, has a lot to do with getting people to see and hear anew. There really isn't anything new under the sun in the broadest sense, so what you have to do is to reinvent it, to say something a little bit differently than it's been said before. I'll give you an example: let's say there's a scenario where there's a political prisoner in a cell, waiting to be interrogated. And the interrogator is coming down the hall and you can hear the echo of his boots. There are two dilemmas here: the first is that, in terms of art, that scene has been captured over and over again. It's almost cliché. However, the second and greater dilemma is that the scene is real—that it happens all the time and it's probably happening right now. And so the challenge for the political artist is how to render that in such a way that people's sensibilities don't skip over that scene, so that ultimately they can really empathize with the prisoner in that cell.

SR: That points to what I find is the second presence that pervades, even dominates, much of your work: after history is anger. It runs almost like a like a bass note through all of your collections. Of course in our society, anger is a taboo—to even feel one's anger, let alone express it. But the danger, as I see it, in having this feeling prominent in so many poems is that, in the end, they might all blend into one extended scream.

ME: I think you're right that there's a danger in having anger overwhelm a poem or group of poems so that it becomes the only thing a reader takes away. But it becomes a matter of tone—that anger can be a recurrent feeling in the poems as long as you vary the tone. . . . I play many different melodies across that bass note. If you flip through the book you'll see poems like "Two Mexicanos," which is a very bitter piece, . . . but you'll also find poems like "Revolutionary Spanish Lesson" or "The New Bathroom Policy at English High School," where the whole thrust is humor. All those poems share anger and yet they are so different in terms of their realization because of tone, and that's a deliberate choice, to create that variety.

SR: I love the wild exaggerations you concoct. The image of the poet in "Revolutionary Spanish Lesson"—it's like a shrewd hysteria.

> Whenever my name
> is mispronounced,
> I want to buy a toy pistol,
> put on dark sunglasses,
> push my beret to an angle,
> comb my beard to a point,
> hijack a busload
> of Republican tourists
> from Wisconsin,
> force them to chant
> anti-American slogans
> in Spanish

In some ways yours reminds me of the poetry of Kenneth Patchen, who also used humor and satire as a leavening agent for his angry social commentary and antiwar poems. It provides us with a way of thinking freshly about our own experiences.

ME: And I have to agree, parenthetically, that anger is something we're "not supposed to have," in no small part because if you started to examine why you had such anger you would start to figure out who is responsible for it and that might mean challenging the status quo in a way that would change it.

So there are political reasons for the suppression of our anger. . . . For me, if I were to leave the anger out of a poem where I think it belongs, it would be the same as if I were writing a poem about a street that was filled with red cars and not mentioning any of them. It would be dishonest.

SR: And yours is not an intellectualized response; it is a direct and visceral experience. Where does that come from in your own life?

ME: I think that anger is expressed for the first time in this book [*Rebellion*]. In the past, what I'd done most of the time was to write about other people. And that's the poetry of advocacy—it's still what I do primarily. But I began exploring a new vein in this book, which was writing about my own experience in the first person. And there are some poems in the book which show very clearly where the anger came from. There's a poem called "Niggerlips," which I know you're familiar with, where it's obvious where the anger came from. It came from having to deal with racist abuse at a sensitive time in my life, high school. And what that poem expresses was just the tip of the iceberg. It also comes from having been raised in a household with my father who is a brilliant man, who is also brown-skinned, and seeing how that has injured him. And the things he went through were far worse than anything I ever experienced, in no small part because he encountered Jim Crow segregation in the South during his time in the military. So there is reference to that in my work as well. . . . He sensitized me to that and passed on, not only the stories of his own experience, but his own anger.

SR: But for many people, such profound anger would result in self-destruction. Yet it looks as if you've made a conscious choice to take that anger and transform it into something else, partly for your own salvation but also for the sake of the art.

ME: Well, there are many who share my experiences, who might think my same words, but who never have the opportunity to express them—to be able to write the poem, get it published, read it to an audience. I get to do that. And it's part of my responsibility as a poet to do that, for those who do not get the chance to speak. That's poetry of advocacy.

SR: This points to the third aspect that is central to your poetry. There is a sense of transcendence, that something exists which carries us beyond the bitterness of personal trials and the burden of history—and that always seems to involve the family, the redemption possible in the deepest human relationships.

ME: That's because I see, not only history, but personal experience as a dynamic rather than a stasis. There is a dynamic between oppression and resistance, between victimizer and victim. There is not only struggle but triumph. And seeing that dynamic, that tension, that conflict, that's where I try to go for my poems, that place where those elements meet and combust. For me the essence of expressing our dignity, our defiance, our resiliency, our potential for solidarity is in the family.

SR: There's a perfect example of that in your poem "La Tumba de Buenaventura Roig," where you journey back to Puerto Rico with your father and search for your great grandfather's grave.

ME: First of all, one of the ironies of that poem is that, in the end, we don't find the grave. . . . But we do gather plenty of evidence of my great grandfather's presence—including finding a grave digger who was actually at the funeral, which is amazing because it took place in 1941. On the journey, what you find is not always what you set out to find. . . . Because the poem is not only about Buenaventura Roig but about the Puerto Rico of his time which was a harsh place but also a beautiful place, a place that does not any longer exist. So there was a very powerful, profound sense of belonging to something bigger than myself, as I say in the last stanza: "we are small among mountains, / and we listen for your voice / in the peasant chorus of five centuries." I felt I was in the presence of those centuries and it was an overwhelming feeling.

SR: Because then, even in our limited perspective, we begin to get some sense of the design that we are part of, of where and who we are. And that can't help but affect us as we push on with our lives and choose our direction.

　　That brings me to the poem that I think is perhaps the loveliest in the collection: "Colibrí." It creates a palpable moment where the ties of family and love counterbalance both the individual's pain and the burden of history. It begins:

> In Jayuya,
> the lizards scatter
> like a fleet of green canoes
> before the invader.
> The Spanish conquered
> with iron and words:
> "Indio Táino" for the people
> who took life
> from the rain
> that rushed through trees

> like evaporating arrows,
> who left rock carvings
> of eyes and mouths
> in perfect circles of amazement.

ME: That poem came about as a direct result of an experience I had with my wife on our honeymoon. We were in Jayuya staying in an old converted hacienda, which is essentially a hotel . . . a very beautiful spot. We came out of our room and found a hummingbird trapped in the hallway. And the bird was crazy, smacking off the walls, desperate to get out, obviously a wild bird. And my wife, quite instinctively, managed to calm the bird down, get her hands around it, which as you can imagine is almost impossible. And while she was doing that, I pushed open the wooden shutters of the window, and in one motion she pushed out. And the bird disappeared into the dusk. . . .

The whole scene to me was so miraculous, I knew I'd eventually write about it, but it took a while before I found the context for the poem, which was simply the ghosts of that place. Fifteen minutes from that spot you could go to a place called "la piedra escrita," literally "the written rock," where you can see the carvings left behind by the Taíno Indians who had been there when the Spanish arrived and were quickly disposed of by them. The Spanish, in conquering the Taíno, did it by slaughtering them with swords and cannon but also did it by taking away their culture, their language, changing the names of everything. One of the themes that also runs through this book is the power of naming: who gets to name your experience. Do you do it or does someone else do it for you and impose it on you? And that is a reflection of the relative power you have in a given society.

So what the poem deals with is that legacy of conquest, and making the connection with this hummingbird and his panic:

> Now the colibrí
> darts and bangs
> between the white walls
> of the hacienda,
> a racing Taíno heart
> frantic as if hearing
> the bellowing god of gunpowder
> for the first time.

And the poem ends with a tribute to my wife, really, but a tribute to all people who are kind, and wishing that the world were that way.

SR: But is it just wishing? Aren't you pointing to something in the world that is capable of redeeming the personal and historical trauma—not only quieting the bird but setting it free?

ME: The reason I have hope—and this is one of the hopeful poems in the collection—is that people like that still exist. That, in spite of everything, we are as human beings still capable of being gentle, still capable of kindness, of generosity. . . . Given the cruelty of history, there is virtually no reason in the world any of us should have those qualities. Yet they persist. I am always astonished at the kindness of oppressed people. That, despite what's put upon them, they can resist—and one of the ways they resist is to become more human, deliberately choosing to contradict the image of dehumanization which is foisted upon them, by exhibiting those human qualities of dignity and grace and gentleness.

10
Marge Piercy

—THE COMMUNAL VOICE

At a party recently, we were discussing the funding crisis in the arts, and one practical-minded businessman complained, "But tell the truth: what good is poetry? What does it really do for people?" I wanted to say: it marks off occasions of beauty in the midst of our daily struggles—though I realized this argument would make little impression on "the bottom line." But if one would like to examine seriously what good poems bring about in our lives, a fitting place to begin might be with the writing of Marge Piercy. Through fifteen collections of poetry (and a symmetrical fifteen novels as well), her passionate voice has been embraced by diverse groups of readers for its political fire, feminist determination, spiritual questioning, and not least, for the sheer pleasure of its music.

As you read *Circles on the Water,* her selected poems, or collections like *Mars and Her Children* and *The Art of Blessing the Day,* you will see how the various threads of her work are braided together to form one expansive journey. More than feminist polemic, her poems contain visions of a woman's struggle to take responsibility for her own life, and describe the fierce honesty necessary in a loving relationship. Her political poems make human faces and recognizable neighborhoods of what would otherwise be merely abstract ideas and cold statistics. At readings, rallies, study groups, and celebrations, her poems are used like hammer and nails, basic tools for building new lives.

In the last several years, many of her poems have become part of the liturgy of the Jewish Reconstructionist movement in which she and her husband (the novelist Ira Wood) are active. Her "poems of praise" are pure lyrical affirmations of the simple experiences we tend to gloss over amid the "important" business of our days: the first salad of March, the heron glimpsed in the marshland, the sweet ache after working in the garden, the lighting of the Sabbath candles.

The couple has also embarked on a new venture together: in 1996, they established Leapfrog Press, a small publishing house committed to championing "books that tell a strong personal story" whose catalog includes diverse fiction, nonfiction, and poetry titles.

Secluded in her Cape Cod home, surrounded by the incredibly lush gardens she has terraced into the hillside, Ms. Piercy's labor makes wild words grow as abundantly as the mounds of zucchini and the tide of orange poppies. Through fair weather and violent storm, her growing season persists. Savoring the poems, we too feel the re-creation that is at the center of our lives—and that, in all truth, is good enough for me.

SR: A good deal of your poetry is built upon a communal voice. Reaching beyond the purely subjective, you seem to be speaking both *to* and *for* your audience. There are even a few of the poems in the new collection that start out with "I" but wind up speaking "we."

MP: One of the functions of poetry has always been to articulate for people, to give dignity to people's experiences, their sufferings, their pleasures, the dramas of their lives. Utterance gives us both a sense of "Oh yes, it was that way for me too." And that sense makes people feel less crazy, less alienated, less weird. There are some poems which are very strongly communal poems where what I am doing is saying in a poem what a lot of people have thought and think, and giving expression to it. And those poems tend to get used a great deal, like the pro-choice poem called "Right to Life," [as have] a number of the poems from *My Mother's Body* about my mother's death. And of course there are also the wedding poems—they make their way into some people's lives.

SR: I love the idea of poetry being used, like a tool or a marker. Is this because certain groups feel your voice represents their perspective?

MP: Used by groups, by individuals. There are also the poems people use as liturgy. A lot of my poetry is used by Jewish Reconstructionist and Reform groups. I have a strong sense of *we* and there are those poems that very obviously are communal poems. They are as carefully wrought and crafted as any other, but there is a great need to create a simpler surface in those poems. The prevailing aesthetics is such that if you create what appears to be a clearer, simpler surface, somehow that takes less art, but it actually takes an awful lot more work. Other poems that are just as useful to people are very individual and specific. They require crossing a certain boundary of shame to write them; what you are going into are stranger, more private experiences—and you hope they will resonate for other people, but you don't know, you have no idea.

There are still others where the writing of the poem is a journey and you can't know if it's public, private, where you are going, or what you are doing with it. You know the poem is important, but the poem itself is a journey that has a very uncertain outcome until the poem is really finished. And I don't mean the first draft. Often times the first draft doesn't really go where it has to go; such poems can take a week to write, a month, a year, five years, ten years, twelve years. I think there was one poem that took twelve years because I couldn't get to the end of the poem until I had arrived at a different vision, different knowledge, a different place. Typically such poems take a year.

SR: Is it your assumption that if you can work your way to the end of the poem, then that is the thought passage the reader can navigate as well?

MP: Poems are different. The genesis of the poem is irrelevant to its success. There are poems that come as if dictated. That you write through once, and there it is. And there are poems that take a year or two to write—but neither is better. The genesis of a poem has nothing to do with whether or not it ends up working.

SR: A lot of contemporary poets maintain a certain distance from their readers, but your role seems almost shamanistic.

MP: I think that my readings are often at their best in strengthening an emotional public experience. I know that people laugh or cry . . . and that seems perfectly appropriate. I want people to go with the poems and experience them almost bodily. . . . I think that if a poem is emotionally coherent, [it] can carry quite a freight of complicated thought and imagery and structure.

SR: Do the changes in your audience over the years alter the way you write or speak? Certainly, between a typical audience in the 1960s and the 1990s, there are dramatic differences in their daily experiences, their political awareness, their expectations about life. And your own situation has changed as well.

MP: Your life changes, the situation changes, everything changes. I feel that since my second book there has been a consistent voice in my writing but it varies enormously from poem to poem. My experience varies, what I am writing about varies. The audience I reach is an audience containing quite a range in age and experience. So something in the poems obviously works— but people are attracted by different poems. In a lot of poets' work, you know what kind of poems you are going to get. I write a lot of different poems. I am a very curious person. I write a lot of poems about the natural world. I write about relationships between people. I write religious poems. I write political poems. I write philosophical poems. There are love poems, poems of all sorts. People may like one kind of poetry. There are people who are crazy about the poems I write about cats. People take what they need. The different parts of books are often well loved by very different audiences.

SR: But from the beginnings of feminism until now, in what the journalists are calling "the postfeminist era" . . .

MP: Is this the postfeminist era? Then why are so many women dying every day? If this is postfeminism, why are women being killed in very large numbers?

SR: My point exactly; because of the situation at the time, many of your early poems seemed almost like battle cries. Now, when they are talking about the end of the movement . . .

MP: They first announced the end of the movement in about 1970. Actually, I think that this election campaign, on the Democratic side, is very strongly riding on women's energy [Bill Clinton's 1992 presidential campaign]. And there is a resurgence of women seeing what they can do.

SR: Clearly your poems are not aimed exclusively at women, but I think that the creation of the women's movement was a strong impetus in your early work.

MP: If you go back to *Hard Loving,* you'll see that it's is not a strongly feminist collection. A lot of those poems are about the antiwar movement, being in SDS, and the civil rights movement. By the time you get to *Living in the Open* certainly, or *To Be of Use* even more strongly, it's true that feminist concerns played a large role.

SR: I think that physicality is one of the real strengths in your writing. We climb inside moments we'd otherwise have no access to—both the pleasurable ones as well as those we'd normally avoid at all costs. "Woman in the bushes," about a homeless woman, or "Rape poem" are perfect examples.

MP: There often are one or two men who leave about two thirds of the way through that poem, feeling what it's like to live with the fear of rape. Sometimes when I read the pro-choice poem "Right to Life," a few people get up and walk out. I feel that it is political; you can understand that. But it makes me wonder, during the rape poem, just who gets angry and leaves.

SR: I heard you read that poem to a packed auditorium in the Boston Public Library. I remember it rolled across the audience like a nor'easter. There is a great difference between thinking you understand a situation and suddenly feeling the body bringing you a new awareness. Do you trust the senses more than the intellect to bring you information about the world?

MP: I don't live in the university like most poets do. I live in a place where I am very rooted into the land. In some ways I am a peasant. I am very aligned to the seasons and the weather and my body. I do write very strongly out of a women's body. I am not a poet who ever pretended not to be female.

SR: A line that struck me in one poem spoke of the way we shield ourselves from feeling: "the pain of others is the noise of traffic passing." That emotional buffer seems to be a contemporary survival mechanism: the more horror we confront—in the daily news, in the communities where we live— the more we attempt to overlook the lives of others around us.

MP: Example: in Boston there was a tremendous outpouring of sympathy for the poor Russian sailors [during the Tall Ships celebration] who did not have enough to eat. Now these are people who pass hundreds of homeless people every day in the streets of Boston and their response to [them] is "Get them out of the way. Clean them up, clear them out." It is simply that somehow sailors on a Russian ship who need food are much easier to sympathize with than people sleeping on grates. *They* are always there. They are always around in the cities now. You go down Fifth Avenue in the morning in New York and every doorway has a homeless person in it.

SR: Right across the street from the White House in Washington, D.C.

MP: But poems are not political platforms. You don't, at the end of them, say, "Give your excess clothes to Rosie's Place." That isn't what poems do. I guess I share that eighteenth-century belief that feeling for something . . . [enables one to act] more ethically. If you believe that other people are human also, you will not sweep them off the streets. You will not feel that hostility towards having to share your city with people who do not have anything left. It isn't that I think poems are a good way to get people to act, but that I think they are a way of getting people to feel, to think, to experience. I guess I believe out of that identification comes more appropriate action.

SR: Is the writing of the poems part of a mental discipline, so you don't slip into that oblivious state of mind?

MP: One of the things you learn as a poet is to pay attention. It's the quality of attention you pay that makes the poetry alive. . . . Attention is love. I wrote a poem about that too, about blessings; it's in *What Are Big Girls Made Of.* That's a concept that interests me a lot—that blessing things is a way of paying attention to them. It is a way of forcing yourself to experience freshly.

SR: In contemporary literature, isn't such "poetry of praise" almost a taboo? As if such feeling runs counter to what it means to be modern?

MP: Neruda wrote them. . . . It is a certain quality of attention to things. I do live very much in my body and in the natural world and in the social world and in the political world and in the economic world. All these different webs—they all relate to me. They are all part of the vision.

SR: And then is your writing about them a way to unite the webs, to create a center from which they may interweave?

MP: Poetry is in its nature a very centering activity. Reading poetry is too. It basically lines up a whole lot of different ways of binding consciousness. The part of the brain that deals with words and meaning. The part of the brain that deals with sounds and patterns. The parts that deal with rhythm, with sense, with imagery, dream imagery, surreal imagery—all of these different levels. All of these different ways of knowing come together in poems. That is why the sound is so tremendously important in poems. A lot of poems are written for the eye only and they come apart when they are spoken.

SR: Since so many of your poems delight in the experience of the body and the physicality of experience, it was all the more poignant to read some of your new work depicting the failing of the body. I'm thinking of poems like "Thinking of Homer at twilight," which deals with your diminished sight.

MP: I do face the possibility of blindness. Now my vision in my right eye is good, but I went through several years of increasing blindness before the last, successful operation. But I feel that it is very important to integrate into our experience the knowledge that we are mortal, the experience of aging. I don't want to pretend that I am thirty. I do not like how women are swept out of the way in this society, how there is a pretense that older women do not exist. The establishment is always looking for a new young woman to be the discovery. And as you get older, instead of accumulating dignity and honors, you're suppose to go to the back of the bus and keep your mouth shut. There is a real hatred of older women in our society. It comes from both men and women. Women are terrified of getting older. It is such an amazing thing we have created for women—that their bodies are not suppose to show they have lived. Or they aren't suppose to demonstrate any accumulation of weight or experience. The ideal woman is just like the woman at the end of *A League of Her Own.* Her friend says, "But you look just like *you*," and she answers, "Oh yes, I married a plastic surgeon." . . . That is all you can do because otherwise you have to be prepared to spend hundreds of thousands of dollars on maintenance of the perfect body. What we admire is less and less *woman* and more and more an android that is created. It is so stupid.

I learned a lot from elderly people when I was a child. But very few children learn anything from old people anymore. They generally don't have much contact with them. The elderly have become these caricatures you laugh at or shrink away from. I hear women in their thirties talking about how awful old women look. It is a form of dumb self-hatred. You can't fear getting older. There is no point to fearing it. You have to find something positive in it. You have to find some growth—of strength or wisdom or spiritual experience or political savvy or something. You have to believe that experience teaches you something. What you need is a set of exercises that constantly make things new, that constantly cause you to re-experience things. I think, as you get older, it is more difficult on some level and easier on another. You learn these mental disciplines that make you . . . pay attention. I pay much better attention now then I did when I was younger. When I was younger I was constantly distracted. I had a very short attention span.

SR: In your poetry, there is one strain that involves the experience of being at home within the body, the self. But there is another that seems to be centered on the struggle to be grounded within the natural terrain or even the urban landscape. Several of the most potent depict the terrible feeling of dislocation so many of us feel from our own surroundings.

MP: There is a longish poem called "Up and Out" in *Mars and Her Children* that is about our loss of a sense of rootedness, our inability to love where we come from. That so many of the places we create in our country are really quite ugly or bland, that somehow they don't hold us, they don't feed us, we don't love them, we want to leave them. Success means moving up and out. Success means leaving behind your roots, getting rid of the people you knew. . . . The whole poem is about the cost of that dispatching of one's own past.

SR: One stanza says

> How can we belong to ourselves, when home
> is something to pry yourself out of
> like a pickup stuck on a sand road;
> when what holds you has to be sacrificed
> as a fox will gnaw off a foot to be free.

If we have no home in the world, it's difficult to feel at home inside ourselves.

MP: I am also talking about the kind of assimilation which America has demanded of people and the loss that occurs when you forget where you came from. The forgetting in families of where they came from, why they came, who they were, how you came to be here. . . . The whole idea of retiring to a new place, for example. I saw that with my parents. There is nobody who knows who you are; . . . there is nobody who remembers your family history or the work you did or what you were in the community. . . . Both my parents were very rooted in their working class communities in different ways, and when they went to Florida they were nothing, they were nobody. There is a tremendous loss of context.

SR: Though this idea is present in earlier books as well, *Mars* seems to devote a lot of energy toward reclaiming your own Jewish identity and history.

MP: I have been very involved in Jewish renewal, probably since my mother's death. I said kaddish for her for a year, and I was going "blah blah bah"—since in my family, only my brother had Hebrew instruction. I wasn't bat-mitzvahed until I was fifty. I have been learning Hebrew in the middle of my life. It was recognizing that I had a need to say rituals that were meaningful. It was wanting to recreate these experiences from the inside, as Reconstructionists do, to re-experience them, to find a sense of my own continuity with my mother and my grandmother.

SR: The writing was a sort of reclamation—of unexplored parts of your life?

MP: That has been a long process, a conscious process for maybe fifteen years.

SR: It's striking because, in contrast, much of contemporary poetry seems intent on the experience of *now*. Your incorporation of an historical element deepens the voice of the poems and increases their range. One of the lines that comes to mind is "for she is a tree of life."

MP: That is a phrase out of the liturgy.

SR: The poem depicts a modern scene—you, your mother, and grandmother, around the table preparing supper. And the image of the woman, your grandmother, becomes a manifestation of "the tree of life"—"I see her opening into flushed white / blossoms the bees crawl into. I see her / branches dipping under the weight of the yield"—these lines suddenly connect the scene to centuries of individuals who've witnessed this vision at the core of the family.

MP: It's not just the family, it's *Torah,* it's the whole living tradition. But you have to understand that in the *Kabbalah* there is a description of a living *Torah* that is constantly being added to, constantly being re-experienced. At Sinai when the revelation came, each Jew that ever lived was present, and each one heard something slightly different. And the final truth is the truth of everyone who has a piece of that truth, putting it all together.

SR: There was a rabbi I spoke with once who said that no prayer is complete unless it includes some portion of improvisation. I like that sense that any spiritual expression must combine an ear for the tradition and awareness of that truth we embody at the present moment.

MP: Yes, and I have a very strong sense of a very rich tradition. When I am lighting the candles, I am doing something people have done for thousands of years, and there is a whole line of women behind me that are briefly alive as [I] do that. I have a very strong sense of that in a lot of parts of life, that we embody the past in us as we contain the future that we are creating.

You know, in this poem, the tree image also represents the world-tree which we are busily destroying. . . . The "tree of the world" is a very old image. Like most people that have studied myths, I am very aware when I hear these things, of the resonance in other cultures. It is the same reason that tarot cards are interesting because they have such a rich storehouse of Western imagery. We are all using these images when we think and read. I use them very passionately, but at the same time there is a part of my brain that makes all the connections. I always figure that whatever you are doing you bring the full intelligence to it. If you are being religious, you bring your full intelligence to it, you bring everything you know cross-culturally, you bring everything you know scientifically—you don't shut off part of your mind. . . . Whenever you shut off part of your mind and don't *know* what you know, we are always making messes then. We pretend we don't know that if I throw a can out the window, that it doesn't go anyplace except down where it lies for the next person. That what we put in the water is *in* the water, what we put in the air stays *in* the air, what we put in our bodies is *in* our bodies. Everything we do we have to do with as much awareness as possible and I think that is what poetry aims for.

SR: You are making the assumption that we possess this storehouse of knowledge, but that we don't always have access to it?

MP: We need a lot more knowledge always than we have; we are always knowledge hungry. But yes we know a lot of things we don't always want to know; we don't want to think about them. I was talking about the consequences we know exist but we don't want to recognize exist. We don't want to acknowledge.

SR: The poem "Amidah" creates that experience very powerfully. "We reach back through two hundred arches of hips / long dust, carrying their memories inside us / to live again in our life." It's as if you are speaking through a larger self, one that takes in many times and experiences.

MP: I believe the self is largely an artificial construct, that we flow out into other people. We are trained to think of individuals as very discrete and as if you know exactly what you are. But we are very fluid beings. Our consciousnesses touch each other. We are influenced by the place, the place enters us, the era shapes us, what we think we are. . . .

SR: The note at the bottom of the poem explains that it was written as part of a Reconstructionist siddur.

MP: It is a part of the service. I haven't collected in my poetry books much of the liturgical writing I've done. I was on the committee that worked on the siddur for B'nai Or, and that was one of the parts of service I wrote.

SR: It seemed as if poems like this represented a new development, a new voice in your poetry.

MP: I don't think it is new, but I think it has been much sharpened by my liturgical work. I have viewed myself operating within the web of history for a long time. It's part of the way I look at the world; it involves balancing all of these different forces. I am both someone who lives enormously in the moment, lives very fully in the body and the senses and in my relationships— but I also try to maintain the sense at the same time of being active in history. Both forces lead to me and the values I try to incorporate and embody. . . . For example, look at the people in Sarajevo who thought they knew what they were doing with their [lives], what was happening with their lives. Suddenly, everything changes—even who you think you are. I have observed how extraordinary people can be—either extraordinarily good or evil, in circumstances that make great demands upon them. They are far different from the people they get to be in daily life, that they permit themselves to be. All sorts of things impact us at once; we live out some of the selves we could be, but there are huge numbers of selves that we never get to live out, except in unusual circumstances. Sometimes a poem can speak out of those other selves. . . .

I think that having been politically active, I've been given a strong sense of the untapped capacities in ordinary people, because I have seen it come forth. . . . You see people, who never thought of themselves as brave, rising up in situations of danger to protect [other] people. You see people whose lives had a very narrow compass, who never thought of themselves as intellectuals, suddenly grasping complex ideas. You see them solving problems they didn't think they could solve or coming together with people very different from themselves and finding commonalty that enables them to transcend the prejudices they grew up with or their notions of themselves.

SR: And sometimes a poem can facilitate that new experience. You touch on a curious idea about the purpose of poetry and the poet's task in "Thinking of Homer":

Homer worked in an oral tradition,
as did my story-telling grandmother whose eyes
were white as boiled egg with cataracts,
but I write. Conventionalized dense squiggles
are how I translate the world, how I
transform energy into matter into energy.

MP: The energy that produces the poem becomes matter. *This* is matter [*tapping a copy of her book on the table*], print on the page, books. And then it goes back into energy again when you read them or speak them. Poems are little machines for recreating energy. . . .

But this is not that unusual. I had a marvelous conversation Sunday with Zalman Schachter, who is a very important Reconstructionist rabbi. A lot of the metaphors he was using, and which I was responding to, were metaphors out of the world of computers. He was talking about spiritual eldering and he [used] expressions like "downloading yourself and your knowledge onto the hard disk of the world." I love metaphors out of the modern experience. I use very ancient symbols but I also use very contemporary ones. I am very much a part of the electronic world and I like that, I like to feel connected to that. I am totally dependent on a computer.

SR: If the poem is an energy transformer, it must also serve as a bridge between worlds of experience—from the natural world to the poet's consciousness; from the written poem to the reader's imagination; from the reader, reshaped into some new experience of the world.

MP: Of course it is. But words alone don't do anything—if words are all there is. Words can't hurt or heal or do things out in the world. I have an orientation, which is at the heart of Judaism, toward actions: it is what you do that matters. But now, speaking is an act, artistic creation is an act, artistic production is real production. I guess what I am saying is that you have to lead a more balanced life; it is incumbent upon you to do things as well as talk about them. You also have an obligation to be active because you are a complete human being and you are connected with other human beings in a social web and an economic web.

SR: Can you tell me about the daily process you use to allow for the energies around you to become part of your writing?

MP: I write every day. That consistent effort is important to the process. It's partly about learning to concentrate—so, yes I work every day I'm home. Mondays are the days I don't write. Mondays I try to handle all the interface with the world. The rest of the week, I write—except when I am traveling, and I do travel a lot to give readings and workshops, and to do research and promote books—the British and European market for my work is very important to me. . . .

My husband and I get up about 6:00 A.M., we drink coffee, we do some stretching exercises, and then we walk four miles. When we come home, we eat breakfast and go to work, and we don't deal with each other.

SR: You go walking in the woods?

MP: It depends on the season—season, wind, flies, all sorts of things. We have a number of walks, and they are chosen by wind conditions, weather conditions, ice, snow. There are some you can't do in wet weather, some you can't do when it is windy, some that are good when it is windy but not good when it is too hot. There is one that is closed this month because of flies, but it will open next month.

SR: And then you each retreat to your cubbyhole?

MP: We each have an office with a computer in it. We go off and go to work.

SR: Do you share what you're working on during the course of the day?

MP: We don't share our work everyday, but we share it at certain intervals, when we think it is ready to share, when we want some feedback and criticism. Then depending on the time of year we might work 8:00 to 3:00, 8:00 to 4:00 P.M.; it varies.

SR: Looking at all you've worked on, around your house and the beautiful gardens, I get the sense of a marvelous synthesis between the building of home and the unfolding of work. Can you tell me how it feels being rooted in this place, to this life?

MP: It has been very important to me. It has been good for my health; it has been good for my poetry. It's caused me to pay attention to a lot of things I had never noticed much: the seasons, I knew nothing about the sea, I knew nothing about the moon, I had never paid that much attention to weather. Do you know how people in the city say "it's not yet spring" unless the thermometer reaches the sixties? Well, spring to me starts with the first crocus in February; and March is a spring month, whether there is snow on the ground or not, because everything is moving, developing. I live with a different sense of the seasons here.

SR: You feel that this now is finally home?

MP: Yes. I am very attached to this. We are very connected to the town as well. My husband is active in town government. I am active in a grassroots women's group started after the Brookline clinic murders. We are both active in the Havurah. . . . It's a term that means "friends" in Hebrew. It should actually be *havarim,* but the Havurah Movement is what it's called. It's a gathering of Jews here on the Cape.

SR: Would you say this place is almost a necessary element in your life and your work?

MP: What do you mean by necessary? We had a hurricane here this year. I lost a friend. We were without water or power for six days. There were people whose homes were totally destroyed. I live in the fallout zone from Plymouth [nuclear power plant], which is not a real comfortable place to live. What do you mean necessary? . . . You never know what you are going to have to do without. You can't ever make statements like that because you have to have a sense of the things that happen to people and the things that happen in this society. You can't define yourself so rigidly. You can say, "This is what I want, this is what I like to have, this makes a good life"—but you don't always know you are going to have a good life.

SR: By "necessary" I guess I was thinking about the way your contact with this place in some way enables the poems to come about. Is there a way, for example, that the morning walk or your time in your garden will feed your writing?

MP: It helps. Of course it does because it provides metaphors. Any kind of activity you undertake with real attention provides very rich metaphors for who you are.

SR: Which is the part you cannot do without, that is essential if you are to feel "at home" in your life?

MP: Writing is what I *have* to do, that is what I am required to do. [*Laughing.*] If I don't do that then I really feel guilty. . . . That is the most basic connection that I have to the world. I am this thing that turns energy into matter that is turned back into energy.

SR: And then sing it loud enough so that we can hear it too?

MP: Well, that is where the energy comes in; the energy is created in you.

11
Rita Dove

—A CHORUS OF VOICES

FROM THIS SLIGHT and solitary woman, what a chorus of voices—bold, sly, anguished, determined—each one spotlighted briefly on the darkened stage of story or poem. Even during conversation, characters from her memory or art appear and disappear, adding their particular slant to an anecdote, spicing the talk with echoes from the past. It's almost as if Rita Dove, poet and novelist, is at the height of her craft when she is giving voice to the collection of presences that have, subtly or dramatically, shaped her life.

The recipient of numerous fellowships and awards, Ms. Dove is currently the Commonwealth Professor of English at the University of Virginia. In 1987, her collection *Thomas and Beulah* made her one of the youngest winners ever of the Pulitzer Prize for poetry. The book encapsulates the history of the twentieth-century African American migration to the North by focusing on her grandparents and the family they created in Ohio. In collections like *Grace Notes* and *On the Bus with Rosa Parks,* the poems have perhaps become more personal, but they still ring with the voices of friends and family, still captivate us with her vivid imagery, her startling sense of the particular.

Dove's first novel, *Through the Ivory Gate,* had just been published when I interviewed her during a reading tour in western Massachusetts. The book explores the way the chords of memory and imagination are blended in the composition of a life. After a few minutes of studied reserve, the poet seemed to relax with me and the questioning opened and expanded; here was a writer, precise but unguarded, anxious to share her stories and her ideas. Her stature among American writers, though, increased immeasurably the following year, when she was selected as Poet Laureate, the youngest our country has had. That the high-profile position did not dampen her effusive spirit or veil the intimacy of the poems is a testament to the way she has learned to direct those inner voices or be directed by them.

Music is a motif that runs throughout Rita Dove's writing, coming to represent the pure realm of spirit and imagination at the core of our experience—though it is too often masked by the brusque business of daily life. Whether they are rooted in pain or triumph, Dove transforms our moments through the act of creation into something that can sustain us, further our journeys. But the great pleasure of Ms. Dove's writing is the sheer musicality of her language, which, by turns, wails like a jazz riff, soars like a gospel choir, and simmers with a classical elegance. She reminds us of the communal power we inherit along with our spoken language and the beauty of the voices that are, perhaps now, singing within us as well.

❖   ❖   ❖

SR: One of the central features in your poetry and fiction is the power of history and memory. Where does that drive to tell the story originate in your life?

RD: Well, it really begins with two feelings I had as a child: First, that *I* wasn't represented in History—I'm talking of History with a capital H— neither as a female nor as a black person. And second, the nagging sense that ordinary people were not represented in history, that history gives you the tales of heroes, basically—and not what happens to . . ."ordinary" people who live through the events. You are right that the twin poles of history and memory have certainly not only fascinated me—I'd almost say haunted me all these years. Because I think history is a very powerful weapon. If you can edit someone out of history, then the next generation—those who do not have a personal memory of certain events anymore—won't have anything to go on.

And cultural memory is remarkably short in our day and age because communities are disintegrating, so there is no oral or communal sense of carrying on a tradition. Everyone is focused in on media, which means that media has the power to tell them what to remember—which brings us to memory, that other focus. I use memory more in the sense of personal recollection—although there is the power of communal memory too. It's intriguing how particular yet inaccurate we are in remembering things; we remember what we want to or need to remember. Put five people in a room who have seen the same traffic accident, and you'll get five different versions of the story. I find this process fascinating.

SR: Are you consciously trying to preserve glimpses of history for the next generation? As a poet, are you a carrier of history?

RD: A carrier of history of a particular sort. In *Thomas and Beulah,* I was hoping to hand down a sense of two very normal people living through a period of incredible change in the United States. . . . I am very interested in how an individual behaves in the flux of the larger history, but also I am interested in recovering the sense that we—as individuals, as human beings—can connect to the universe. The heroic sagas that we get in history books may be necessary to provide the overview, but they do make you feel like you don't count.

SR: What I love in your writing is your astounding sense of the particular. We feel we can almost live through the experiences of the poems. And some of the moments provide us with a small glimpse of a black America we'd otherwise never see.

RD: I believe we live our lives in the particular; we blossom through detail. We don't walk down the street thinking: here I am, forty years old, walking down a Midwestern street. We look at *that* flower, smell the breeze. Sensory detail is how we experience the world; and the deepest way to convince someone of your reality, that [you] can understand someone else's world, is through the particular.

SR: But there are things that I can never experience—especially being white, being male—and suddenly to have some small entrance into this other life is quite a moving experience.

RD: Well, that is marvelous, because I believe if, as human beings, we can enter those other worlds even for an instant, then it becomes a little more difficult to hate that other person simply because they are different, to treat them badly or to kill them.

SR: But you mentioned specifically the way history wields a certain power. Tell me a little bit more about that. I know poets shy away from proselytizing through their poems, but I can't help but think that your intention was more than making the beautiful object on the paper.

RD: Definitely. My primary intention has never been to make the beautiful object on paper, although I think that beauty beguiles us so well that no matter how horrific the topic, if the poem is beautiful, it convinces. It's true, poets tend not to proselytize. Let me approach it this way: in my first book is an entire section of slave narratives; what had impressed me about the slave narratives I had read was the fact that they were a witnessing, a witnessing of horror. Some of them had been written by ex-slaves, others dictated and transcribed by abolitionists.

Yet how modest the language was! All they wanted, it seemed, was simply to get it down on paper, so people would know what happened. That feeling of not being able to trust any larger power to do the right thing—that you just have to bear witness to the experience—that, I think, is the extent of the proselytizing I am doing. Witnessing is very powerful; in a way, each poet does exactly that every time he or she writes a poem—witnessing a little piece of life. I don't think about the poems in terms of the grand sense—well, I am going to remake history or revamp it—but perhaps more a feeling of chipping away at history as a whole; I don't think of history as orderly, as some kind of entity that we can even understand.

SR: Your poems, with great delicacy, bear witness to the lived experience of history. Two examples from *Grace Notes* come to mind: "Summit Beach" seems to bring back the figure of your grandmother Beulah again; and "Crab Boil" centers on a girl I took to be a young Rita Dove.

RD: Yes, I am the speaker in "Crab Boil." I will admit that poem as autobiographical, though that recognition is not necessary to an under-standing of the poem.

SR: In each poem, a small personal experience is depicted center stage with just a hint of the larger historical forces churning in the background. The phrase "the Negro beach" is enough to conjure the racial climate in the 1920s. But Beulah seems hardly aware of this when she "climbed Papa's shed and

stepped off / the tin roof into the blue, / with her parasol and invisible wings."
If not the tide of history, there must be something else that supports this
woman, gives her the confidence to take that brave step.

RD: In that particular poem, the "something else" is a sense of self, a
wellspring of love that comes from family and the community. I keep
coming back to the community. . . . What will always keep you going is that
sense of being supported by others, others who understand, others who care,
who have been through similar experiences. The girl in "Crab Boil" doesn't
quite understand the segregated beach business but she has learned, even at
that young age, to look and pay attention to her elders. Elders are very
important in African American families; in fact anyone older than you in an
African American community has the right to tell you what to do, to
dispense lengthy advice. But this girl has enough acumen to look around and
to watch and so learn how to behave, how to survive in a world whose rules
are absolute for her. On the one hand, such alertness can cause you to become
very reserved and distrustful; on the other hand, you learn to rely on those
around you who have "been there," and then you are strengthened by this
support system.

SR: But you create an interesting tension between the communal sway and
the will of the individual. The girl keeps questioning, "Why do I remember
the sky / above the forbidden beach, / why only blue and the scratch, / shell
on tin, of their distress?" She almost empathizes with the crabs captured in
the pail, especially after Aunt Helen's comment, "Look at that— / a bunch
of niggers, not / a-one get out 'fore the others pull him / back." They tell the
girl the crabs will feel no pain in the boiling water, and she finally accepts
their claim. "I decide to believe this: I'm hungry." There's a conflict of two
sorts of knowledge: the wisdom of the culture set against the girl's innate
understandings, almost a wisdom of the body.

RD: But we get the feeling that she goes along with their wisdom yet she
doesn't believe it totally. She decides to believe for the moment, and in this
moment, as you said, the individual comes into conflict with the community. I think, really, she bows to the exigencies of the situation. Even so, I
think it's the best possible relationship between individual and community.
We are all individuals who may share certain things which make us feel that
we are a community—but the individual should never be obliterated or even
blurred by that connection with the community. Even Beulah in "Summit
Beach, 1921"—she wants to fly!

SR: Although at the end of the poem, the girl thinks of her aunt and reasons:

"After all, she *has* / grown old in the South. If / we're kicked out now, I'm ready." What has changed inside her?

RD: What has changed is that she now understands how to gird her loins in a moment of survival. She understands when to stop feeling in order to get through the moment. It is a sad epiphany, because this kind of revelation dulls children's eyes when they are faced with injustice that doesn't make sense—unless you just give up on people, declare the human race evil. And this is especially tragic for her, a little black girl [who] is extremely perceptive, who looks at everything, the sky and sand and even hears the sounds of the scratching claws—who was like one big nerve ending. She decides to muzzle her emotional responses because she must survive; she has to eat, she is hungry. Whereas at the beginning of the poem she might have been devastated if the whites had come and chased them out, now she is ready to not feel a thing and go.

SR: I wonder if that dramatic break with the world is particular to minority experience in this country? Does that moment dovetail with the scene [in *Through the Ivory Gate,* Dove's first novel] where young Virginia is thrilled over her first straight-A's report card, and the response of her white friend is to push her down, call her "nigger." With that one word, her sense of the world is shattered, and you describe the beginning of that survival mechanism the girl will adopt.

RD: Well, yes. Of course it would be ideal if it had never happened to her, but it does. And I don't think it's something particular only to racial minorities; it happens to all of us on some level as we grow up, as we change from children to adults. I think it is more consistent and perhaps less explainable when racism or sexism is the cause. It really is horrible, but it happens. So to try and make others see how betrayal shatters reality and how one may shut down in order to survive would bring us a long way toward explaining adult behavior in certain situations. It all depends too when this shutdown occurs. For people not in the mainstream of society, it may happen at a younger age, which is potentially more damaging.

I remember a poem by Yehuda Amichai in which he talks about his grandson using the metaphor of a hatching egg—how he has come out whole and how miraculous that is, until some tragedy, some hurt occurs. Then, says Amichai, the boiling begins; we just don't know if he is going to come out hard-boiled or soft. You see children of all ages, all colors: you see them at age five and they are glorious; and you see them at age eight, and half of them are still wonderful but somewhat muted. I've seen this because I've watched my daughter grow up; she's nine now. But I also see older kids when I visit classrooms to teach poetry, and when they get to be about eleven, there is very little openness left. It's just incredible; but something has happened along the way.

SR: You've talked about the intellectual discipline in your household, the knowledge that your parents tried to armor you with as a girl. There's the father's admonition in "Flash Cards": "What you don't understand, master."

RD: It wasn't a rule that was laid down, though there were other kinds of rules—a prescribed amount of television per week, and always doing your homework first thing after school—but there was a feeling in our household that the only ticket to a happy life is to do the best you can no matter what you do. You can't cheat on that kind of commitment. But it wasn't a stern warning; it was an expression of love.

The one place we were allowed to go practically anytime was the library. The only stipulation was that we had to have read all the books we got before returning for more. I remember my parents asking, "Have you read all these books?" And then they would say, "Well, you aren't through yet; you can't go back until you finish reading these books." You know, finish what you have done.

My siblings and I, we enjoyed learning—maybe because we weren't allowed to watch too much television. In the summer that was agony! We had to find other things to do: so we read a lot, and wrote radio plays and rock 'n' roll songs. My brother and I started our own summer newspaper. He was always the editor-in-chief because he was two years older, and I always quit to form my own magazine called "Poet's Delight." I never got further than designing the cover; I'd spend a week drawing every single autumn leaf on a maple tree. And then I would write one poem, and that would be it. We went through this summer after summer, the same scenario. But it forced us to invent entertainment, to use our inner resources. On the other hand, there was this great feeling of trust our parents instilled in us, as if to say "Well, we raised you this way and we'll stand behind you."

And I remember once coming back from the library nearly in tears; I was about eleven or twelve or so, and they wouldn't let me check out François Sagan. I had read something in a magazine about this seventeen-year old girl who had written this risqué novel, and of course I wanted to read it. I think it was *Bonjour, Tristesse,* and the librarian said, "No, you can't read it, you are not an adult." It was the first time anyone had forbidden me to read. So I went home and told my mother, who wrote a note that said, "Let her check out any book she wants." I think my parents felt if any book was too old for us, we would get bored quickly. That moment made a great impact on me; I realized they trusted me.

SR: Turning your mind loose—that's quite a brave step for parents, a test of faith in the learning process. And neither of your parents—am I remembering this correctly—had been to college themselves?

RD: My mother had a scholarship to Howard, but wasn't allowed to go. She was sixteen when she graduated high school. She had skipped two grades and her parents were afraid to let such a young girl go to Washington, D.C., alone, so she didn't attend college.

My father was the first person in his family to go to college. There were ten brothers and sisters, and they were poor, so during the Depression when they didn't have shoes, they made sure that my father had shoes in order to go to school, because he was intellectually inclined and they believed he had *the chance.* I didn't learn about this until I was an adult. This was his burden, and he carries it still—all hopes were pinned on him. He got a masters degree in chemistry and became the first black chemist in the rubber industry in Akron, Ohio, so he became the battering ram that opened the door.

SR: That has become a common immigrant tale—parents pinning their hopes on their children. So there is the communal handing-on of their dream. And even if it were never mentioned, you knew you were being given not only a chance but a responsibility. Were they happy when you turned to poetry for your life's work?

RD: It wasn't the career they expected. I don't recall any conversations where they tried to steer us toward a certain career; I just *knew* I was suppose to be a lawyer or a doctor, you know, that kind of profession. But doctors had to cut people up, so I thought, "Okay, a lawyer, then." When I entered college, I declared a pre-law major until my first class in government, and that was the end of that! I guess I felt sufficiently afraid of what my parents might say so I claimed an English major as preparation for law school, and I kept up this pretense until I was a junior. That was the point I decided to try and become a writer. I went home at Thanksgiving and said to my father, "I want to be a poet;" and to his credit, he simply put down his newspaper and said, "Well, I've never understood poetry, so don't be upset if I don't read it."

I remember feeling immense relief at that moment, as if he were handing me the reins. He was saying, "I accept that this is what you want to do; I just want to let you know that I am not showing any disapproval by not reading it." Since then he has read my poetry, of course, but at the time I considered it a perfectly honorable pact.

SR: For any family, the prospect of their children pursuing a life in the arts creates a certain anxiousness: how will they make a living, and will they be safe? Let me ask you, then, about the burden of family. There are many times, especially in *Grace Notes,* where you talk about the pain you carry as a result of the family experience. One that caught my attention was the wonderful "Poem in Which I Refuse Contemplation." There is a skipping back and forth from the speaker's consciousness to that of a letter from her mother. And the letter blends all the anguish of family life with the comforting business of everyday life. Along with news about the onions and Swiss chard in the garden, there's

> *Your cousin Ronnie in D.C.—*
> *remember him?—he was the one*
> *a few months younger than you—*
>
> *was strangled at some chili joint,*
> *your Aunt May is beside herself!"*

RD: It is a difficult burden. When you move out of the family's physical reach, you begin to grow into a different person. And every time one returns to the family, one slips into an old role only partially; a subtle feeling of alienation occurs. In that poem, I am the one who went away. My brothers and sisters all still live in Akron, Ohio; they're professionals in chemistry and computer science but they stayed there in the family, while I went off to all these places. I always felt they didn't really understand why I needed to see the world. "What is she doing out there?" That's what I imagined them thinking. So I think there is a sense of . . . not really alienation, but a sense of difference, of distance that experience creates—and though one may long to go back home, to return to the womb, it isn't possible.

SR: And even if memory attempts to bridge that distance, something has been surrendered. The poem contains the lines "but I can't feel his hand . . . /" and the closing "I'm still standing. Bags to unpack." And I just wondered if it seems to you that language is the way we can unpack our bags, let go of some of the burden, and at the same time re-establish some kind of a bond?

RD: Language and poetry are not going to save anybody. Poetry can make the hurt a little bit more comprehensible and hence bearable, but it is not going to "make it all better." I have never felt that. Poetry can bridge some of that distance, but the distance is still there. In that poem the invisible bridge of support, a remedy for alienation, is the way in which the mother's words reverberate and inform the thoughts of the woman standing there with her bags. In the end she can say, "I'm still standing. Bags to unpack."

In a way, the mother's letter has given her a lesson. In one sentence, she mentions that the cousin has been strangled; the next, she complains about those raccoons in the crawl space—so life goes on. "I want to let you know what is going on in our end of the world," the mother is saying. "Take care." So there is a connection; there are people out there who love you.

SR: I think I skipped past that meaning too quickly. I was struck by the weight of the bags, the burden, and not the reassurance of the mother's love. I guess that double-edged sword is present throughout. I think of the poem "Flash Cards," with the father drilling the math lessons into his children's brains. His injunction comes in the line, "What you don't understand, / master," but the weary child counters at the end, as if it were the answer to one of the arithmetic problems, *"Ten,* I kept saying, *I'm only ten."*

RD: My brother and I would get together to figure out our math home-work. We would spend hours trying to figure out a difficult problem on our own before giving up and approaching my father because, well, he was a *real* math whiz, and if we had a question about algebra he would say, "Well it would be easier if we used logarithms." We would protest, "But we don't know about logarithms!" but out would come the slide rule nevertheless and two hours later we'd learned logarithms, but the whole evening was gone. So it did force us, number one, to try and do it on our own. And in the end, you also realize that they love you, since they are spending all this time on you. My father was very stern in those days; right before bedtime those flash cards had to come out. I hated them then, but I'm glad now.

SR: But his challenge, "what you don't understand, master," goes beyond math homework. I thought that was one of those examples where he was trying to armor you with a way of approaching your life.

RD: Yes. And yet there is still that individual spunkiness of the ten-year-old who says, "Yes, you are supposed to master it—but give me a break, I'm only ten years old! Let me be a child a little longer." On the whole though, this advice has served me well. I don't have any real sadness about that. I am grateful that my parents were as strict as they were, because the mind is at its most malleable and absorbent at that age; you can cram as much into it as you can bear. It gets harder and harder the older you get.

SR: Knowing how you feel about this, I thought it was curious how often you touch on the sense of "forbidden experience" in your writing. There are Uncle Millet's stories in one poem, the sort of racy tales of women and whiskey, which you weren't suppose to hear but somehow memorized. Then there is the sense of unbridled fantasy in another ["Fantasy and Science Fiction"], where you say,

> Sometimes, shutting a book and rising,
> you can walk off the back porch
> and into the sea—though
> it's not the sort of story
> you'd tell your mother.

There seems to be this tension between the civilizing influences of family and community versus the sheer forcefulness of the imagination which asserts itself through language.

RD: Forbidden stories are powerful stories. They are forbidden for certain reasons, and those reasons are keys to navigating the maelstroms of human relationships. Forbidden stories can change your life.

Now in the poem, "Uncle Millet," the forbidden quality lies in the idea that one can actually step out of the boundaries of rules and survive. And as wonderful as my childhood was, there certainly was a sense that the adults were watching carefully to make sure we would not stray from the narrow path. To think that one could escape blame by running off to Canada and still slip back home every once in a while to say, "Hi!"—you don't want to let children know that such a thing is possible! . . . But in the poem "Fantasy and Science Fiction," the kind of dreaming that takes you out of the influence of the family is not something you would tell your mother because you instinctively know she will start tightening the reins. The individual's imagination can be a dangerous thing for the community. I'm not trying to say communities are all like this—it's a give and take.

SR: In the last several years, we've had an experience where the larger community wants to censor individual imagination. Society is not willing, as were your parents, to turn over complete responsibility to the individual. Instead, governments attempt to control, not only what kind of art you can make but what kind of art you will be permitted to view.

RD: It is extremely dangerous. It is dangerous for the spiritual health of the world. You cannot keep a mind sequestered; it will break out some way.

SR: And by offering a mind its freedom—even if it entails a certain element of danger—what does this confer upon an individual?

RD: It is offering people a certain faith that they will be humane. First of all, what is danger? This is something everybody defines in their own way. The idea is that if a child is brought up with honesty and compassion and discipline, then no knowledge is dangerous because that child will take that knowledge, think about it, and be able to decide what is wrong or right.

SR: This would seem to be an argument for poetry, the arts, as a vital element in the health of the individual mind as well as the society at large.

RD: The arts *are* vital. In an age when we find ourselves being increasingly compartmentalized, where information bombards us but meaning is practically nonexistent, or expendable, the arts are perhaps one of the most necessary elements in society to remind us of our humanity.

When photos can be altered so that you can not even tell whether it is an original image or not, we need to be connected to—all the words sound corny—but we need to be connected to our soul. We need to remind ourselves why we are here on this planet, what kinds of responsibilities we have—not only to the planet but to each other as well. And no other discipline that I can think of is doing that work except the arts.

The poet began as the person charged with carrying on the legacy of the race; she was present at all official functions and rites of passage; he provided the songs and the music for these rites of passage, and so served as a conduit between ourselves and to the universe. And that still holds true today; that is what a good poem or a novel or play or dance or musical composition does—it connects us again.

SR: I'd like to ask you about music, which is another pervasive presence in both your fiction and poetry. Was that also something inherited from your parents?

RD: Music was always being played in our house. There was Bessie Smith and Josh White, but there was also Fauré's flute sonatas. . . . My maternal grandparents both played instruments, the mandolin and the guitar. My parents never learned an instrument; it was understood, though, that when we reached the age of ten, it was time to pick an instrument. So I chose the cello, as Virginia does, and played cello all through college and even beyond. I've since switched to the viola de gamba. Music offered me my first experiences in epiphany—of something clicking into place, so that understanding went beyond, deeper than rational sense. Since my parents were not musicians there was no one to ask, "How do I get this melody to sound right?" So I just kept plugging away until the things my music teacher had said made sense. At a very early age, music was my private sphere of discovery. It was a journey I was taking on my own. For a brief time I considered a career in music, but I knew I didn't have the kind of discipline necessary for a concert performer. But music remains a great source of pleasure to me.

SR: In the novel, when the character of Virginia plays the cello again for the first time in years, you write that "the high notes in each phrase insinuated themselves into her blood: above the treadmill of chordal progressions a luminous melody unscrolling and floating away, high in the upper ether, where there was no memory or hurt." How does music or art accomplish such transformation?

RD: If I knew how music did that, I would be one up on everybody! One of the magical things about music—and you're right it's not just music, but any art—is the pleasure of its making. The journey that it takes you on transcends not only the painful memories, but the pain contained in music's very expression as well. An incredibly sad piece can be exhilarating. One of the secrets of art is how it can help us not exactly digest the pain, but accept it. It lifts you up, over the pain, but it doesn't let you forget it.

SR: So there's no question about the music as an escape or a suspension of the gravity of daily life?

RD: I don't see it as an escape. I don't see escape as very desirable because if you escape history—if you escape anything—then what you are actually doing is abdicating a part of your humanity. You are saying, "I don't need this, I want to forget that"—but to me, part of being human is precisely this push and pull, this ambivalence. It makes life three-dimensional.

SR: How does this connect with the ideas in a poem like "Dedication," where the speaker says, "What are music or books if not ways / to trap us in rumors? The freedom of fine cages!"

RD: Poetry is a wonderful "fine cage" because a poem, particularly a lyric poem, has as its cage all of its sounds, even its shape on the page. And to fashion a full-fleshed poem in as tight a space as possible is, to me, the real electricity of utterance. Of course narrative poems take larger spaces but even so, there is no room for fluff in that context, either. To me, poetry is very musical. It is a sung language; it is also a way of—not capturing, not reminding us—no, letting us *relive* the intensity of a moment. Moments slip by as you go through life and sometimes a moment is sharp enough and arresting enough to make you stop and remember it; but the smaller moments, even the ones that affect us, are followed by yet another moment, so they get lost. Poems recover those moments—a very small moment, perhaps just an instant, but in a fine cage indeed.

SR: So the word cage does not carry with it the connotation of imprisonment, loss of freedom, in that poem?

RD: That poem is a tricky one because the narrator is duplicitous; you can't trust a person who begins, "Ignore me. This request is knotted— / I'm not ashamed to admit it." Although she says "ignore me," she actually insists upon the opposite. The narrator chafes a bit at the things that music or books can't do. They can't do everything, obviously. We still need human contact; we still need love. So that quote is a poke in the ribs at those who would insist that music and art are ethereal and can make you a better person. This poem is saying, "Art? It's not so hot."

SR: It reminded me of a Bill Stafford poem entitled "The Day Millicent Found the World," where the girl travels into the woods until she finally reaches the longed-for state: "Lost. She had achieved a mysterious world / where any direction would yield only surprise."

RD: Oh, that's great!

SR: Your speaker declares, "I wanted only to know / what I had missed, early on— / that ironic half-salute of the truly lost." I thought it was a delightful concept, this unspoken brotherhood or sisterhood of people hopelessly immersed in experience.

RD: You don't even have to do a full salute! [*Laughs.*]

SR: Let me ask you about the music of your writing—not just "music" as a motif but the musical textures you create with your words. There's one passage [in "Definition in the Face of Unnamed Fury"] where Thomas was speaking:

> "How long has it been . . . ?"
> Too long. Each note slips
> into querulous rebuke, fingerpads
> scored with pain, shallow ditches
> to rut in like a runaway slave
> with a barking heart. . . .

It almost feels like a tenor sax belting out a bebop phrase. Tell me about the music you hear when the words are coming to you.

RD: The music is so important to me; I can't stress that enough. A poem convinces us not just through the words and the meaning of the words, but the sound of them in our mouths—the way our heart beat increases with the amount of breath it takes to say a sentence, whether a line of poetry may make us breathless at the end of it, or give us time for contemplation. It's the way our entire body gets involved in the language being spoken. Even if we are reading the poem silently, those rhythms exist.

There are times in fact when the music of language guides me as much as any plot or meaning. In the poem you mentioned, Thomas is frustrated because he tries to go back to the mandolin after long absence; he is rusty and can't make it work the way he wants to. It's one thing to say that in plain old language, but to make the rhythms jagged, the lines full of stops and starts and aggravations that can explode in, as you said, a sax riff or a little bit of blues—this conveys a deeper sense of frustration. So I pay serious attention to a poem's music. "It don't mean a thing, if ain't got that swing"; if there's no music, what's the point of a poem?

SR: If there is a down-and-dirty feel of the blues in that poem, one of my favorites from *Thomas and Beulah* has a completely different musical sense and, with it, a different emotional sweep. I'm thinking of "Gospel" which begins

> *Swing low so I*
> *can step inside—*
> a humming ship of voices
> big with all
>
> the wrongs done
> done them.
> No sound this generous
> could fail:
>
> ride joy until
> it cracks like an egg,
> make sorrow
> seethe and whisper.

The poem flows with the rhythm and insistence of gospel, and hearing it spoken aloud does seem to carry a listener away, rising up on that ship of voices. It set me wondering if you—like Beulah stepping off the roof in "Summit Beach"—feel as unbound and protected by the presence of this music.

RD: True, I am carried by it, I am buoyed by that music, absolutely—"No sound this generous can fail." But first you have to get there, you have to reach the point where the sound is that generous, no one can help you. It is comparable to Garcia Lorca's description of the *duende;* he has a wonderful essay which mentions a famous singer who comes back to her native Andalusia to sing in front of her people. She has this beautiful, well-trained voice, and yet they all declare they don't want to hear merely beautiful singing: where is the *duende?* they ask. So the singer gets back on stage and tears up her voice in order to achieve the *duende*—and I think this is soul— the moment when the song, the words and the emotion are wedded unto death and nothing, not beauty, nor propriety, nor genius, can get in the way. A great poem is possessed by the *duende;* you cannot dissect it.

SR: Let me shift the context a bit. Yours is an interracial marriage, am I correct?

RD: Yes.

SR: If I may, I'd like to ask a question about how that experience has altered your perspective as a writer. One of the rare criticisms I've heard about your writing concerns the lack of raging anger in your work. I heard one poet say, "Of course Dove's poetry can be accepted comfortably by white academic society because she doesn't have the edge, the raw angry passion of a poet like Ai. So her work doesn't threaten the safety of that intellectual distance." I wondered if being in an interracial couple—and probably having to deal with more challenges day by day than most of us are ever confronted with— if that hasn't tempered the old angers, rechanneled that energy toward some other end?

RD: Oh, the anger is still there. The way I function best in the world is not through anger but, as the father says in "Flash Cards," to master it, to be on top of situations. It is very hard to think when you are angry. That doesn't mean that you aren't angry, but it means you are trying to find a way around the anger so you can do something about it. Certainly, as a partner in an interracial relationship, I have had my share of things to be plenty angry about. But the best revenge is to be as clear as possible in my poetry. I agree that it may be easier for the literary society to accept poems like mine rather than those of, say, Ai. There is a point, of course, where I cannot control how someone wants to use or interpret my poems. Most of the poems, though, are differentiated enough; they are not easy answers.

My feeling, my mission if you will—though I don't usually think of it in those global terms—is to restore individual human fates to the oeuvre. Literary portrayals of women and African Americans have been flat, and since the sixties they've been predictably angry. This stock characterization allows the reader to fall into certain categorical thinking. I want to resist that. I don't want you to think of a particular character simply as "this black angry person"; I want you to think of him as Joe or Mary or Martin. Take the speaker in the poem "Genie's Prayer Under the Kitchen Sink": He's been summoned by his mother to unclog the pipes; he's angry because his life is going nowhere, it's as clogged as his mother's sink. I want you to see him not as "just another angry black male," but as a man with a stultifying job, who suffers from a paralyzed leg, whose sister died of cancer, whose anger is against fate and circumstances but who is so possessed with the urge to create that he pours his energy into building cheesy rec rooms for prurient entertainment. Now—if you can see this man as an individual, then he cannot be lumped into a group and dismissed.

I think the poet Ai's dramatic monologues also insist on individualities, very distinct human predicaments—most of them angry personalities, perhaps, but distinct nonetheless.

SR: And to my reading of it, both poetries offer us different tools, different approaches.

RD: Exactly. We needed a Martin Luther King and we needed a Malcolm X.

SR: But when I heard that comment, I had just gotten your new novel and I came across the scene where Virginia says, "I didn't ask for respectability. I can't help it if it dogs me wherever I go." I thought this might be biographically accurate. Maybe it has to do with the quality of your family background. It seems to have given you a very stable base from which to speak, and if your voice is not going to be the one putting the torch to certain old ways, perhaps it is implicating a new ground on which to build something new.

RD: Yes, we do need fire, but we need more than fire, too.

SR: Some of that difference involves a motherliness, if I can call it that, that appears in some of the new work. There are three or four poems in *Grace Notes* that are specific explorations of a woman's body, and often the focus is on passing that knowledge on to your daughter.

RD: I have gotten very surprised reactions from readers too: "Can it be that Rita Dove is actually writing about *that!*"I had gotten a reputation for being a genteel poet; I've never understood how. But I am deeply grateful to the women who really blazed the way—poets like Anne Sexton and Sylvia Plath and Maxine Kumin.

When I was in graduate school and just beginning to write seriously and send out my work, a good poem was one that sounded like it had been written like a man. It had to have a certain toughness, a certain screening-out of emotions, clear and linear writing—which went absolutely against the way I lived my life. In fact, one of the reasons I wrote so slowly when I first began writing seriously was because I had this mistaken notion that I had to finish each poem before I could go on to the next—sort of like finishing your plate at dinner. When I finally began looking at the way I live my life, I realized that I never did anything linearly. I would juggle several tasks at once: If I was walking downstairs, I would pick up a couple of things along the way, talk on the phone, make a mental note to thaw out the chicken. "Wait a minute," I thought. "I don't live my life that way, why am I trying to write that way?"

So I began allowing all those errant voices, those scraps of poems and stories, to surface in what ever fragmented form they chose, and my work method found its balance. It's a method, I think, that women find more comfortable than men, perhaps by virtue of the way most women have been trained to manage our lives. I really think it is much more akin to the way our minds work, in starbursts—the way we walk down the street and see a thousand different details at once and yet contain them all, so that they kind of bounce around inside.

SR: Instead of creating an organized map to where you are going.

RD: Right. Just studying the map in order to head straight toward a prescribed destination. How boring!

SR: I also wondered, in a political sense, whether this was a way for you to reclaim the body, to repossess things that were perhaps barred from the way you were allowed to think, to write?

RD: Absolutely. It was liberating to be able to write about the body, childbirth and breast-feeding, without reticence or lingering.

SR: Was it an act for your daughter's sake as well? We've talked about the giving-over of knowledge from one generation to another. Was this a writer's need to hand something down to her daughter?

RD: Yes, it is intended to be handed down. And my daughter has read those poems; she is nine now, so she thinks they're pretty neat. I can't guarantee what she will say when she is fifteen—teenagers are usually mortified by such personal confessions—but I hope the idea of a mother and daughter being able to share these kind of intimacies is something that will sustain her.

SR: This idea of passing things on extends beyond the mother-daughter exchange to the way we attempt to educate the younger generations. With all the debate about educational priorities, I would think the arts possess one of the most vital sets of learning tools we could offer. The challenge is to pass on to young people this sense of the tradition—poetry as a place for discovery, as the reservoir of our common story. How do we do that? How do you pass on the intangible, those openings where music takes you to another reality, where a lyric poem can perform its sound-work, its sense-work all at once? How do you introduce someone to these transcendent experiences without resorting to that rational linear map?

RD: You do it, I think, by going at it in as many different ways as possible. I really don't know how the mind grasps the intangible, why something clicks. We make educated stabs in the dark until something ignites. It's important not to be afraid in these situations—to read the poem and let it linger in the air, without engaging the left side of the brain. Instead of saying, "Isn't it wonderful how this certain image fits into the general conceit?," we should first simply read the poem aloud and let them claim it for their own.

Another way is to connect the act of writing or reading poetry with other kinds of art. Show the student that there is indeed music in poetry, and a kind of a dance of words. More than anything else, when students see that you are exhilarated by the language—when they see you lose your shyness, the reserve a teacher adopts in front of a class—then they know something is there, some secret worth unearthing, and they want to get in on it.

SR: I've even had the question framed this way: What good is it? Because students have been taught that something is good if you can make a lot of money doing it, or because it carries a certain prestige. So I'll hand that question on to you: When you make a poem—what good is it in your life, and what good do you hope it might create when a reader receives it?

RD: As human beings we are endowed with an incredible gift: we can articulate our feelings and communicate them to each other in very sophisticated ways. To write a poem in which the almost inexpressible is being expressed is the pinnacle of human achievement. So, in a sense, it's silly to ask what good is it to reach the pinnacle!

Every time I write a poem I imagine a solitary reader—the reader that I was as a child, curled up on the couch. I remember the moment of opening a book and feeling the world fall away as I entered an entirely different realm; I remember the warm feeling of another voice whispering to me, a voice that was almost inside of me, we were so close. I write a poem and offer it to you, the reader; and if, on the other end, you can look up from the page and say: "I know what you mean, I've felt that, too"—then both of us are a little less alone on this planet. And that, to me, is worth an awful lot.

12
Bei Dao

—RECLAIMING THE WORD

BEI DAO IS THE PEN NAME of China's foremost dissident poet, Zhao Zhenkai. Reading about his work, one is hard-pressed not to conjure up an almost-mythic image of the man. He is hailed internationally, in both literary journals and the popular press, as one of China's most extraordinary young talents and as a driving force behind the 1976–1979 Democracy Movement. It is said that literally millions of readers in his homeland know his poem "The Answer" by heart. Any of the young students massed in Tiananmen Square in 1989, struggling to bring democratic reforms to their nation, could have recited it as easily as any member of the Woodstock generation could muster the lyrics to Bob Dylan's "Blowin' in the Wind." Bei Dao currently lives in exile in Denmark, but the Chinese government refuses to allow his wife and young daughter to join him. The tacit choice he was given: come home and be silenced or live apart from everyone and everything he loved. The precepts of conscience are not without their price—this is only one of the axioms that have become part of the poet's education in the politics of twentieth-century literature.

I spent several afternoons talking with Bei Dao when he visited Boston to take part in Oxfam America's annual Voices of Dignity poetry benefit. We met at the home of Iona Man-Cheong, a visiting China scholar at Massachusetts Institute of Technology. Although the poet had some command of English, Iona served as translator for our talks. A tall man, slender and fine-featured, Bei Dao greeted me with the gentlest of handshakes. Rather than the impassioned firebrand I had come expecting, I found a quiet spirit, extremely shy and intensely private.

I began by asking the poet about the significance of his pen name, which in Chinese means "North Island." It seemed a simple enough starting point. If, when the question was translated, the poet winced, I was not yet focused enough to detect it. "The name itself was accidental, with no great significance to it, except that it was chosen twelve years ago with the first publication of the 'unofficial' literary magazine called *Jintian* (*Today*)" which he edited with his poet friend Mang Ke. In a society where all information is tightly controlled by government agencies, these underground publications provided a new kind of public forum for the Chinese people. Handwritten or typed, they were mimeographed and distributed by hand on the streets of Beijing or pasted as broadsides on what would soon come to be known as "Democracy Wall." "Because we knew there was some danger involved with this publication, we wanted to avoid any attention from the authorities, and in order to do this, we chose pen names for each other. And so Mang Ke chose my pen name, Bei Dao, and I don't know what was the inspiration for the choice. But there is perhaps a more symbolic level to the name because, in 1976, when I first began translating poetry, I brought out two books of translations of the Northern European poets. And, in fact, since I've been in exile beginning in 1989, I've lived in Northern Europe. There is a sort of traditional belief in China that one's name and one's fate are linked together."

Born a mere two months before the formal creation of the People's Republic, it is perhaps too easy a metaphor to compare the drastic developments both man and nation have gone through. But I asked him to talk about the huge shift in vision that changed him from a young member of the Red Guard during the Cultural Revolution into a leader in the Democracy Movement that is attempting to wholly remake Chinese society.

"To repeat a Chinese slogan," he began, "'One was born under the Red Flag and grew up under the Red Flag.' From my childhood onward, right up to the Cultural Revolution, there were never any doubts in my mind because we grew up under the Communist system. So with our education—at school and at home—it was taken for granted we lived in the best of all possible societies. No doubts about Communism, the Party or the system itself." Indeed, Bei Dao was born into a prosperous, well-educated family; he attended the same secondary school as many of China's political elite and seemed destined to attain the comfortable life the Party accorded to its loyal professionals. "The greatest turning point for me came during the Cultural Revolution when I was sixteen, with the call for youth to go down to the countryside and to participate in production. Up until that point, I had received the best possible education. In a sense we were at the top of society. All of a sudden, we saw the bottom of society, the reality of most people's lives, and it was a complete contradiction with everything I had experienced before.

"So from the late sixties until the eighties, this was a period I examined Communism and had enormous doubt. It was also the time I began writing poetry."

But Bei Dao was quick to take issue with one premise of my question, denying that he is a leader of any movement. When he and Mang Ke began their poetry journal, they were careful to make it a purely literary forum. "It contained no political statements whatsoever. Naturally, I met people from other magazines who were much more political. But if I saw myself as a leader at all, it was as an artistic one. The problem for China in the last half century has been [deciding] what exactly was the definition of 'politics.'

"On the other hand, it is also true to say that everything that I have done has always been interpreted politically. And this, for me, is an enormous problem to deal with. . . . Naturally, for Western readers, they're very happy to feel that I belong to the Democracy Movement as a leader. But I see myself, first and foremost, as a creative artist, as a poet." He was taking great pains to make this distinction clear to me, studying my face as I listened to Iona's translation. "What I really feel is that I'm in the middle of a conflict between art and politics, between art and power. And the result of this conflict has enormous political implications. As a writer and a poet, I am part of a search to find a new language of expression [within the Chinese]. Naturally the state feels this search as a positive threat to their powers."

Was this just a problem of semantics, modesty, or something deeper? After all, a poem like "Résumé" begins

> Once I goosestepped across the square
> my head shaved bare
> the better to seek the sun

> but in that season of madness
> seeing the cold-faced goats on the other side
> of the fence I changed direction . . .
>
> —from *The August Sleepwalker*

If this was not the voice of rebellion, then what was it? His anthemlike poem "The Answer" was written shortly after the first Tiananmen student protest in 1976 (dubbed the "April Fifth Movement" because it took place during the days preceding *Qingming,* China's traditional time of mourning), which also met with a violent response from the police and military. It begins

> Debasement is the password of the base,
> Nobility the epitaph of the noble.
> See how the gilded sky is covered
> With the drifting twisted shadows of the dead.

By the third stanza, the poem nearly explodes with the spirit of defiance:

> Let me tell you, world,
> I—do—not—believe!
> If a thousand challengers lie beneath your feet,
> Count me as number one thousand and one.
>
> I don't believe the sky is blue;
> I don't believe in thunder's echoes;
> I don't believe that dreams are false;
> I don't believe that death has no revenge.

When a poet's words are capable of moving great masses of people into action, how can it be seen as anything but politics?

Bei Dao turned to the philosopher Wittgenstein for his response. "If you look at his later writings where he discusses the influence of the 'daily language,' the point he makes is that language itself *is* politics. This is particularly true of China where literature is completely encompassed within the whole framework of politics. The example you gave me of the students using my poem in Tiananmen Square. This gives me a very complex mixture of feelings. On the one hand, of course, I feel incredible pride. But on the other hand, I also feel quite strange because this popularization of poetry on a mass level makes me feel doubts as to what this sort of usage means. I think of myself as a nonconformist but not a revolutionary. . . . It makes me feel that the meaning of my poem may be misunderstood. Especially by Western audiences . . . I don't see myself as a representative of such-and-such a trend or political opinion. I see myself as an individual who is trying to create a new form of language, a new mode of expression.

"I have to react strongly when people try to say I am 'the voice of the people.' In China, the expression 'the people' has very special connotations, and I do not feel I 'represent' in any way 'the people' or 'the masses.' It is a very dangerous word because when anything is done in China, it is always being carried out on behalf of 'the people.' And who *are* 'the people?'"

Of the many trials Bei Dao has undergone in the West, this is perhaps the most threatening: the power of what he calls "mass culture," the ubiquitous and unstoppable media machine that is constantly grinding lives into story lines and human voices into carefully polished sound bites. No matter how attractive one's media image might be, Bei Dao's feeling is that it robs you of your hard-earned humanity.

"A few years ago I read at a poetry festival in Rotterdam. When I was interviewed, things went very well. But three years later, I read there again. And the reporters asked me the exact same questions again—about 'The Answer' and the meaning of my name and so on. I became fed up and began to resent the interviews. It's a problem I've encountered quite often in the West, and I think it's connected with what you said earlier about the 'commercialized image.' You're slotted into an image, into a sort of representative story angle, and you can never leave it. You're stuck there for the rest of your life. And it doesn't matter what you do afterwards, you're always going to be whatever it is they've decided you are.

"It's like with computers: you get 'entered' as certain data, and every time this data is called up, *you* get called up with it. You become this one spot of data in the cultural memory bank, and it's the only use, the only function you have. And this is very much connected with the idea of commercialized images, mass culture, and it's created an enormously negative reaction within me."

By this point, I could see how I had already fallen into the same trap, carried the same sort of preconceptions to this conversation. I folded my sheets of prepared questions, slipped them back into my notebook and tried to listen harder to the unfolding strains of the conversation.

The irony in Bei Dao's complaint, of course, is that many Western artists would probably feel nothing but envy for his predicament. We've become so much more adept at cultivating and marketing our images in order to acquire a larger audience and gain some measure of financial freedom. The danger we face is of losing track of the *genuine* in our experience and in our work, of becoming a parody of what was once our selves. "I feel, as do many exiled writers, that we are caught between a rock and a hard place. On the one hand, we're absolutely against the sort of state control of literature as is seen in China, the dictatorial approach to the arts. On the other hand, we feel just as oppressed by commercialized literature in the West. And in a sense, there's very little difference in the end result of both."

I tried to steer toward some of the fundamental experiences all writers encounter so that, poet to poet, we might find some common ground from which to examine the conditions of an artist in exile. I told him that, certainly, my first experience and first responsibility in writing a poem is to my private self and the integrity of the language of the imagination. But as the process continues and I begin to consider a poem for publication, I become increasingly aware of audience—of those you hope the piece will speak to. Surely he did not wish to create his poetry with no audience whatsoever?

"Of course, I don't differ from you, in first writing for myself and then for readers. But your definition of 'readers' is probably very different from mine. When I first started writing twenty years ago, it was not possible to think of 'the general public.' When I thought of an audience, it was really a small circle of friends. Because it was a time of great repression, it was dangerous to have one's poems go too far afield." I got the impression that, had the Chinese government not interceded, Bei Dao might have remained content within these narrow borders. "When I write poetry now, I still think in terms of that small circle. But of course, now the reaction, the reflection that returns to me is quite different. It's much broader. Before I left my country in 1989, I could count on a larger audience within China itself. But since then, this has been cut off completely. My works are forbidden in China. So now I have to think more in terms of overseas readers, and this of course has created a major change for me.

"When you write poetry in China, you work within the context of a national entity with a very well defined cultural background. Leaving that behind, joining an international context, the language changes and [the experience] muddies the whole concept of national backgrounds and cultural boundaries. And I see this not only for myself but as a phenomenon that has happened to many writers and artists in the twentieth century."

Indeed, with the proliferation of technological advances, the global communication of ideas is virtually instantaneous, and mass media has accelerated its drive to flood the international community with all manner of imagery and information. But the writer removed from his own culture, even from his own mother tongue, becomes a curious specimen; he is both extremely sensitive to the generation of new iconography and susceptible to the cross-pollination of what were once distinct cultural forms.

"This phenomenon is, on the one hand, a restriction, a limitation. On the other hand, it is a way up, a new growth. The development of modern literature in China has always been this conflict between East and West. But in the past it's been the case that either people overemphasize Western influences or they overemphasize the traditional. Now it's more the case that there is room to mix the cultures. On the other hand, I don't like the idea of 'international culture.' Even to define Chinese culture is a very complex question because you can talk about popular culture, mass culture, the culture of the court, the culture of the Chinese minorities. There is no purity of cultures[in China]. So what I prefer to look at is the idea that there is a further mixing of cultures, which I see as a very interesting occurrence—one of the most interesting cultural phenomena of our century.

"If you look at a writer like Paul Celan, for example: he was Jewish, born in Romania, wrote in German, and was later imprisoned in German concentration camps. After his release, he went to live in Paris. It's very difficult to say what sort of 'cultural background' he came from. I myself feel that this group of people now, this exiled literature, has its own mixtures of culture, and is making itself increasingly evident."

> True, this is spring.
> Pounding hearts disturb the clouds in water.
> Spring has no nationality.
> Clouds are citizens of the world
>
> Become friends again with mankind,
> My song.
>
> —from "True"

I recounted to Bei Dao the story of the great Russian novelist, Alexander Solzhenitsyn, who was living in exile at that time in a rural area of Vermont. When he was first banished from the Soviet Union, Harvard University invited him to deliver the commencement address at that year's graduation ceremony. Because I so admired his work, I snuck into the courtyard to hear his speech. The writer sat stony-faced through the long litany of million-dollar donations from the alumni and then, when it was his turn to speak, launched into a harangue about how spoiled we've become in the West. To his mind, we've been made so complacent by the wealth of our society, we've forgotten the real value of the freedoms we enjoy and the responsibilities they demand of each of us. Depending on which section you were seated in— among the silver-haired alumni in the front rows or the recent undergraduates toward the rear—the remarks were greeted with expressions ranging from outrage to wild applause.

Bei Dao seemed to be pleased by the irony of the situation. "When I first went to Europe in 1985, my friends warned me: 'You be very careful! Don't let this American culture take you over.' But in fact, I discovered that it's very difficult to define American culture. That it isn't just the commercialized images, but it exists on more levels, a very complex phenomena. You give the example of Solzhenitsyn: he lives in the U.S. and the majority of his readership is in the U.S. and the West—and look at how he was able to speak out—so what does that say about American culture?"

The novelist's cautionary speech bared the double-edged sword of Western society, where radical expressions of freedom are everywhere apparent while the borders and restrictions are often invisible, embedded in the very structure of politics and the marketplace economy. But my conversation with Bei Dao was underscoring the idea that the invisible walls we tolerate can box us in as surely as the more concrete ones in China. Though the question was rife with contradiction, I asked Bei Dao what he felt about the freedoms he now experienced in exile. He struggled for a moment to find a response, then quickly flipped through the pages of *The August Sleepwalker,* the English translation of his poems. His finger came to rest on the lines from the poem "Accomplices" that said, "freedom is nothing but the distance / between the hunter and the hunted."

But the poem goes on to say, "we are not guiltless / long ago we became accomplices / of the history in the mirror," and it contains some of the same sting as Solzhenitsyn's rebuke.

"It is a universal predicament. Initially when I wrote this poem, I had the Chinese audience in mind, that all through history, the Chinese willy-nilly end up supporting the dictatorship. But it is just as applicable to the West too; you become accomplices to the commercialization of your culture. In China, . . . many people complain about the dictatorship and the government repression. But on differing levels, everyone also cooperates [with the repression] because it is part of your everyday culture—and this is something one can't ignore.

"And in the West, particularly in America, every creative artist and every intellectual is also responsible for the creation of this commercial culture— because they themselves participate in it. It does not occur accidentally. . . . I think it is the responsibility of every person to, first of all, acknowledge that this contradiction exists in life, that we are all a part of this contradiction and it cannot be avoided. And it is the responsibility of each individual to struggle against this in the best way that he can."

I wondered whether this wasn't, in the end, poetry's deep-rooted power: to stand as a language separate from that of the political slogan and the television commercial; to underscore the vitality of free thought by refusing to be used by either "hunter or hunted." In Bei Dao's conception, the poet's voice must attempt to remain like a still point amid the tidal forces of politics and history, reflecting the individual's perspective. Perhaps the most radical act one can perform—in China or the West—is to think one's own thoughts, to stand apart from the crowd.

"There is a joke in China about how poets must be worthy of incredible respect because the government sees them as so important that they even put them in prison. I do understand that in the West, for a poet to have some social consciousness, some social representation, is a very important phenomenon. But you have to understand that the social background in China is so very different. In a country like mine which has suffered for such a long time under government repression—where, in order to maintain its power, it feels it must control not only politics but also all art and literature—there is a great imperative for a Chinese writer to escape from this sort of control. And the danger in being a so-called representative is something that strikes at the very root of creativity itself. The struggle among artists and writers in China has been to separate writing and creative impulses away from politics. So the debate in the past few years has centered around how to create a pure literature, something like what you've called art for art's sake."

Bei Dao was born in Beijing but his family roots are in Shanghai and the area where the Yangtze River pours into the East China Sea, a place combining the influences of traditional culture and international trade. His early experiments with poetry and fiction show a willingness to draw from both ancient Chinese literature and the modern voices from the West. He helped pioneer a new style of verse called, by its critics, "a poetry of shadows" because it intentionally employed dark and dreamlike imagery, a retreat from traditional forms, broken syntax or sudden leaps of reference. It was Bei Dao's way of fulfilling two contradictory needs: to comment on the totalitarian abuses that plagued his society, yet to do so in a manner that was somewhat shielded by the obscurity of his symbolism; and to explore a personal dreamscape where feeling and imagination could be given free reign. Even written in exile, his work maintains a certain distance from his readers; it presents a door that requires a bit of imaginative effort to open and even then only permits entrance one person at a time.

"The most important struggle in China has been who has control over the language. There are writers in China who have criticized the government openly in their work. But if you look at their language, if you look at the style in which they write, it is the same as is used by the government. So they are still restricted in that very narrow area. And for creative writers, the goal has been to create a new language that would put some distance between them as members of the literati and the government in power.

"I don't want you to mistake my meaning: I think that the modern language in China is a very beautiful thing. But in the forty-odd years since the establishment of the People's Republic, language has very gradually been taken over completely by officials and by the government. It is very frightening. People have no means of free expression."

I couldn't help think of the many official languages we confront every day in America: the vocabulary of pop culture and advertising, of diplomacy and the political campaign, the military-speak so prominent during the Iraqi war coverage. A catch phrase like "Just do it!" can as easily be interpreted as "Don't be afraid—risk your dreams!" or "Damn the costs—buy this product and have what you want." It doesn't take a great stretch of the imagination to realize that one man's "collateral damage" is another man's "slaughter of innocent lives." Through the lens of language, even the reality of our days is altered. But in Bei Dao's experience, the massive machinery of government was the sole arbiter of message and meaning.

"This phenomena really took off in the late stages of the Cultural Revolution, when all our word groups became fixed by the Party—and this was seen in newspapers, broadcasts and in the language people used to speak with each other. As a simple example, take the word *sun* or the word *red*. *Sun* really means 'the leader' and *red* means 'the Party.' I had a friend from middle school who was asked, 'What color do you like?' His response was, 'I like blue.' And this boy was censured for having the wrong political attitude, for being politically incorrect. In this way, the language has become so fixed and so controlled, there are no outside means of expression."

Hearing this, I began to appreciate in a new way why this Chinese poet fought so faithfully over the territory of words. The poems in *The August Sleepwalker* are arranged chronologically, and you can witness the poet's focus becoming more personal and inward, his style increasingly opaque and surreal with time. It's as if he were pulling the poems further and further away from easy interpretation, struggling to keep them far from anything that could be taken as mere cant or co-opted as a slogan.

And just where does this leave a poet like Bei Dao, living far from his homeland, watching it struggle for the character of its future life? Does his aesthetic position mean the artist may abdicate his or her responsibility to play a role in revitalizing a culture, in supporting the well-being of the larger community? If anything, this conversation was underscoring the contradictory impulses every thinking person—of the West or East—must eventually confront: what good is a free individual if he has no sense of his place in the human community? Yet what good is the social order if it must eradicate the individuality of its members in order to survive?

"There is a Western outlook towards China that ought to be corrected. The West tends to see China in oversimplified terms, especially when it comes to looking at the June 4th incident in 1989. The West looks at the overall mass movement as a sign of change. But when you look at poetry, it's a very delicate, minute thread that underlines everything that goes on. In a way, you can see poetry as a sort of silent revolution in China. But it is there in the consciousness of many different types of people. It does have a function to play but it is never broadcast in broad terms." Such a perspective is in marked contrast to the two-minute dramas we watched unfolding on the evening news. Bei Dao was pointing to the levels of complexity in all areas of his nation's daily life where incremental steps forward will go unnoticed.

"Generally speaking, I think democracy is inevitable in China. It's just a question of time. But during this time, there are huge problems that China faces that could damage the outcome of democracy. These problems are very basic, for example: population, food resources, energy, education. These are challenges that will have a major impact on what kind of democracy one sees in China in the future and will determine how quickly it arrives."

I couldn't help wondering how the prospect of this slow evolution felt for a young man living several thousand miles from the home he wishes to enter, from the faces he would give almost anything to touch again? Did he think he would see this new China in his lifetime? "The process of bringing democracy about is not like a revolution. It's not like democracy is going to appear all of a sudden one day. It's a long slow process. And within that development, one of the most important things to bear in mind is that the Democracy Movement in China is not at an end, because already there is a phenomena growing called 'civil society' [and] the government itself is able to control less and less of society. It's not able to reach down quite as far as it used to. The growth of civil society is a basic foundation that is necessary before one is able to see democracy come about. And the process of democratization itself is like that of the poetry revolution: it's silent, it's slow. But it will come."

The Art of Poetry

in the great house to which I belong
only a table remains, surrounded
by boundless marshland

the moon shines on me from different corners
the skeleton's fragile dream still stands
in the distance, like an undismantled scaffold
and there are muddy footprints on the blank paper
the fox which has been fed for many years
with a flick of his fiery brush flatters and wounds me

and there is you, of course, sitting facing me
the fair-weather lightning which gleams in your palm
turns into firewood turns into ash

I had a last question for Bei Dao. When James Joyce lived in self-imposed exile from his homeland, he used newspapers, street maps, and photographs to create a Dublin-of-the-mind that his stories could live inside. It would seem, I told him, you have been deprived of most of the essential elements you need to continue your work: family, fellow writers, the language and the landscape. As a poet, how are you able to persist?

As my words were translated, a shadow of sorts swept across his expression. "That is a very interesting question," he responded slowly. "The relationship between a poet and his homeland is very complex—at times, very close, at times in conflict. I think we Chinese have a very special relationship with our land. It's difficult to leave that behind. I think I've created an inner world, an illusion of China . . . very abstract but highly specific. It's a summary of experiences that includes the back streets of Beijing, the look of certain places, the sounds of people quarreling on streets or exchanging the time of day. . . . I still carry my Chinese address book with me because it helps me to recreate situations. Because without concreteness, there can be no illusion, no dream-China. Sometimes my dream-place is so real. . . ." After a pause, he added, "If the conditions in the real China eventually change, it might still be hard for me to return."

By this time, I could see that Iona was somewhat exhausted; in this linguistic tennis game, her role was to play on both sides of the net, leaping rapidly from one language, one mind-set, to the other. I clicked off the tape recorder and our host graciously retreated to make us some tea. Now Bei Dao and I conversed with our own limited resources, hand and facial gestures counting for as much as the broken phrases. We exchanged poems and Bei Dao gave me copies of the selection he would read the following evening at the Oxfam celebration. Two of the newer pieces caught my attention immediately; considering all that was said, "Requiem" was a surprisingly straightforward elegy, subtitled "for the victims of June Fourth." He spoke of the sadness he felt to hear news of the massacre in Tiananmen while living so far from the event. Each of the three stanzas began with the word "Not" and, in its negation, seemed to attempt to erase a portion of grief and remake the memory of the tragedy that occurred. Still, he was careful to make the distinction that "One may be giving voice to feelings other people hold— but that means the poem represents feelings, [and] is not a representative of how people feel." Yet he also offered that "a poet does have the responsibility to be the memory of his people, to remind them of past events—and this is especially true in China where there is a state policy of national amnesia. The government would like the people to forget that Tiananmen ever occurred."

Requiem

Not the living but the dead
under the doomsday-purple sky
go in groups
suffering guides forward suffering
at the end of hatred is hatred
the spring has run dry, the conflagration stretches unbroken
the road back is even further away

Not gods but the children
amid the clashing of helmets
say their prayers
mothers breed light
darkness breeds mothers
the stone rolls, the clock runs backwards
the eclipse of the sun has already taken place

Not your bodies but your souls
shall share a common birthday every year
you are all the same age
love has founded for the dead
an everlasting alliance
you embrace each other closely
in the massive register of deaths

The second was a brief poem entitled "A Picture—for Tiantian's Fifth Birthday." The voice in this had little of the elusiveness, the abstract imagery that created a safe distance between poet and reader. This was as intimate as a love note and, Bei Dao explained, was written for his daughter; Tiantian, her nickname, is written in Chinese with two characters which look like a pair of windows and also forms part of the character for the word "picture."

A Picture

Morning arrives in a sleeveless dress
apples tumble all over the earth
my daughter is drawing a picture
how vast is a five-year-old sky
your name has two windows
one opens towards a sun with no clock-hands
the other opens towards your father
who has become a hedgehog in exile
taking with him a few unintelligible characters
and a bright red apple
he has left your painting
how vast is a five-year-old sky

—from *Old Snow*

Bei Dao and I took a walk outside to shoot the photographs for the interview. The great warmth and openness that animated his face in the midst of our talk vanished before the gray stare of the lens. "It is like a gun," he said, "aiming at me." And, sadly, I understood too well what he meant by these simple words.

But we walked and chatted, he straining to summon his words of English, I struggling to simplify mine. It was a warm spring afternoon and the forsythia were already blooming. We found a spot for him to stand and I searched in my case for the lens I wanted. Finally he asked me, "Are you married?" and I was shocked to realize it was probably the first question in our long conversation that Bei Dao had posed. "Yes," I told him. "And I have a son, fourteen, very big!" I added, gesturing with my hands. Bei Dao smiled. He told me a bit about Shao Fei, his wife, and little Tiantian, now a six-year-old. "I speak to them on telephone, but not often. Dangerous," he explained in a quiet voice. We were thinking—each in his own way—of the incredible distances words are able to travel sometimes, when they are clear, well tended, and fitted for the journey.

POSTSCRIPT

When I first met with Bei Dao, he had been in exile from his homeland for only two years and was still trying to come to terms with his new life in the West. Throughout the 1990s, he would wander between European and Scandinavian cities, eventually settling in the United States. He survived by taking temporary teaching positions, searching for—if not home, at least refuge—a place and a community where he might gain some measure of peace. It was through the generosity of friends and strangers—the network of Chinese expatriates and the loose-knit family of poets—that he began to remake his life, a process he has beautifully detailed in his recent collection of prose pieces, *Blue House* (Zephyr Press).

All the while he continued to write and publish his poetry—*Unlock* appeared in 2000—creating over time that "new language" he had spoken of when we'd first talked. Less overtly political or even personal, the new poems are filled with luminous images and unexpected associations, creating a dreamlike intensity. Still, all it takes is a word, a turn of phrase, to anchor the poem suddenly in the lived world or to hint at the burden of memory never far from his attention.

Preparing this collection of interviews for publication, I met with Bei Dao in Cambridge, Massachusetts, and brought him a copy of the expanded conversation. After reading it, he shook his head mournfully; speaking now without the aid of an interpreter, he struggled to express his reaction and could only come up with the single word: "Naïve." Was he embarrassed by the certitude of his younger self—or by the grand terms in which I had outlined the importance of his work? Had a decade's education in the realpolitik of the literary establishment (not to mention the machinations of national governments) chastened his outlook? Or was he just feeling the wear and tear that the long journey had exacted upon his life? He made several attempts to find words for his feelings but, in the end, felt he had simply "spoken too much." Still, I explained to him that the interview was an important record of this transition in his life and, with characteristic generosity, he gave me his blessings for the project.

Over coffee, we chatted about the changes in our personal lives. I found out that, after great effort to preserve their relationship, his marriage to Shao Fei had sadly ended. But paradoxically, divorce from the poet finally allowed his wife and daughter to obtain travel documents and to visit Bei Dao in the United States. A teenager now, Tiantian may even be able to attend high school in America and be reunited with her father. I watched as these words animated Bei Dao's normally placid face and reminded myself of how I must always try to intuit the inner spirit of this poet and not merely rely on outward signs. It is the very same method, I realized, required by the landscape of his poems, which, suddenly, seemed not so very foreign at all.

13
Donald Hall
—WITHOUT AND WITHIN

Tₕₑᵣₑ ᵂₐₛ ₐ ᶜₑᵣₜₐᵢₙ ₛʸₘₘₑₜᵣʸ about it. My first visit to
Donald Hall's home at Eagle Pond had been in autumn, though in the
New Hampshire hills winter announces its approach early on. Hall's wife,
the poet Jane Kenyon, had been away that day but as I was given a tour of
the house and its surroundings I noticed signs of her presence everywhere I
looked. She too was an exceptional writer, someone I hoped eventually to
include in my interview series. But I didn't worry; there'd be time.

With Hall, I discussed how rooted to this bit of the earth he and Jane had
become over the years, how it was a presence in much of their work. Work,
weather, memory, the resonance of place, and of course love—we spoke of
how these elemental experiences seemed even more precious now that his
cancer may have drawn a boundary line on what he might expect to enjoy.
Yet it was a wonderful conversation, one that led to a friendship through
correspondence and occasional visits as the years passed.

Now, once again, I drove along the twisting country road and saw the farmhouse and barn come into view, snow-sheathed this time, a dark December afternoon in 1997. Once again, Donald Hall appeared on his porch to greet me—only this man barely resembled his earlier self. He'd grown a scruffy beard and his hair was long and wild. His face seemed marked by his long period of grieving. He wore a sweater with a hole prominent in its side (and I instantly caught myself thinking: if Jane were alive, I wonder if she would have prodded him about that—"You're going to be photographed today; put on a nicer sweater.")

As it turned out, he had come out of doors to smoke a cigarette, something Jane preferred he not do in the house. And though it was approaching five years since his last operation, a period after which the doctors had pronounced him cured, and nearly three since leukemia had erupted, claiming Jane Kenyon's life—Donald Hall was in no hurry to reestablish the license of a solitary life. He was acutely aware of what was now absent. After all, the new book of poems detailing the year of his wife's dying and the series of letter poems that followed bore the simple title: *Without.* But he was trying to live with as much of Jane's presence as imagination could bear.

He still had the rooms they shared and their painted bed, the hill paths they walked with Gus, their old dog who still traipsed beside him. He had poems and journals that preserved something of her voice, and a tiny shrine he'd erected in his study: photographs, an old driver's license, a passport, the small intimacies of a shared life. And chiefly, he had the daily routine of a full-time writer, a discipline that had sustained him for decades and something he was now struggling to reclaim.

Later on, it didn't surprise me when I found that both of my interviews, six years apart, had culminated with similar statements (though the tone of the two lines revealed a world of difference). The previous one closed with the poet declaring, "Find what you love, and do it"; this one, with the pronouncement, spoken two times for emphasis, "Get back to work."

SR: One of the reasons I wanted to come back to Eagle Pond to talk with you again is that, of all my interview subjects, your life has changed most dramatically in the intervening years—a change that, as the new book makes clear, has had an equally dramatic effect on your poetry. Our earlier conversation focused on home and place-making, and the role language has in that process. You described the many ways this house, this terrain helped form you as a writer—when you were a young boy visiting your grandparents and especially when you came back to live here with Jane. Before I get into the more crucial changes, I wanted to ask about differences in the way you look—something I remarked upon when you greeted me on your porch. I'm curious whether this was a conscious choice—trying to make the outside match the inside, so to speak.

DH: Well, I think I'm restless without Jane and perhaps the change in my appearance is part of floundering about, flailing about, trying to find it—and I don't know what "it" is. But I'm traveling more than I used to. At the beginning, after her death, I couldn't leave the house, I couldn't even go away overnight for a couple of months. Now I travel more. I'm very glad to get back because place is very important to me and I wouldn't want to move, to get away. People have counseled that, people make all sorts of suggestions, you know, "Go away, take a trip, get away from Jane." I don't want to. She's more *here* than she is anywhere else. The first year or so she was very present—and I don't mean supernaturally. All her clothes were here, her study was untouched—and still everywhere I look, her handwriting is on all the herbs, in the telephone directory and so on. I don't want to be away, but I am restless. What I want I do not have.

I haven't let my hair grow by deciding to; I just haven't been going to the barber. And I'm aware that Jane was my barber for twenty years of marriage and more, perhaps that's why. When people ask me, I tell them that. Growing the beard was again something. Life has totally changed, my life has totally changed and it's as if with the beard I've acknowledged this change. I had a beard the first half of our marriage, a different kind of beard, a big bushy one. But I suppose a sort of seeking after change, looking for something, that may satisfy me—as I am not otherwise satisfied—may explain the change in appearance.

SR: I mentioned to you in my letters how pleased I was that you still included Jane in your readings. Just a few months back when you read in Cambridge, you began with a few of her pieces even before you read your own. You weren't hiding your grief or your pain—it was acknowledged as part of all that you were doing.

DH: I tell you, far from wanting to hide from it, I wanted to scream it. In the days and weeks and months after Jane died, I couldn't talk about anything but the last eleven days [of her life]. We knew she was going to die the last eleven days, and then there were the details—of Cheyne-Stokes breathing, of the eyes stuck open, of closing her eyes. People often say, "How courageous of you to speak of it"; well, it wasn't courageous at all, I couldn't *not*. I felt like the Ancient Mariner, who had to tell his story. And I made up a story about myself—not as a truth but as illustrative—that I go into a diner and I have a hamburger and say "Could you pass the ketchup?," and the man passes me the ketchup and I say, "My wife used to like ketchup; she died of leukemia," and I tell him the whole story. . . .

I would meet somebody, an old friend or anybody I hadn't seen for a long time and I couldn't talk about anything else. Or I'd meet somebody for the first time—often this still happens—and I tell it again. For a long time it was, say, the last eleven days that I'd talk about mostly, and then it would go back over the whole illness. There are a million stories, many of which are in the book *Without* that you have read, but there are others as well. There are subsequent poems. . . . I cannot *not* face it; I think it does me good to face it. I don't believe in hiding things and tamping things down—but it's a matter of temperament, not a matter of the right choice. Henry Adams, after Clover's suicide, lived forty or fifty years and never mentioned her name, not in any letters that survive. I don't know that he ever mentioned her name to his dearest friends—but if he did they didn't say so, John Hay, and so on. But that was his way, and it was an enormous grief and an enormous mourning for him that he expressed in silence. I don't think he denied it (I'm an Adams freak). But my way, far from denial, was proclamation. . . .

The worst day was not the day she died, which was April 22nd, but April 11th, which was the day we were told that she was going to die. For fifteen months she struggled to live and had a bone marrow transplant; and suddenly on April 11th—a week earlier her blood work had looked good— the leukemia was back and there was nothing to do. That was the worst day. And a year after her death, I arranged to give a talk on that day. I didn't have to do it that day but I knew that if I could talk that day—and I would talk about her—that would relieve my mind or my heart. It is as if to spread my grief out onto the world is a form of relief for me. I think, *I know,* it makes some people very uncomfortable. I think *Without* will make people uncomfortable, people will find it—some one or two people have—relentless, and insistent upon horror, and that is my way. I don't apologize for it nor do I say it's the only way to be. But it's my way.

SR: Actually, the poems had something of the opposite effect on me. A first reading involved, as you said, a profound welling of sadness. The horror to me centered on the medical technology surrounding the act of dying— having to deal with the hospitals and medical procedures and drugs. But as I went back through the manuscript, I was struck again and again by the ways you were forced to savor the littlest things in life, the sorts of experiences that we squander thoughtlessly.

DH: That sense is common. Of course, I had had cancer twice before Jane had her leukemia, and I was supposed to die. She had cancer first—ten years before she died she had—what in retrospect was a minor thing—she had a genuine cancer totally enclosed within a salivary gland. That was removed and there was no chance, we were told, of metastasis, and it had nothing to do with the leukemia. But of course we faced possible death for one of us then. And then probable death for me when the right half of my liver was removed, which was just two years before Jane took sick, less than two years before Jane took sick. We faced the possibility or even probability of one of us dying over those many years. And then of course in fifteen months we knew. . . . Leukemia is a dreadful disease that kills half of adults who have it. Jane's type, I won't go into it, but because of the particulars of a cancer cell and Jane's type of leukemia, her chances were far fewer than most leukemias, her percentage was lower. We knew that the probability of death was high but we did everything to make her live. Out in Seattle, where she had her bone marrow transplant, Janey was in terrible pain—from the treatment, not from leukemia—and she used to say again and again, "Perkins, am I going to live?" And what she meant, of course, the rest of the sentence was, "Or am I going through all this shit for nothing?" I never answered her cheerfully. She wouldn't want false cheer. I said, "That's what we're here for." And when we knew she was dying, she didn't talk a lot. But I could see her thinking a lot and at one point she said, "It was worth it. I'd do it over again." Despite the earlier thought, she just followed the process toward possible health. Wouldn't you, at this point or at that point, have given up? We did savor things. Her dying was of course the worst thing in my life. Taking care of her, however, was one of the very best things in my life. I'm very happy to say that it's the best thing in my life. I loved taking care of her.

SR: That comes across quite clearly in the poems, even though the imagery may be somewhat frightening to us.

DH: And she loved being taken care of. She was a depressive—had suffered through profound periods of depression—and I don't think that she could always believe I loved her as much as I claimed to, but she finally did. I don't mean it's compensatory, for one moment, but taking care of her was a joy. And when I was sick over a much less extensive time, but possibly mortally ill, she was wonderful taking care of me. She was my model. I didn't have any struggles about taking care of her; it's absolutely what I wanted to do, what I wanted to do every day. When she was in the hospital I was by her bed by six or before every morning and at night she'd get really tired by seven or eight and I would put on a record and leave, but come back in the morning early.

When she was here—she was probably here half the time or more of the fifteen months, and the other half in one hospital or another—here, I worked by her side most of the time. I was able to do a great deal of work while she was sick. I read to her when I could, I did every errand for her I could do, I brought her blankets or whatever, hot blankets, I fed her when we were home, I learned how to program pumps and deliver material into her bloodstream—but still there was a lot of time left over. The only thing that could take my full attention was writing. And I wrote about her a great deal; the first half of *Without* was all or virtually all drafted while she was alive. I read her some of the things I was writing about her. But I also wrote about other things; I wrote three or four short stories, some poems on other subjects, some children's books—or I'd work on things that I'd already begun.

SR: I'm remembering the time when you were ill, the things Jane and you discussed during the television interview you did with Bill Moyers. It was as if you were talking this out in order to make life ready for your absence, for Jane's sake. It must have been terribly hard to make the switch when suddenly it seemed as if you were given a reprieve from your cancer, but almost as quickly Jane's illness appeared.

DH: I was terrified of course that my cancer might return while she was ill. If I had died before she did, if my cancer had come back early on, God knows who would've taken care of her or taken care of me! I was worried about that a lot. The irony of her death—she was supposed to survive me by twenty-five years—and the loss of someone you love and you've been married to for a long time . . . It's horrible in any case, but I felt outrage as well! It just could not have happened. When we left Ann Arbor and moved here, I was forty-seven years old and most people think that was when I began to be a good poet (if they think I'm a good poet at all). When she died she was forty-seven. It's just outrageous, outrageous. When the Moyer's [interview] came out, the *Boston Globe* did a long article—the Moyer's show had quite a bit about my cancer, my "imminent death"—and the *Globe* article actually had the title, "Happy For Now." One month later, Jane was diagnosed with leukemia. The irony is with me every day. When I write poems about her now, I cannot help having that thought: *she* should be writing these poems about *me,* not me about her. A pointless thought, but I cannot get rid of it.

SR: In one of the letter poems after Jane's death, you speak to her saying,

When you wrote
about lovemaking or cancer,
about absences or a quarrel,
I loved to turn up in your poems.
I imagined those you'd make
after I died; I regretted
I wouldn't be able to read them.

—From "Midwinter Letter"

But the very act of imagining such a thing used poetry to infuse this place with some sense of continuity.

DH: Right, right. When I wrote some of the letters, when I was moving along in the letters, I would consciously think, "If Jane were writing this what would she do?" I wanted to learn from her. In the absence of Jane Kenyon, I wanted to write Jane Kenyon poems. I don't think I did.

SR: In my last letter I asked you about just that. I felt, in various ways, that her influence was there in this manuscript. In some of the clipped rhythms, the simple but striking images, the restrained tone.

DH: Well, I'm glad if it is. I don't think I could really sound like her if I tried. But if I could be influenced—because I admire her so enormously, her work—I'm happy.

SR: But somehow, now that the situation is reversed and *you* are the one left to make these new poems, you don't seem at all comforted by that vision— Jane taking pleasure in your continued work. How do you cope with the burden of the poetry?

DH: I have no choice, if I'm to write at all, but to try to cope with it. These are the thoughts that haunt me as I write.

SR: No sense there must be joy for her, knowing . . .

DH: No, no, not really. I would love it if I thought she could read them and she'd like them. I want her to like them: "Pretty good, Perkins!"

SR: By the way, where did "Perkins" come from?

DH: The story's not particularly interesting. When we were first living here, we drove over to Maine and we went to Perkins Cove and we seemed to see Dr. Perkins and Perkins the lawyer and Perkins' drugstore—and Jane just laughed and said, "This Perkins must be some fellow!" And she started calling me Perkins thereafter. But I thought, why this—and I realized that when she first knew me I was her teacher; I was a poet at Michigan, and Donald Hall was kind of an institution. And this was the sixties and all the students called me "Don," for that matter, and I think Perkins was more comfortable for her probably. I asked her this and she said, "Well, maybe."

Only last April, two years after her death, was I able to begin to work on her archives. When she was dying, one of the first things she said was that she wanted her papers to go to the University of New Hampshire, where mine are. But I couldn't touch them for two years. And I found amazing things—diaries, the journals from when she was fourteen and fifteen—she never threw anything away—and all the drafts of all the poems of all the books, even the ones that weren't extraordinary. But I also found a notebook from the time when she was taking my class. She actually took a big lecture course of mine and I didn't know her. The following term I let her into—not knowing her, not interviewing her or anything—I let her into a small writing class, which was how I really got to know her. I admitted her on the basis of reading her work only. That class would meet for the first time in a classroom that was [listed] in the catalogue. But thereafter we would meet in my living room. We'd find one night a week when we could all get together, and so at the first meeting of the class in the classroom, I told them where I lived. Jane had never known my address. I found a note in her notebook, which must have been written that day: "When I discovered that Donald Hall lived not three doors from me, it was as when I heard that Dublin was a Viking stronghold or when I went to take the goldfish out of the bowl but discovered that the water was too cold to sustain life." I was pretty scary. No wonder she called me Perkins.

SR: The earlier poems in *Without*—they're clearly autobiographical, following the experiences as they came, yet you choose to refer to the characters as "he" and "she" instead, distancing yourself from them. Only later on the "I" appears and . . .

DH: It's "he" and "Jane" or "she." I originally wrote it "I"—and it was just a forest of I's, trees of I's. I didn't know what to do about it, I had no idea. And one friend of mine—many people read through this manuscript, several as much as three times, and did me an enormous amount of help—one friend in particular . . . About fifteen months after Jane died, I had a draft and I knew I was going to change every page, and I did, but I was ready to show it to some people and she was one of the first readers. And she told me change "I" to "he." I thought she must be wrong, but one thing that I've learned to do often is to try something out. With a computer (which I don't use, but I have someone else use it) it is easy to do. So I changed all the I's to he's to see what it would look like, and tried it out on other people. And it turned out right. I would never have thought of it, but she was right. No one is deceived—or is supposed to be deceived. The "I" was not just egotistical; this intimacy in such dreadful situations was painful. When she's gone, she's dead, and I'm writing her, I feel that the intimacy of address absolutely requires "I." The first poems are not addressed to her or to anyone. They're descriptive; they're narrative. And the use of "he,"—no one has actually objected to it. I showed it to ten people the first time and then I rewrote the whole thing entirely, largely based on what people had said to me but also on ideas I had, and showed it to another ten people. . . .

SR: A different . . . ?

DH: A different ten people, yes. So they wouldn't notice the change about a "he"; they would see "he" for the first time, as it were, among other things. So I would get a clean reaction to it. And nobody objected to "he," nobody was puzzled by it or anything. So I really think that was a good thing. It was Caroline Finklestein who came up with the "he" instead of the "I." Ellen Voight helped me enormously with the structure, and had great effect on the structure of *Without*. Galway Kinnell, Sharon Olds . . . actually, I shouldn't list people because I'll leave some out . . . Alice Mattison, Jane's great friend—these people were enormously important to it, and I've left out two or three names that were as important as them. I won't try to list because it's invidious when you leave people out. Anyway, I always have had a lot of help, beginning with Jane, going on to Robert Bly and old friends, but also younger friends—Liam Rector has helped me and Cynthia Huntington. I call them young—they're in their forties, but that's young compared to me anyway. I had a tremendous amount of help and a sense of validation from these people.

SR: Getting a whole separate reading of the text—ten different responses to the poems—I assume you couldn't simply incorporate other people's readings into one in order to produce a whole? How could you respond...?

DH: Oh, I listen, I listen, I listen. I correct for the veer of particular winds. And always it is true that somebody will say, "This page is wonderful except for that line, take that out of the stanza." And somebody else will say, "Now most of this page isn't very good, but *that line,* that's really good, don't lose that!" Opposites. It's frustrating at first. There are various things that you can do. Sometimes a stanza didn't belong there; it belonged to another letter. I moved parts of letters back and forth. And the little postcard on the nine-month anniversary of her death was part of a letter originally, but it was a false climax, making it an anticlimax in the letter. So I removed it and made it a separate item. There were numerous and enormous changes. There was the Thanksgiving letter which became incorporated in a Christmas letter. The midwinter letter was probably a third again as long originally and I cut it down considerably, so you can never . . . I don't suppose that anybody's reading is represented all the way through there, but everybody is represented in places all the way through.

SR: Some poets resist so strongly incorporating outside influences, other writers' opinions or viewpoints—for Stafford, I remember, it was almost a matter of religion that no one be permitted to look at the poem until it is complete and ready for submission.

DH: I know, I think it's foolish, I think it's self-protective (even though I love Bill Stafford's work). There are some people who simply can't work my way. But I can't really work without it. I've always had a lot of friendly help. And I've given a lot. By and large, it doesn't work unless it's reciprocal.

SR: Like the sort of partnership you've described with Jane.

DH: Oh yeah, yeah.

SR: In many of the poems from your earlier collections, you celebrate the life of the body, sexual love, pleasure. In *Without,* you still seem to be celebrating the life of the body, even when you're humbled by the destruction of the body. Two come to mind. There's one that begins,

> Alone together a moment
> on the twenty-second anniversary
>   of their wedding,
> he clasped her as she stood
>   at the sink, pressing
> into her backside, rubbing his cheek
>   against the stubble
> of her skull . . .

It's only with the words, "stubble / of her skull," that we see this as other than an ordinary erotic poem, witnessing the effects of the chemotherapy. And, later on in the book, there's a parallel scene but with quite a different emotional tone. It's one of the poems after Jane's death where you say,

> [I] wash my hands at the sink
> as I look at Mount Kearsarge
> through the kitchen window

where you stood to watch the birds.
Often I came up behind you
and pushed against your bottom.
This year, home from unwrapping
presents with grandchildren
and children, sick with longing,
I press my penis
into zinc and butcherblock.

—from "Letter at Christmas"

DH: Oh yes, "zinc and butcher block." And at first I didn't notice—you may not have noticed it either—*butcher, cleaver,* cutting off your prick. There's castration in the word *butcher.* I didn't realize that when I wrote it at first but over time . . .

SR: I felt the harshness of it. Actually I heard that poem before I read it; it was one you read at the Blacksmith House, I believe. But you're right, the word delivers a sort of covert violence that punctuates the longing of the poem.

DH: But there's a lot of sexual reminiscence in there, and then there's sexual lamentation. There's this happy memory of sex, but then there's something like the butcher-block poem focusing on the loss of it—and the loss of the particular with her. The erotic life was very important to both of us and it was almost at the center of our lives. So the loss of her as a lover, and the memory of all the lovemaking, was very much on my mind—not while she was ill so much, when we couldn't make love, but afterwards.

SR: But it's as if it has significance beyond simple pleasure and beyond also the bond of husband and wife. It becomes a symbol of something larger. I thought of the Yeats quote you use in one of the pieces: "The sexual intercourse of angels . . . is a conflagration of the whole being."

DH: Actually, I rewrote the quote a little bit—and Yeats was quoting Swedenborg. I'm happy to foul things up a little bit for my purposes. But Yeats did write Florence Farr—who was an old lover of his—when they were both very old people and he said, "The intercourse of angels is a conflagration of spirits," or some such quote. And I said in my poem, "I want to fuck you in paradise." There's anger in that too. There's anger in the gesture of using the word that a lot of people won't want to hear. But it was a word that Jane had no objection to. I think that some of my outrage is embodied in some of the sexual detail of the poem. Even in "Letter With No Address," the first one in the series, there's the detail about her, me putting her on the potty and her saying "Mama, mama," closely followed by the image of the cars, the automobiles, suggesting an encounter dog-fashion. It's affectionate, funny, and angry, I think. It's supposed to be, all together. Jane would have roared.

SR: You mentioned, before I started the tape, that some people had responded negatively to just how revelatory the poems were—not only concerning your grief and the details of her dying—but in those most intimate aspects of the relationship. Is that some sort of boundary that needs to be maintained in poetry?

DH: I don't feel so. I have been sometimes upset by the intimacy and revelations of other people's poems, but I don't think that being upset by art is a bad thing. People will say glibly that art is to disturb us, to upset us. Well, that's one of the things art can be for. I believe generally in not holding back, letting it be out there. I'm not embarrassed by these things. If other people are, too bad. Go your way, I'll go mine.

SR: But it's not as if you think such intimacy needs to be there in the poetry. Isn't it simply where you are now in this particular experience?

DH: Not every poem is autobiographical. I've written lots that are not. This book is enormously autobiographical. Details may be inaccurately collapsed together—two events collapse into one, I mean it's not history—but this book of Jane's death and my grief afterwards either exists as intimate document or it doesn't exist at all.

SR: It makes me think about the way our lives, when examined through the poet's eye or an artist's eye, become understandable to ourselves. Something like a scrim is removed and we see events as if for the first time. There's a funny passage concerning this. You mention an album book of photographs that someone gave you, that Roger "took / in his documentary passion— / inside and outside our house, / every room, every corner— / one day in September 1984." And the furniture looks odd and out of place, the art on the walls. And then it ends: "The kitchen wallpaper shone / bright red in Roger's Kodacolor; / it faded as we watched, / not seeing it fade."

DH: I'm looking at it right now. . . . It was bright red in the photograph, brand new.

SR: It seemed to me that, again and again, what you were doing here was taking the elements of your life together . . . and remaking those experiences, recasting them, so to speak, on a new stage. And under this intensified light, we witness what was there all along.

DH: You know, when other people died who were close to us, Jane and I went to poems. I mentioned, just talking with you, Bishop King's "Exequy" about the death of his young wife. I remember reading that to Jane when a dear, close friend of ours died in her seventies—for the companionship of grief. And Gilgamesh has it! Gilgamesh, the oldest poem we have. The strongest part of it is the shrieking, howling grief of Gilgamesh over the death of Enkidu. Companionship in grief is all we can have. It is not consolation; it is a hug and a shared tear. I've talked to people who've had things happen to them like the death of Jane—people who have lost a younger spouse like me or people who've lost a child. We don't tell each other that it's all right or that there's any compensation for it—we just hug each other, as it were. That's what the poem can do. I went to Jane's poems of grief—Jane had a good many poems of grief—for companionship in my grief over her.

Of course I didn't write *Without* as an altruistic act to help other people, but I always knew that if the poems were good they would, in fact, help people who were in the place where I was. I wrote them, I began them, not out of a literary necessity, except that it is the habit of a lifetime to reach for a pad of paper when I am moved. I can't imagine not doing it, on any subject—joy as well as sorrow—but sorrow is more intense than joy, alas. So I would necessarily write about her death. And then, having written the first letter, I found comfort in addressing her. I wanted to write more letters. Then I realized the letter form, the epistolary form, was marvelous, the way you could leap from topic to topic. Something could remind you of something else, then you could remember something that happened twenty years ago and you could tell her the news of the day and keep moving, moving, moving. Representing the mind at work with grief, processing its grief and attempting to hold on to an intimacy with a lost one—it was ideal. Every day I could get up and work on them and try to make them poems and make them better. This was in the service of wanting to make art, and my material was the death of my wife, who loved art and wanted to make it and would applaud me wanting to make these feelings into art.

SR: That was a part of my thinking when I asked about the issue of "he" earlier; I was wondering if you had to create a separate self, if that was the only way you could bear to depict Don Hall, the husband, by the wife's bedside.

DH: I think that after I changed from "I" to "he," the poems continued to change. I think the change . . . allowed me to make them better, in fact. That wasn't the only thing I changed in those poems because that change started probably in '96, almost a year before I stopped tinkering with the manuscript. I tinkered for about a year after that change. That was one of the early changes.

SR: Let me ask you a question about the idea of the letter as a form for the poems in the book's second half. After I received the manuscript of *Without*, I began coming across a number of other examples. Allen Dugan has letterlike poems spoken to his dead wife, some dealing with the anger and shame associated with desire when one survives the loss of a partner. But the ones that reminded me most of yours were [Eugenio] Montale's *Xenia* sequence. They too create an ongoing conversation with the memory of his late wife. I was surprised you weren't familiar with them. In one of the letters, he writes: "But it's possible, you know, to love a shadow, / we ourselves being shadows." And I wonder, in some sense, if the very nature of the letter form was a way of purposely trespassing across the boundary of the grave.

DH: Oh, perhaps not accepting it exactly. I knew she was dead. I think perhaps it took two years for the last cell of my body to admit that she was dead. I stayed with her body a long time, about four hours, before they picked it up. And I kept touching her and kissing her, she got colder and colder. And I knew what I was doing. I wanted to know she was dead. And I had "calling hours," which people don't like so much anymore but they do it in the country.

SR: Calling hours?

DH: That's where the body's displayed in the funeral parlor the night before the funeral. Very few people have the open coffin at a funeral anymore—that used to be common—but I knew that would freak out certain people close to me, so I didn't do that. But I had calling hours the night before. Knowing that she was dead was very important. Still on the day of the funeral, when everybody left—my children volunteered to stay with me, of course, but I wanted to be alone—the minute everybody left, I went down to the graveyard and stood at her grave.

SR: At night?

DH: Yeah. And the next morning I was there by six. I talked to her. I didn't think she was listening, but I talked to her at the grave and it comforted me to talk to her at the grave. I needed to do it. *Comforted* is much too comfy a word. I talked to the dog about her a lot. But I also talked to her photographs. The letters were the written versions. It was not that I felt really in communication with her; it was a one-way conversation all the time. But it helped to be able to do it. One of the things that happens as the years go on is that she's no longer "you," she's no longer *y-o-u;* she is "Jane," she is third person. But it took at least a year before that happened. She recedes, she diminishes. I had a dream in which there were, at the end of the room on shelves, like bookshelves, something like 269 small corpses, about the size of dolls—all of Jane. And I realized I had not yet buried them all, that this was a task that was ahead of me. This was a little over a year after she died that I had that dream.

I had some wowser dreams, goodness knows. Everybody believes they're somehow responsible for a death. And I had dreams where Jane had abandoned me, running off with another man—which was not a part of our life together or an anxiety in our life together. Ridiculous, you know, but you can't call a dream ridiculous. My mother died when Jane was two months sick; and then Jane's mother, who was very close to both of us, died three months before Jane did. I had a dream in which Jane had died, and our house was deep in the woods, not right on the road, and I was aware (without seeing them) that the townspeople around where we lived were very saddened for me because Jane had died. But they were also sad because they knew the sheriff was coming to put me in jail. And the sheriff was coming to put me in jail because, in my caring for Jane, I had neglected the old women who lived in the woods in their little cottages and they had all starved to death and died. That one was clear enough.

SR: I wonder if these poems then aren't about trying to bear this huge weight of responsibility, to apply a verbal remedy to the real-life heartsick pain you were experiencing?

DH: In the poems I do talk about taking care of her. She knew it; there was no doubt in her mind that I was taking care of her, but perhaps I need to say so to the world.

SR: Let me ask you a question about your sense of time. In one of your books that was always my favorite, *The One Day,* you talk a lot about this altered sense of time; time is portrayed as being quite fluid, expanding or compressing in response to our activity in the world. And the purest joy is to be wholly immersed in some act of labor, some *now,* to the point of where time seemingly disappears altogether. Here's a passage from the third section of that book:

> Here, among the thirty thousand days of a long life,
> a single day stands still: The sun shines, it is raining;

we sleep, we make love, we plant a tree, we walk up and down
eating lunch: The day waits at the center when I reached out
to touch the face in the mirror, and never
touched glass, touched neither cheekbone nor eyelid,
touched galaxies instead and the void they hung on.

And there's a parallel to that expressed here in the new poems, though with
a shift in tone. There's the bleak compression in the poem "Without":

no spring no summer no autumn no winter
no rain no peony thunder no woodthrush
the book was a thousand pages without commas

Later, there are the lines that say,

The hour
we lived in, two decades
by the pond, has transformed
into a single unstoppable day,
gray in the dwelling place
of absence.

DH: Now it's transformed, changed because of Jane, yeah. I've also been
working on a poem which is sort of the fourth part of *The One Day*. A year
after Jane died, I went into mania for three months and then I plunged into
the worst depression of my life. I had seen Jane be as bad as I was, but I had
never been so bad. I had been up and down like everybody, a little more so
perhaps, but I went into mania and depression for the first time in my life.
I was not delusional but I'd sleep two hours and roar around like crazy for
twenty-two hours, and this went on for about three months. Then abject
despair, abject despair. At the onset of this abject despair, the movement
between mania and depression was a rapid cycling where I would go from
euphoria to despair to terrific, murderous anger, not directed toward anyone
in particular. It was awful. It was just terrible. The murderous anger was the
worst. I read *The One Day* again—and the third part, which seems to allow
that people can be happy together, I hated, I really hated it. Because it was
a lie. Because somebody dies. [*Hall's words were coming slowly, as though he
were struggling with emotion.*] So I wrote at this time, a long time ago now,
of coming out of depression into anger. I wrote something, which at the
moment is called the "The Dead Day" but I think I may call it "Dead Days,"
in which I'm repudiating that complacency. I'm saying that "day" that I lived

in was an illusion, a complacency, and that really everything about human life is rotten. [Entitled "Kill the Day," this poem eventually appeared in *Gettysburg Review*.]

SR: Well, that's a lie too.

DH: Tell *the poet*. Don't tell me. [*Laughter*.] You know I'm not going to argue with you.

SR: This isn't Steven trying to play devil's advocate; I'm responding to a person I know—through your words and your letters—and as a reader responding to the body of your work. There are moments even in *Without* where you're coming very close to Jane's death and still we are given a sense of being—perhaps *redeemed* is too strong a word. Something still survives, surpasses the dour limits of the situation. Tell me if I'm reading this incorrectly, but there's the passage that describes your first winter together at Eagle Pond—"It dropped to thirty-eight below— / with no furnace, no storm / windows or insulation . . ."—and you describe making love on the floor beside the fire burning in the wood stove. Then the stanza concludes:

> You were twenty-eight.
> If someone had told us then
> you would die in nineteen years,
> would it have sounded
> like almost enough time?

And her answer in the end seems to be, "It was enough." It's not something she'd have parted with, even for the terrible twists life has in store for us.

DH: I think what is implied, at the moment of asking the question, is that however long it would have seemed back then, it sure as hell wasn't. But of course the next question, which you're asking for, is eternal life, a kind of eternal present—but *The One Day* made a kind of an eternal present. And you know—the present is not eternal. Anyway, I'm not arguing intellectually against *The One Day*. I do feel in some of that third part a sort of complacency that now I resent.

SR: I understand where you live inside this experience. But I'm speaking now to the effect it has on a reader, someone outside the actual event. When the manuscript of this book arrived in the mail, I was sitting on my couch, going through the poems and I got to this one brief passage. I read it over three or four times—and the day was suddenly different. I was compelled to

put down the poems, to go in to see my wife Karen, just to talk to her about
it. It was a very simple passage, not overtly poetic. Again, speaking in the
third person, the verse reads:

> Why were they not
> contented, four months ago, because
> Jane did not have
> leukemia? A year hence, would he question
> why he was not contented
> now? Therefore he was contented.

If that sense of things becomes obscured for you perhaps in light of what
came to pass, understand that, as language, it is a taste of the eternal day. At
that moment, I looked around my room, I looked at my wife, I looked at my
son—and I experienced that moment in a different way.

DH: Incidentally, that bit came out of correspondence. I wrote Wendell
Berry—he and I write each other all the time; he and Jane were close too.
And I wrote Wendell and said, "Why weren't we totally happy six months
ago?," because Jane didn't have leukemia then. I know it's a silly question.
When Wendell wrote back, because Wendell looks things in the eye, he
doesn't kid around, he said something like: "Maybe a year from now, you'll
wish she had leukemia." If she had leukemia, she'd be alive. That wasn't his
wording. . . .

SR: That experience of being so wholly immersed in a moment that it
almost dissolves time—if that bliss is one pole of the human experience,
maybe the feeling moving through *Without* is the polar opposite, a
counterforce, a movement toward complete dissolution. And it serves as a
warning—to steer clear, as much as we can, of that complacency that would
have us drift unthinkingly between those two extremes. What about the
poem entitled "Without"? It's an amazing description of that collapse of
logic and order in life.

DH: I originally wrote it—you know, it was in *The Old Life*—I wrote it
when she was alive. It's changed somewhat in the new version; I put it in the
past tense, for one thing. When people reviewed *The Old Life,* who knew that
Jane was dead, they said that this was a poem about her death. Well it wasn't,
but I saw that it could be, and perhaps it does better as that. So I changed
it. One day in Dartmouth Hitchcock, seven months or so after she was
diagnosed, and she was back in for some reason or another, I looked out the
window and the leaves were changed. Probably it was that they had started

to turn red, but it could have been that leaves had come. She first went up there in January and there was snow. I saw her look out the window and I saw that the season had changed, or it had changed twice, and I had not noticed. And I thought, "This was a year without seasons; it's a year without punctuation." Then I began to write and I wrote without punctuation, often avoiding syntactical connections, and this was what it seemed like—a headlong stream of denial, of subtraction, of nothingness—not nothingness quite, but removal. I wrote a draft—probably I have 100, 150 versions of that poem, but I think that by the tenth version it was essentially there. That's often true. With the "Letter After A Year," the last of these, I started to write it, and I thought it was going to be a poem. It was the eleventh draft [that] I knew, "I've got it," but I had to write another 150 versions, something like that. But with the eleventh draft I knew it would be there.

SR: The next 150 were necessary to confirm it?

DH: The next 150 were, well, some big changes, a lot of little ones. Eventually it's a dash instead of a semicolon or a colon instead of a dash, or a change in a line break—do I want more or less of a pause here? Do I want a break between the adjective and the noun or end-stop it after the noun? I try it one way one day and try it back another way the next day. So the word *draft* comes to means a retyping of something with very few changes in it. I use the word that way. There is a time in which I know that the material and the shaping of it is all here—it's just that the words are wrong. [*Laughter.*] With "Without," most of the words were there, soon, but there was a lot of minute changing after that. I read an early "Without" to Jane maybe in September of '94. Of course, it's a poem which if someone glances at it superficially, he thinks, "Oh, this is surrealism or something." Jane said, "That's pure realism. That's exactly what it's like. You got it, Perkins."

Fairly early on I realized that in order to have this sameness of absence all the way through *Without,* I had to have near the end a kind of false dawn. And it's true, it's realistic. There are days when the pain is less. And the counts are good, and so on. Also for the point of view of the poem and the feeling of poet and reader, there has to be some contrast against the gray barrenness of the regular day. The moss takes on greenishness; that doesn't get very brightly colored, but it suggests it might get greener, then no, no, no, no . . .

SR: The possibility that slowly reemerges—that you could take up a pencil again, shape a line of poetry again. Interestingly, it has a parallel in one of the sections when Jane comes back home from Seattle [and the bone marrow

transplant]. There's that same small incremental step *toward* something—
I think it mentions something about being able to walk a few hundred yards
with your dog Gus, and dictating a few lines of poetry.

DH: She dictated that, "The Sick Wife," sitting over here, March 8th—and
she was dead April 22nd. We stopped at Crisenti's on the way back from
getting blood work. Crisenti's is a market in New London.

SR: I know now, compared to the magnitude of loss, those "false dawns"
or those small possibilities, they don't seem to balance out. But from the
outside view, working through the text, there is some balance. Between those
two polar forces, we renew our understanding of the simplest visions, the
minute pleasures.

DH: Oh yeah, yeah, yeah. Gussie's happiness when we came back from
Seattle—oh God, it was just extraordinary. And I wrote about that in the
letters, I think.

SR: I'm not sure if I've got this right, but there was the line she wrote for
your gravestone and instead . . .

DH: She didn't write it for my gravestone, the two lines on her gravestone.

SR: She wrote them *about* you, I didn't realize . . .

DH: She wrote a poem called, "Afternoon in McDowell." It's in the first
part of *Otherwise.* We went down to McDowell in the summer of '92 when
I was having chemotherapy. My liver went out on May 1st '92; I've made it
more than five years now. In August, I was skinny and chemo was
unpleasant—it wasn't terrible, it wasn't like her chemo. We went down to
see Dick Wilbur get the gold medal. And we heard music; we heard him read
poetry. The sun goes in and out and she says, "Thin after your second
surgery, you wore the suit . . .." And so she plants it, and then the last stanza
begins, "After music and poetry we walk to the car. / I believe in the miracles
of art but what / prodigy will keep you safe beside me?" And then "as you
fumble with the radio dial / to look for late innings of a Red Sox game."
That's how it ends. It was Galway Kinnell and Bobby Bistol, his wife . . . who
suggested I take these two lines and put them on her tombstone. I was going
to do, "Let evening come," which everyone knows, and which she didn't
even write about death—but the lines on the gravestone are, "I believe in the
miracles of art but what / prodigy will keep you safe beside me?" And it reads
Jane Kenyon next to *Donald Hall.* I'll show you a picture of it. You can't get
in there right now because the snow will keep you out.

SR: Where is this?

DH: Four miles down in Andover, Proctor Cemetery. It's where my grandparents are, and some of my great grandparents. We bought the plot when we lived here, in 1981 or something. We lived here for years, we were very happy, we knew we were going to stay here until we died, and as a kind of affirmation of our love of this place—and in our mutual morbidity, which was certainly there—we bought a grave plot for ourselves in a place that was very pretty down there. Maybe some time you can see it. Then after she died—we had talked about everything except what the gravestone would look like. We planned our funeral, wrote her obituary together. We did her book [*Otherwise*] in the first four or five days when we knew she was going to die. After that she began to lose her powers of speech. You've read all about that. We didn't talk about her gravestone. I don't know why I didn't think about that; but at any rate, I made it up after she died. I got black granite, polished black granite, with both our names on it and three out of the four dates, and then these two lines that she wrote, that Galway and Bobby suggested for her tombstone. I think it's perfect. The ironic answer is, *here* is where we will be safe beside each other, in this ground.

SR: I'm asking, not suggesting this: Does something in the world that she's made with her words and the world that you're making with yours—is that not a place where you feel that you are also together? Is that something of the "prodigy"?

DH: Oh, I feel we are together there. And our archives will be together at UNH [University of New Hampshire]. People will write about us together, and read us together.

SR: You don't see the poetry itself as some sort of—maybe *spiritual* is too unfocused a word—a sort of conjoining in a realm beyond the physical? That's what I wondered about the letter poems—whether you thought they were one way to secure that union.

DH: It's the *act* of doing that. It's an act of being together with her, the writing of the letters. Writing the letters, I was attempting to learn from her in the poetry. I was addressing her and it felt, not supernaturally but actually, as if I were talking in her ear. And now her ear is further away and I can't do that so much, but that distance is just inevitable. I can't feel guilty about it. I do date other women; I feel no guilt about involvement with other women. She would have had other men.

SR: When you mentioned the feeling that angers you about *The One Day,* that sense of time, I remembered two or three places in *Without* where you seem, not to be repudiating that but actually experiencing that again.

DH: I don't deny that, you know, Steve. When I talk about repudiating the third part of *The One Day,* I'm really talking about its relative comfort. I had an intense sense of that false comfort in July of '96, but I don't pretend it was literary criticism. Notions or attitudes toward time that are in that poem are also in the letters. I don't deny it. I don't find it contradictory because my desire to present a despairing and angry alternate ending comes out of another experience. And I think it's probably worth recording. I don't know if it's a poem I'll ever publish. I've been working on it now for a year and a half, on and off, and just the last few days I've done a lot of work on it. But I'm preserving it ["Kill the Day"]. This is what I intend to do with poems. I'm not revising it according to my later feelings. When I look at this poem, I am back in July or August or September of 1996, which is a bad place to be; it's hard to work on it, but I want to represent and embody *that* emotion.

SR: I think the level of commitment to say you're not going to be less honest, you won't soften or sweeten that, you're going to represent who and what you were . . .

DH: Right. And I'll write another poem. And I have written other poems. I've written lately some poems about more nearly accepting that she's dead. I *know* she's dead but the question of accepting it in the sense of not wanting to, oh, burn the house down, not wanting to be bombed or something. There's something I've been working on called—I don't know if I'll keep the title—but it's called "Distressed Haiku." It's haiku in the sense there are two parts, but there're not seventeen syllables. I have, let me see, one of them is, "The Boston Red Sox win a hundred games in a row. / The mouse rips the throat of the lion. / And the dead return."

SR: The passage I was going to point out actually touches on that very idea. "Letter At Christmas" opens with "the big wooden clock you gave me"—the one you and I are hearing right now, ticking away as we talk. It goes on:

> In Advent
> for twenty years you opened
> the calendar's daily window;
> you fixed candles in a wreath
> for church; you read the Gospels
> over again each year:
> the child would be born again.

This concept of time isn't the same as in *The One Day,* but that represents ritual time, spiritual time, a time *above* time—I wondered if that wasn't pointing to a redemptive experience, something that holds life together. "The child" does come again.

DH: But in that poem, the child is irreparable. That child is going to die on the cross in less than thirty-three years, thirty-two years. If Christmas is here, can Easter be far away? This is my first tree and my first Advent calendar since Jane died. Nancy gave me the Advent calendar and Nancy insisted I have the tree, and I got Philippa and the girls to come out—my daughter and her daughters—to come out and help me with it. And it's okay. I wouldn't have done it otherwise. But I couldn't possibly have done it last year. Forget it! I'm trying to approach the life I once led, only with this terrific absence. And recently, only in the last month or so, I have been going to bed early and reading a lot and waking up at five-thirty—and I had gone to staying up until eleven and sleeping until seven. I took note that I was moving back to the old schedule but without Jane. That's a rather large "without." There's a curious way in which—it will be three years in April—this is the third Christmas without her, and she doesn't know about TWA 800; there's so much that has happened that has separated her from the living. This has the effect in my imagery of her shrinking, diminishing, getting smaller, like the telescope reversed. There's an image of grief becoming drier. I weep every day, but I don't howl. I howled and scared the dog all the time, for a long time. And I've probably only howled once in the past six months. And there's some regret in losing it. You remember "Home Burial," or you remember the similar thing at the end of "Out, Out—": "And they, since they / Were not the one dead, turned to their affairs." That's such an outrage. That the world should go on is such an outrage—but it does.

SR: Using the image of the Christ child as an example, don't we have something like that mixture here? In new life we already accept that death and sacrifice are part of its destiny? And yet within it, joy somehow persists, something is affirmed. I felt that joy slipping through in certain places of these poems, as bleak as some of them are.

DH: There are moments of recollection of joy, of great joy. I can even take joy in the birds—but that was an identification with Jane too; I'm not sure if that's clear. I used never to pay attention to birds, and after Jane died I started loving the birds. I tried taking over her characteristics; unfortunately, I took over manic depression—two years in a row. I've been manic in April and depressed in November when the light changed.

SR: Is that when she had it too?

DH: No, she wasn't manic very often. In 1984 she had quite a bit of mania and occasionally she had it. I never connected it with the light. She did have trouble with darkness, but that was depression. This fall I had mania for awhile in November, not very extreme; then I had a very brief depression, very much like the summer of '96 but it was only about thirty hours long. Jane had a light box, and I've been using it.

SR: Full-spectrum light?

DH: I think it really helps. I'm also on Wellbutrin, an antidepressant, but it's also antimanic. . . . I never had a problem with darkness; I used to find it cozy. I used to argue with Jane, mildly. I didn't expect her to change. I'd say, "Oh no, I find it cozy"—she'd find it depressing. Then the November after she died, I crashed. But I didn't get manic until the following April. It was one year after she died when I went manic. In April '96, I remember thinking, "Am I manic? Ha, ha, ha . . . ," and just this November I said that to someone, "Do you think I'm manic?" I didn't really believe it because you don't want to think there's anything strange going on. But when I'm manic I lose weight, and I don't sleep and feel fine without sleeping. . . .

Jane was mostly depressed—but she was bipolar, not a pure depressive. Some of those ecstatic, religious poems are manic. The saints were all manic-depressive—and why shouldn't God work through blood chemistry? I think the survival value of manic-depression is perfectly clear because in mania you can do great things for everybody, and in depression you hurt yourself or people close to you, but not everybody. With mania you can write *Paradise Lost* as it were.

SR: I think maybe some of the questions I'm posing about *Without* seem to duel with you because I'm still viewing it as a literary document, on the outside as a reader. Your commentary reveals how the making of the poems affected who you were day by day. For example, when you talked about taking on Jane's characteristics I immediately thought about the last poem in the collection, "Weeds and Peonies." When you describe bringing in the flower—"One magnanimous blossom . . ."

DH: " . . . and float it in a glass bowl . . ."

SR: And that image not only recalls your wife, it also takes on a gardener's sense of time. Like the earlier Christ child image, we see a thing that is born to die, yet its beauty is what reaches us.

DH: They "lean their vast heads westward / as if they might topple. Some topple." That was actually the first poem I wrote after Jane died. I put it last. It was Ellen Voight, the structure genius, who suggested that. She was absolutely right. It is not a letter, but it ends the letters. It puts a cap on it. Having all the letters addressed to her, this one—which has a lyric structure, not a letter structure—provides a kind of cap to end the poem. It could've led into it, I mean, I think I originally put it chronologically, then ended with "Letter After A Year"—"not seeing it fade." But I think that this is better because it's less crepuscular than the "fading" ending. I think it's a strong poem, and it's a whole and coherent poem. The letter poems are coherent finally but they appear to wander, and in a sense you need them all rather than one of them. And "Weeds and Peonies" is a single poem. It provides a coda—I keep saying cap, coda might do. . . . Of course, I did change a few words in it after I knew it was going to be at the end. An early draft was in the *New York Times* at the end of '95. The *New York Times Magazine,* in the final issue of the year, writes about the notable dead of the previous year. I was thrilled when they called me up and asked if I could write something about Jane. Could I write a poem? Well, I couldn't sit down and write one, but I had been writing poems about Jane. And I had parts of "Letter With No Address" at that point, but "Weeds," a slightly earlier version, was, I knew, complete enough. I knew I would make it better, but I knew it wasn't bad. So I printed it there and it was printed on Sunday, December 31st, 1995, the year she died.

SR: Let me ask you two more questions.

DH: Absolutely.

SR: There are two questions I thought of immediately when I knew we'd have this chance to talk. But I didn't know if it was fair to ask them—until I read the manuscript and saw the ways you'd already stretched the boundaries. The first question is about place and the second is about the place you've built within your work—books, poems, and stories. We've come to see your life as wholly enmeshed in this place, this farm house. In one of the poems here, you describe attending to your mother's belongings after her death, "preserving / things she had cherished—and in late years dreaded / might go for a nickel at a sale on the lawn." It's both wonderful and somewhat frightening to think of how much of ourselves we invest in mere things, and then to imagine them without us. But then, in another poem, you contemplate setting a fire and burning Eagle Pond to the ground.

DH: Right, I mentioned that. Partly because I didn't want everything dispersed. I didn't say anything to my children, and finally they realized it and got together and said they wanted to keep the house after my death. I know they mean that, and yet it could become financially impossible and so on. There are one or two people who want to keep it as a trust. If my grandchildren want to live here, fine. Otherwise maybe it could be used for artists or something like that. But I don't know where the money would come from to keep up a trust. There might be answers to that too. The notion of it being a museum, as it were, like the Frost place—that's not a pleasant notion. My favorite notion would be that a grandchild, or great-grandchild or great-great-grandchild might continue to live here in the house where Jane and I lived—in the house where my grandparents and great-grand-parents lived—and really *live* here. But I cannot control that. I can just imagine that and hope for it. The notion of it being stripped and auctioned off is, of course, a bitter and horrifying notion, but I can't control anything.

Whatever I can control, in the sense of working out contingencies for what to do with the books, the objects, and the photographs, I will do. My children can keep them as long as they want for the grandchildren. Otherwise, UNH has what it wants because UNH has my archives. These are practical matters I work out with my lawyer. I haven't yet done a new estate and will, so I will have to do something new. So I have to do something new. But it requires the cooperation of a lot of different people, all of whom are very busy and it's hard to get going. This was my grandparent's place; it became Jane's and my place; and it's still the old place with the "string too short to be saved" objects around here. Many of my grandchildren are fascinated by it. When my grandchildren come here—they are five, five, seven, nine, nine (that means there're five of them)—they love to explore and see things and so on: "Let's go upstairs!" I take them up to the barn—I've just had the place cleaned out and fixed up—and we explore that. They're not living here the way I did in the summers, but they're enjoying it and knowing about it and hearing stories about it.

The place is very important to me. I can go away from it longer now. I take on more travel than I would if Jane was here because I really didn't like to leave her very much. But I don't want to move somewhere else. It would be very hard to think of another woman moving in here, in Jane's shadow—it would be hard for another woman; I don't mean hard for me to accept.

SR: It would not be a conflict?

DH: Well, I haven't found a woman. I think I really would like to live here with a woman in monogamy and quiet. When I start working on the job description, it sounds a hell of a lot like Jane. It's not as if I'm trying to duplicate her. That's highly unlikely. I know it would be hard on a woman who was a poet, but even on a woman who's not a poet. When I go out with a woman, people will tend to say to her, "Are you a writer? Are you a poet?" That is a complication. And there's the gravestone with my name on it with Jane's. I'm not advertising for a wife. But I am lonely. And I'm lonely for the female. And I *have* many female guests—I'm not speaking of lovers only— old friends and so on, and it's nice to have them come here; it would be nice to live with someone. But I am in my seventieth year; I'm sixty-nine years old. I'm vigorous now and healthy, but how long will I be? And what am I asking someone to put up with?

SR: You've talked about this place as almost a spiritual entity, and I can understand your wish that some grandchild could eventually be like the child you were and take emotional ownership of this house. But, as you said, those decisions aren't of your making. I wonder now whether you think of your own work—maybe even your poems and Jane's together—as another kind of ground, a tangible place? And do you have a hope for what will become of that place and who will visit there in the future?

DH: I hope for it. I feel clearer certainly about the value of Jane's. I also know, with my brain, that I don't know anything about what is going to happen. I've seen literary reputations rise and fall. *Otherwise* sold twenty thousand hardback in the first year; it's remarkable, and there's a remarkable amount of tribute to her since she died. That does not mean that she's going to be read in a hundred years. When I look at the poems, I find it hard to believe they won't remain. I read them aloud to crowds, I read them to myself, I read them to my friends. They seem, if anything, better than they did before she died. From the time of, say the mid-eighties, when she was writing the best of the poems in *The Boat of Quiet Hours,* I have admired her enormously. We were very careful not to compare each other. We didn't like it when other people compared us. When we were first married, she got condescended to—"isn't it nice that you write poems too." Later on there'd be people who would tell us, when we were together, that she was better than I was. That was sexist too because it was "man bites dog"—"Isn't it weird: she's better than you are, the woman is better than the man, the younger better than the older." She didn't like that, either. Even after her death I don't like to make comparisons. I know that, if you put a gun to my head, I would think I like her poems more than my own. But I also would laugh at anybody who said that, because how the hell would you know? You don't know. I would love to have the poems, as it were, walk hand and hand into the sunset and be together and terrific, and people loving them together.

And I think sometime someone would like to make a book of our work together, write a book about us together, and so on. I don't want it to happen now. If somebody came to me and wanted to write some joint biography or something like that, I think I would run and hide because I wouldn't be able to stand any sentence of it. I'd know ahead of time, no matter what the sentence was, I wouldn't stand it. So let it be after I'm dead and gone!

But I do think of these things. I think this is apropos your question. That's a pleasant thought that we would be remembered together, preserved together, as writers, as makers of poems, and that our poems were thought of in conjunction with each other. They're no parallels; there's Robert Browning, Elizabeth Browning, husband and wife both poets, and we stop there. Sylvia Plath and Ted Hughes—no, it's not quite a good example. Of course there are many poet couples now because of the plethora of poets in the United States, people getting together, meeting each other in MFA programs. We did very well at avoiding bad feeling. One thing, we were different generations—so her first book came out when my sixth book came out. We weren't head on in competition. And we were very good at drawing boundaries. When two people read together, the first one is always the warm-up band. Sometimes with friends we'll flip a coin or draw straws to see who gets first, rather than "out-*modesty*-ing" each other or whatever. Janey and I just alternated. One night in the September of '93—'93 was a wonderful year, the last year of health—we read in Trivandrum on the southern tip of India on a Friday night, and the next Monday night we read in Hanover, New Hampshire, totally exhausted—and we remembered who had started the reading in Trivandrum!

That's just a little example of the boundary-setting. And we had rooms on the opposite corners of the house. We would knock on each others' doors, not to interrupt each other. And we knew absolutely that we could leave manuscript around on tables—and it would not be looked at without the invitation of the other. I would *never* read a poem of hers without her asking me to, or any other piece of print. . . . I think to live with each other all day long and to do the same thing, as it were, we really needed to be careful.

SR: I think that was one of the vital dynamics of your life together, and I can't help but feel it's affected the work that's been written in this house, written about this landscape. But do you think of this word place as its own territory, something enduring beyond the lives of its makers?

DH: The trouble with thinking of it as a place—this would mean to say that something would remain. It's not that I'm modest. I've read literary history,

I've been around a long time; I know that people who seem, at some point in their lives and even at the moment of their deaths, to be a permanent part of American literature—fifty years or thirty years later, are not read. I also know that a hundred years from now they might be read again! I can't say anything about my own work.

There are two books of mine that seem persistent; they're not my favorites among my work. One is *Ox-Cart Man,* the children's book, and another is *String Too Short to be Saved,* my first book of prose. There are others that have their fan clubs, and there are some poems that get reprinted a lot—but I've known since I was in my late twenties that I would never know how good I was (or how bad I was). I also know that, as opposed to younger people, I translate the word *good* to mean "endurance." By good I mean the poem will be read two hundred years from now. That's a long time. The young, Generation X or something, [don't] think about that. When Shakespeare or Milton talked about immortality they meant lasting *forever.* Well, we can't think of that. But if I say two hundred years, that's just as good. . . . Henry Moore was wonderful to hang around—I wrote about him. Every time he began a sculpture, he wanted it to be better than Michelangelo. Every time he finished he knew that he had failed—but maybe the next one would be. There's something like this in Yeats too. Yeats was constantly saying, "Everything I've written is no good, but *now* I'm going to write what's good!"

I don't feel that way about the work I'm writing right now, but I would still hope a year from now I might. There are times when I think that what I'm writing right now, what I'm working on right now, as with *Without,* might be the best I've ever done. One thing that's really true for a writer, for every writer I know—when you want to write well, you really want to write well *now;* you're not interested in *having* written well, you know? Oh yeah, that was twenty years ago, terrific, thanks a lot. What have I done for myself lately? [*Laughter.*]

SR: I hope you realize, from your audience's reactions when you read these poems, you're achieving some of those precious *nows.*

DH: It's good, the responses. But there are ways to discount praise. I tend to discount it—when I get praised, when I win a prize, I find ways to discount it—and I think that's probably more healthy than not. If you start to believe your good reviews, you're dead already. You can be pleased and feel fine for a moment—but then get skeptical and get back to work. Get back to work.

SELECTED SOURCES

Bei Dao

Unlock. Translated by Eliot Weinberger and Iona Man-Cheong (New Directions, 2000).
Old Snow. Translated by McDougall and Chen Maiping (New Directions Books, 1991).
The August Sleepwalker. Translated by Bonnie S. McDougall (New Directions Books, 1988).

Rita Dove

On the Bus with Rosa Parks (W. W. Norton, 1999).
Grace Notes (W. W. Norton, 1989).
Thomas and Beulah (Carnegie-Mellon University Press, 1986).

Martín Espada

A Mayan Astronomer in Hell's Kitchen (W. W. Norton, 2000).
Imagine the Angels of Bread (W. W. Norton, 1996).
Rebellion is the Circle of a Lover's Hands (Curbstone Press, 1990).

Carolyn Forché

The Angel of History (HarperCollins, 1994).
Against Forgetting: Twentieth Century Poetry of Witness (W. W. Norton, 1993).
The Country Between Us (Harper and Row, 1981).

Donald Hall

Without (Houghton Mifflin, 1998).
Old and New Poems (Ticknor & Fields, 1990).
The One Day (Ticknor & Fields, 1988).

Seamus Heaney

Electric Light (Farrar, Straus and Giroux, 2001).
Beowulf (Farrar, Straus and Giroux, 2000).
Opened Ground—Selected Poems 1966–1996 (Farrar, Straus and Giroux, 1998).

Maxine Kumin

Connecting the Dots (W. W. Norton, 1996).
Looking for Luck (W. W. Norton, 1992).
Our Ground Time Here Will Be Brief (Viking Penguin, 1982).

John Montague

Smashing the Piano (Wake Forest University Press, 2001).
The Collected Poems (Wake Forest University Press, 1995).
Mount Eagle (Wake Forest University Press, 1989).

Mary Oliver

New and Selected Poems (Beacon Press, 1992).
Winter Hours: Prose, Prose Poems, and Poems (Houghton Mifflin, 1999).
The Leaf and the Cloud (Da Capo Press, 2000).

Marge Piercy

The Art of Blessing the Day (Knopf, 1999).
Early Grrrl (Leapfrog Press, 1999).
Mars and Her Children (Knopf, 1992).

Charles Simic

Jackstraws (Harcourt Brace Jovanovich, 1999).
The Book of Gods and Devils (Harcourt Brace Jovanovich, 1990).
The World Doesn't End (Harcourt Brace Jovanovich, 1989).

William Stafford

The Way It Is—New and Selected Poems (Graywolf Press, 1998).
Even in Quiet Places (Confluence Press, 1996).
Passwords (HarperCollins, 1991).

❖ ❖ ❖

Poet and educator STEVEN RATINER has contributed poetry and prose to numerous magazines in America and abroad. Two of his chapbooks were published in 2002: a retrospective collection from Pudding House Press's Greatest Hits series and *Button, Button,* an artist's book in collaboration with Marty Cain.